BACK TO

JERUSALEM

CHURCH PLANTING MOVEMENTS
IN THE HOLY LAND

BACK TO
JERUSALEM

CHURCH PLANTING MOVEMENTS
IN THE HOLY LAND

RAY REGISTER

WINEPRESS WP PUBLISHING

Packaged by WinePress Publishing, PO Box 428, Enumclaw, WA 98022. The views expressed or implied in this work do not necessarily reflect those of WinePress Publishing. Ultimate design, content, and editorial accuracy of this work are the responsibilities of the author.

ISBN 1-57921-303-0
Library of Congress Catalog Card Number: 00-102711

What Others are Saying—

"I believe *Back to Jerusalem* is informative, strategic and prophetic!"
—Luis Bush, AD 2000

"This is a very remarkable document. Certainly everyone connected with ministry in Israel should be very familiar with it, and anyone interested in the Holy Land in general should read it."
—Dr. James H. Montgomery, DAWN 2000

"Your material is excellent and very helpful to the new generation of leaders. I think the Holy Land is indebted to you for your many years of faithful service to the glory of the Holy One."
—Dr. Imad Shehada, President
Jordan Evangelical Theological Seminary

"I indeed think anyone interested in Church Planting in general and in the Middle East specifically needs to read it. It also has broad ramifications in that it offers keen insights into how to persevere and actually see churches established among Middle East Muslims."
—Dr. Keith Eitel, professor of Christian Missions
Southeastern Baptist Theological Seminary

"You have done a fine job citing the critical issues a church planter will face in working in the Middle East in general, and in Israel, in particular. An understanding of these issues by new personnel will benefit them immensely in getting started in evangelism and church planting. I like your emphasis on the positive signs and hope for the future which you see now and into the 21st Century."
—Dr. Dale Thorne, former Area Director for
the Middle East and North Africa
International Mission Board, S.B.C.

"All Christians have an interest in Israel and a deep desire for Jews and Arabs there, and everywhere, to love and be loved by Jesus as their personal Savior. Ray Register helped make some to the history he records in this book. He gives helpful understanding of past and current conditions, and wise suggestions for an even brighter future. Read it and pray!"

—Dr. Cal Guy, Professor of Missions, Emeritus
Southwestern Baptist Theological Seminary

"I read *Back to Jerusalem* to find out what was going on at the site of Christ's resurrection. The missionary activity in the Holy Land described in this book reveals much discontent in the area and a yearning for a better life. Christian ministries are offering a better life by bringing the Good News of Christ the Redeemer. The Word is spreading!"

—Rose Hutchinson, Past Regent
Catholic Daughters of the Americas, Bend, Oregon

"If you are looking for a book that weds theoretical with practical, then *Back to Jerusalem* is the book. Dr. Register uses his thirty plus years of experience to give a candid and life-like portrayal of his part of the Kingdom's work in Israel."

—William P. Harrison, Southern Baptist Representative
Nazareth, Israel

"This is a book about church growth in the Middle East, by an author who knows what he is talking about, from more than 30 years of in-the-field experience. Ray Register reflects the work of God and a sense of divine mission that will bless and inspire the reader."

—Jerry Rankin, President, International Mission Board
Southern Baptist Convention

I dedicate this book to the memory of
three great men who mentored me
through my formative years
as a church planter
in the Holy Land

Bevin Woodhead
Roy Whitman
Bill Hern

Acknowledgments

This book would not be possible without the many family and friends who have patiently dreamed, prayed and labored with me in its writing, research and publication. First of all, I owe more than words to my wife and partner in ministry of forty three years, Rose Mary Rich Register who has shared the joys and challenges of ministry in the Holy Land with me for nearly thirty five years. I am deeply grateful to the Drummond Center for Great Commission Studies at the Southeastern Baptist Theological Seminary in Wake Forest, North Carolina and to the students of the class on "Current Topics in International Missions." They gave me the opportunity to present the first half of this book as lectures when I taught as visiting Fletcher Professor of Missions in the Fall semester of 1996. Dr. James Blackmore, professor emeritus, offered valuable assistance on the historical section. I am also grateful to Rev. Brian Steely, pastor of Sahuarita Community Baptist Church near Tuscon, Arizona for helpful suggestions and computer expertise.

Acknowledgments

Stephan Nash, M.D. of London, England and Lynne Abney, M.D. in Nicosia, Cyprus gave invaluable advice in reviewing the manuscript from their expertise of serving many years in the Middle East. Rev. David Smith of Baptist Village, Israel assisted in proofreading and served as a co-laborer in ministry. Roger Mikel from the International Service Corp assisted in graphics. I profited much from those who labored before me and with me in church planting in the Holy Land, especially Dr. Dwight Baker, Rev. James Smith, Rev. Joe Underwood, Dr. Finley Graham, Dr. Bill Wagner, and Dr. Dale Thorne. I am grateful to Dr. Peter Wagner and Tom White who focused my attention on the vital role of strategic level prayer and spiritual warfare in church planting. A special thanks to Dr. Ken Cannon, my second cousin and retired professor of English at Coe College in Cedar Rapids, Iowa for assisting me in correction and arrangement of the manuscript. I am grateful to the leaders of the "New Directions" of the International Mission Board of the Southern Baptist Convention for their patient counsel and inspiration for the final revision. They are too numerous to mention, but I owe a special debt of gratitude to Dr. Jerry Rankin, Dr. Avery Willis, and Dr. Michael Edens for their encouragement and to all the members of the Regional Leadership Team of North Africa and the Middle East. Any opinions expressed or errors made in this book are my sole responsibility. Any good that may come from it should be credited to the hundreds of Christian, Muslim, Druze, Jewish and international partners in ministry with whom God has blessed me through an enriching career as a church planter in the Holy Land. In the end, may God alone receive the glory!

My wish now is to share with those who pray for and support work in the Holy Land and with those who feel the call to take up our labors. My prayer is for a rich harvest!

Contents

Contents

Introduction

World attention remains focused on the Middle East as Israel and the Arab countries negotiate peace settlements. The "Holy Land," or present Israel-Palestine, continues at center-stage of world attention as we begin the 21st Century. Television brings the struggle and agony of Jew and Arab over their claims for the Holy sites in Hebron, Nablus, Nazareth and Jerusalem into our living rooms. The continued threats of Iran, Iraq and other Muslim countries to the peace process engenders fear of an imminent Armageddon. Political and religious dynamics continue to converge in the Holy Land, maintaining it as a pivotal location in the modern world.

Receptivity to the Gospel message of the saving power of God in Jesus Christ increased after the Gulf War. Islam, though a formidable opponent to the Gospel, weakened in its monolithic control over the masses as Muslim fought Muslim. The ongoing Muslim fundamentalist renewal reveals the heart-cry of the Middle Easterner for a deeper relationship with God and a hunger for spirituality. This new window of opportunity has been created not only by military conflict, but by a war in the heavenlies which is being won by spiritual warfare and the fervent prayers of many believers around the world.

Evangelical Christians from numerous churches and organizations mounted a concerted effort of "Praying through the 10/40 Window" in October of 1993, to pray for all peoples living between 10° and 40° North Latitude, which included the majority of the Muslim world population.[1] DAWN International conducted a survey of Evangelical churches in the Holy Land that same year which revealed those who took church planting seriously and those who paid only lip service to the idea. "AD 2000 and Beyond" became the theme of planning and preparation, to reap the harvest resulting from concerted prayer.[2] Strategic level spiritual warfare, spiritual mapping and identificational repentance have impacted the region. The over 100 million Muslims in Israel, The Palestinian Authority, Jordan, Egypt and other Middle East countries, as well as over four million Jews have felt the spiritual fallout of these prayers.

For the first time in recent memory Muslims in increasing numbers are accepting the Gospel and the power of the written Word. They are seeking fellowship with Christians to learn how to pray and to worship God in new ways. Parallel with this new phenomenon, Jewish Messianic fellowships continue to flourish and open their doors, even to Muslim background believers. Christian Arabs are beginning to see the ripe harvest field of the unreached Muslim people surrounding them. They are losing their fear of witnessing to both Muslims and Jews. Persecution and opposition are a result, and many suffer for their faith. Muslim, Jewish and Christian believers are surviving, and their fellowships are growing as they join forces in this spiritual struggle.

The good news that Jesus saves and reconciles men to God and to each other spread from Jerusalem in the first century like wildfire, flamed by the wind of the Holy Spirit from house to house. But the fire went underground and smoldered in traditional churches that dotted the landscape of the Holy City, with the Islamic invasion of the seventh century. Now, with the dawning of 21st century, the fire is breaking out again, fanned by the praise of numerous believers of all nationalities in assemblies, house churches and traditional churches all over Jerusalem and the Holy Land. Hence the title of this book, *Back to Jerusalem,* which is written to serve as a resource for spiritual warfare and mapping to those who pray for the Middle East and as an orientation manual for those called to serve in the area. Jerusalem has returned to center stage, not only in world politics, but of God's activity in planting his church anew in the Holy Land. Is it by chance that as Jerusalem celebrates 3000 years of history, it also experiences almost phenomenal church growth?

New responsiveness in the Holy Land and the Middle East requires new strategies for Gospel ministries in the 21st century. This book maintains that God plants churches in the Holy Land and around the world when his servants, both local and expatriate, incarnate the love of Christ in culturally sensitive witness, humble service, sacrificial sharing, fervent prayer and brotherly love. A time of harvest follows patient rock removal, diligent soil preparation, generous sowing, and God's provision of the rain of the Holy Spirit in due season. God has proven this to us over and over again during thirty-five years of labor in the Holy Land. Those expatriates who join the movement of God in church planting must be willing to pay the price of years of language and cultural acquisition and humbly realizing it is the people of the land who must ultimately bear the major responsibility of leading out in church planting movements. They must increase and we must decrease if God is going to have free rein in planting his church.

A radical and positive shift in missiology from the theme of "church planting" to that of "church planting movements" has impacted the final revision of this book. The dynamic spread of the church in its Jewish and Gentile form in the Book of Acts is the ultimate model for church planting movements. They are a spontaneous act of God that can only be encouraged or impeded by the strategies and institutions of man. The Holy Land is a classic case study of the successes and failures of these strategies which can be applied to other situations worldwide.

Back to Jerusalem shares insights gained from many sources to assist those who come after us in gathering the harvest and to inform those praying for us. Chapter One gives a short history of church planting movements in the Holy Land, to show that God has planted the church in this rocky soil in the past and continues to do so today. Chapter Two describes numerous challenges facing church planters in the Holy Land. Signs of hope on the horizon for the 21st Century are offered in Chapter Three. Chapter Four examines critical issues in planting the church in the Holy Land. I share ideas about preparing for the harvest while in your homeland in Chapter Five. Advice to newcomers for reaping the harvest in the Holy Land is given in Chapter Six, "Down in the trenches and enjoying it!" Methods of church planting are presented in Chapter Seven. Chapter Eight encourages the development of strong churches using proven leadership styles. My vision for church planting is amplified in Chapter Nine. The Conclusions show clearly how the church is growing in its Arab, Jewish and international expressions in the Holy Land as the Gospel comes "back to Jerusalem."

A survey of the Galilee region is found in Appendix A. I offer selected models for church planting in the Holy Land, which describe actual churches in the area in Appendix B. Appendix C presents graphs of the growth of the Baptist, Messianic and Muslim background believers.

Back to Jerusalem is the first in a trilogy relating our experiences in Jerusalem and the Holy Land during the past thirty-five years. We plan to share in more depth our insights into ministry with Muslims in the next book, and finally our personal memoirs. As the Arab proverb goes, "God is with the patient, if they remain patient!"

Factors Impacting a Church Planting Movement In the Holy Land

chapter one

A Short History of Church Planting Movements in the Holy Land

D o not be surprised that God has been planting His church in
the Holy Land throughout these two thousand years. Anyone
who assumes that they are doing something new in this ancient
area of the world is naive. It is equally naive to think that the church
failed completely in its effort to spread the Gospel through these
two millennia. Following is a brief review of many valiant efforts
and some tragic mistakes.

Biblical Backgrounds

Scholars and theologians disagree about when the church
started in the New Testament. A simple reading reveals clearly it
was in the heart of God and the express ministry of Jesus to plant
the church. Jesus' choosing of the twelve, sending out of the seventy, two by two, and declaring to Peter, "I will build my church,"
were clear indications that He had in mind creating a body of believers.[1] I personally believe two plus Jesus is an "embryo church."
The church was born when the Spirit that resurrected Jesus fell on

those gathered in the upper room on the day of Pentecost, as recorded in the second chapter of the Book of Acts. The early church has served as an example of the "ideal church" until today. It developed naturally around the temple and synagogue and nurtured itself in home fellowships. The church commissioned Paul and Barnabas to establish and strengthen other fellowships. They went first to synagogues and then to pagan forums. Persecution eventually sent the church into the catacombs, where both Jews and Jewish Messianic believers were buried.[2] The apostles carried the church to the "uttermost parts of the world" and established it in martyrdom. The Holy Land remained a launching pad for the beginning of the church around the world, at least through the lifetime of the Apostle James, the elder leader of the Jerusalem church. The Book of Acts serves as the manual and model for church planting movements in the 21st Century.

The Byzantine Church

Archaeological evidence abounds in Jerusalem and Galilee indicating that numerous synagogues eventually became churches, as thousands of Jews received Jesus as their Messiah and became "Nazarenes."[3] Many rituals and chants preserved in the present Greek Orthodox Church in the Holy Land bear a strong resemblance to Jewish worship. The presence of the altar behind the veil (now a wooden screen) attests to Jewish temple origins. It is not without reason that the Greek Orthodox Church boasts that it follows traditions of the apostles. The Jewish church inherited the culture of Alexander the Great and took on a distinctly Greek flavor after the days of the apostles. It dispersed into the Greek gentile world, after destruction of the temple in AD 70. Essentially, Alexander's Hellenizing influence in the Mediterranean world served to ease the spread of the Gospel from Jew to Gentile.

The practice of adult or believer's baptism remained in the Byzantine church well into the fourth century. Baptisteries, over a meter deep and shaped into a cross, can be seen at Shivta, Avdat, and Latrun.[4] Ornate church buildings attest to a lively and thriving Christian community in the Holy Land when Constantine legalized the faith in the fourth century. Delegates from some of these churches attended the Council of Ephesus in 431.[5]

Constantine commissioned his mother, Helena, to search out holy sites during her famous pilgrimage in 329. Church buildings, or "basilicas," subsequently built over the ruins of pagan temples, marked many of these locations. The most famous of these was the rediscovery of the tomb of Christ. It lay under a mound of dirt, and over it stood a pagan temple, according to Eusebius, the early church historian. Earlier tradition recorded by Origin attributes the site also as the burial place of Adam.[6] An early Byzantine icon (picture) depicts the resurrected Christ lifting Adam out of his grave. This tradition adds clarification to Paul's teaching in I Corinthians 15:42-47 that Jesus is the second and last Adam. On this location Constantine built the Church of the Resurrection and called it the "New Jerusalem." I recently visited the Church of the Holy Sepulcher and found ancient tombs hidden behind the present structure, built over the site of Jesus' burial.

Recent excavations in the Jewish quarter in the Old City of Jerusalem exposed the "Cardo," the long street pictured on the Madaba mosaic map in Jordan. Roman Emperor Hadrian built the Cardo as part of Aelia Capitolina, on the site of Jerusalem, after its destruction in AD 70. It later expanded to a forty-foot wide road, lined with columns by the Byzantines. The Cardo stretched from the huge Nea Church, constructed in AD 540 by the Emperor Justinian, and was the scene of a magnificent yearly processional of the Bishop of Jerusalem, during the Byzantine era.[7]

Archeologists recently uncovered a rock on which the Virgin Mary was reputed to have rested on her way to Bethlehem. The site was discovered initially in 1992, but the size of an enormous octagonal Byzantine Church constructed over the rock in the fifth century became known when an illegal water pipe was dug through the area to connect the Har Homa housing development. The church measured 43 by 52 meters and is one of the earliest and largest churches dedicated to the Virgin Mary. The church covering the rock known as the *kathisma,* or seat in Greek, was destroyed in unknown circumstances in the eighth century.[8]

A Historical Atlas of the Jewish People indicates that by the sixth century the majority of the population of the Holy Land had become Christian. This phenomenal growth is attributed to permanent settlement of pilgrims and the Christianization of large sectors of the pagan population. Success of evangelism, according to this book, was largely due to efforts of the monasteries which had been established throughout the land. A map indicates 47 such monasteries and Christian centers by the 5th Century.[9] This indicates a church planting movement carried on from the time of the Apostles.

The affluence and political power acquired by the church, under a succession of Byzantine emperors, led to its undoing. Theologically, the church became polluted by debate over the role of the Virgin Mary in the incarnation and by various disputes and rulings of church councils. Inherited traditions took the place of simple heart faith. Many devout believers took to the desert and adopted a monastic life-style to escape decadent ways in the cities. The life of one of the more colorful believers named Euthymius of Armenia is recorded by Cyril, a native of Beth Shean, born about 524. He tells of Euthymius' arrival in Palestine in 405. Not used to desert life, he befriended the local Bedouin shepherds to learn their secrets. Later, he led tribal leader Aspebet to the Lord. A dream in

Arabia led Aspebet's son, ill with paralysis, to Euthymius' monastery. Robert L. Wilkens relates the story of this conversion:

> When Euthymius saw the boy, he made the sign of the cross over him, and he was healed at once. When Euthymius saw the Bedouin's belief, he catechized them and had them baptized in a font in the corner of a cave. Aspebet was renamed Peter. For forty days Euthymius instructed the tribe with the divine word, teaching them they were no longer Agarenes or Ishmaelites but descendants of Sarah. Peter built a cistern and a bakery for the monastery. As the number of Christians grew among the Saracens, Euthymius asked Juvenal to ordain a bishop. Euthymius proposed Peter, who was consecrated the first bishop to the Arabs of Palestine, with the title of the camp of tents. Euthymius' relations with the Arab-speaking tribes can perhaps be seen as a portent. Several hundred years later, when Arabic had become the lingua franca of the region, it was the monks in the monasteries established by Euthymius who would be responsible for the first translation of Christian writings into Arabic and for the beginning of Christian Arabic literature.[10]

In the 1970's, while on a trip to Mount Sinai, I came upon a dignified, elderly Bedouin sheik riding a camel. I gave him a copy of the Gospel in Arabic. He remarked, "Oh, I read this years ago. The monks in the monastery gave me a copy!" The spirit of Euthymius still lives in deserts of the Holy Land.

A terrible Persian invasion in AD 614 weakened the Byzantine hold on the Holy Land. They ravaged churches and slaughtered nuns.[11] This set the stage for a Muslim invasion by the followers of Muhammad of Arabia. Augustine's "City of God" dream almost vanished with the capture of Jerusalem in 638 by the Muslim army. Umar ibn al-Khatab, the Muslim conqueror, graciously spared his army from turning the Church of the Holy Sepulcher into a mosque by refusing to pray in it. He chose to pray outside, instead. The Mosque of Umar in front of the Church of the Holy Sepulcher still marks the spot of his wise and magnanimous decision.

You can understand the attitude of traditional churches to western evangelical work in the Holy Land when you know the glory that was once Byzantium. Most members of Evangelical churches in the Holy Land come out of Greek Orthodox and Greek Catholic Churches. An indigenous perspective of church planting movements forces us to ask, how much of the glory of the Byzantine Church was imported from Byzantium with its Greek priests and monks? Its heavy emphasis on church structures, ceremonies and holy places overwhelmed the simplicity of the early house-church movement and replaced the vitality of faith with symbolism and form. The church had spread rapidly from house to house under severe persecution until it was declared legal by Constantine in AD 312. From that time on, Christianity became the state religion, imposed from above, not motivated solely from the heart. The effect was to stifle the church planting movement of early Christians and lead to disastrous results. The "edifice complex" inherited from the Byzantines continues to this day to limit church planting in the Holy Land.

Did life in the church really touch needs of the local Arabs and the persecuted Jewish population, especially in Jerusalem? It appears the glory of Byzantium was imported to the Holy Land and was not locally inspired. The concept of a church in the Holy Land today, with almost 2000 years of tradition, still means a building with a priest. He wields all authority, with mysterious trappings for divine worship, incense and chants. This naturally affects present day attitudes of traditional Christian leaders toward Western church planting concepts. They see Evangelicals as threats to their system or "status quo," acquired from traditional churches and Muslim rulers. These priests see Evangelicals as subversives who threaten their flocks. Prayer needs to be directed toward the leadership of traditional churches, so that they may free their flocks to follow the Bible under leadership of the Holy Spirit, before the new wine of renewal splits the old wineskins of tradition.

The Advance of Islam

Swiftly invading armies of the followers of Muhammad rode a dust storm to victory over the vastly superior Byzantine army at the Battle of Yarmuk, southeast of the Sea of Galilee, on August 20, 636.[12] Cities of the Holy Land fell to Muslim conquerors in swift succession. The church went from power to weakness despite wisdom and tolerance of leaders like Umar. Many in the general population welcomed Muslim conquerors as liberators, because they spared them from Byzantine taxes and religious-political authority. Jews, formerly persecuted under the Byzantines, were allowed to build and use synagogues. Likewise, Christians built and used churches in the seventh and eighth centuries under Muslim rule.[13] Successive changes of Muslim rulers slowly imposed restrictions on Christians as *dhimma,* or second class citizens, and segregated them into religious communities, or *millet.* Slow pressure of the *dhimma* system on the psyche of Christians in the Middle East is explained by C.H. Malik, former Lebanese ambassador to the United Nations:

> Under the Ottoman Turks, the Orthodox became part of the Muslim dhimma system. According to this system there is a distinction between Muslim and non-Muslim subjects. The former, constituting the umma (i.e. the nation) of Islam, enjoy privileges which the latter, being only dhimma (i.e. held under or protected by the dictates of the conscience of Islam, which includes legal

and political status allowed them by the Qur'an), are not entitled to enjoy. They were thus distinctly second-class citizens. As *dhimma*, the Christians have their own religious, social and political status, whereby they may practice their own religion "freely," but they cannot seek or accept conversion of Muslims to Christianity; they cannot serve in the armed forces; they cannot hold high governmental office; their men cannot marry Muslim women; and they must pay special tribute to their Muslim rulers. If you want to remain Christian, you had to submit to this system. That is why the predominantly Christian Near East became, with the passage of time, predominantly Muslim.[14]

The landscape of Jerusalem changed with construction of the Dome of the Rock and al-Aksa Mosque by Muslim Caliph Abd-al-Malik in 691. These structures not only rivaled the Christian Church of the Holy Sepulcher but also competed with the Muslim pilgrimage or *Hajj* to Mecca.[15] Intense Muslim devotion to these sites on the Temple Mount was inspired by Muslim traditional interpretation of a verse in the Quran. It said, "Praise be to the one who caused his servant to travel by night from the sacred mosque to the farthest mosque, whose surroundings we have blessed, to show him some of our miracles!"[16] In the "night journey" (Arabic: *israa'*), Muslims believe Muhammad rode Burak, a half-mule with a woman's face, from Mecca to the Wailing Wall (*al-mabka*) in Jerusalem and ascended (Arabic: *mi'raj*) from there to the seventh heaven, passing Jesus, who was only in the second heaven! Muslim interpreters still debate if this took place in a dream or in reality, but to this day, "night journey and ascension" (Arabic:*al-israa' wa al-mi'raj*) remains the basis for Muslim claims to the former Jewish holy site on the Temple Mount in Jerusalem.[17]

Arabic slowly replaced Greek as the language of commerce. Spiritually, the church limited its witness, for the most part, to theological arguments between particular Christian and Muslim leaders. The final blow came when the so-called "Mad Caliph," Abu Ali Mansur al-Hakim (996-1021), Shi'ite Fatamid ruler in Egypt, issued an edict which was signed by his Christian Secretary Ibn Abnun, to destroy the Church of the Holy Sepulcher. One of his soldiers literally chiseled the tomb of Christ in the Church of the Holy Sepulcher down to bedrock in 1009. This fateful blow, along with harassing of pilgrims wishing to worship in holy places, and coupled with successive invasions of rival Muslim armies into the Holy Land, led inevitably to the Crusades. [18]

The Crusades

Many question the motives that led Pope Urban in 1095 to call the faithful of Europe: "Enter upon the road to the Holy Sepulcher, wrest it from the wicked race and subject it."[19] Most emphasize the negative aspects of the Crusades and the bitter taste they still leave for Muslims and Jews in the Holy Land. One commentator balances this by indicating, "The Crusades were an attempt to recover by holy war what had been lost by holy war."[20] Reality is that the 40,000 Crusaders who captured Jerusalem on June 7, 1099 perpetuated an indiscriminate slaughter of all ages and sexes, regardless of race or religion. History records: "heaps of heads, hands and feet were seen throughout the streets and squares of the city."[21] Such gruesome acts, perpetrated in the name of religion, explain why Muslims and Jews to this day see the Crusades in a very negative light. Greek Orthodox and Jews alike were often slaughtered, as the Crusaders made their way across Europe to the Middle East.

It is hard to find anything positive from the Crusades to contribute to the subject of church planting! But there were two exceptions. Francis of Assisi studied Islam and braved the Sultan's camp in Egypt to preach the Gospel to Muslims in 1219. Later, Ramond Lull, a visionary and scholar, died as a martyr on a mission to Muslims in Boujie, Tunisia in 1316.[22] Nevertheless, these do little to erase the memory of deeds of the Christianized pagan Crusaders, whose evil actions spoke louder than good words.

The real hero of the Crusades, for the average Muslim, and begrudgingly for the Christian today in the Holy Land, is not Richard the Lion Hearted, who established his kingdom in Acre. Salah al-Din Yusif al-Ayubi, the Kurdish Muslim commander who defeated the Crusaders at the strategic battle of the Horns of Hattin, on the North Western shores of the Sea of Galilee in July 1187, won the day for chivalry and honor. He released his Crusader prisoners after the battle, whereas Richard the Lion Hearted, the Crusader commander, later slaughtered 2700 Muslim captives during the siege of Acre, when they could not pay the requested ransom![23] What a reversal of Christian compassion!

Richard and Saladin ironically made peace in a most unusual way. Richard married his sister to Saladin's nephew and granted the honeymooning couple the city of Jerusalem as a wedding gift! Richard knighted Salah al-Din's nephew on Palm Sunday, May 29, 1192, to seal the peace.[24]

The final end of the hundred-year Crusader reign came at the hand of Baybars, leader of the Mamluk slave dynasty of Egypt. He destroyed a huge church in Nazareth in 1263 and massacred the Templars in Acre in 1291. The Holy Land eventually fell to the reign of the Ottoman Turks whose leader, the "Sultan" or "Caliph," ruled from Istanbul, the former Constantinople of Byzantine fame.

As Hitti said, "The Crusades bequeathed a legacy of ill-will between Muslims and Christians that has not been forgotten."[25] Those who labor in church planting in the Holy Land see constant reminders of the Crusades. Ruins of strategic castles dot mountains bordering the Mediterranean, and blue-eyed, blond-haired children still play in the streets of Muslim villages. Kenneth Cragg observes that the Crusades "left noble piles of architecture on the eastern landscape but seared the eastern soul."[26] It is a lesson Jesus taught, "All they that take the sword shall perish with the sword."[27] Questionable motives, using wrong methods, fail in church planting, as well as in all other endeavors of life. Evangelical Christians who realize the spiritual strongholds Satan has built upon deep wounds of the Crusades are beginning to retrace steps of the Crusaders. They are meeting on locations of various atrocities committed against Jews, Orthodox Christians and Muslims, to ask God's forgiveness. It is hoped, through such identificational repentance, that wounds will be healed and hearts will be open to receive the Gospel in the 21st Century.

18-19th Century Missionary Movement

Napoleon's invasion of Egypt and his subsequent defeat by the British fleet at Acre in 1799 turned attention of the Western world back to the Holy Land. Christian circles in Britain began to speculate concerning restoration of Jewish people to the Holy Land. Joseph Frey, son of a rabbi, came to faith in Jesus in 1798 and encouraged formation of the London Society for Promoting Christianity Among the Jews (The London Jewish Society, or the LJS) in May 1809. The LJS sent Joseph Wolff, a young German Jewish convert, to Jerusalem in 1822. Wolff was preceded by Levi Parsons, who worked in Jerusalem in 1821, under the sponsorship of the American Board of Commissioners for Foreign Missions. Parsons labored among the Greek Orthodox before dying at age 30 in Alexandria, on February 10, 1822. His partner, Pliny Fisk accompanied Wolff on his trip to Jerusalem but died soon after of fever, in Beirut on October 29, 1825. The dramatic story of Parsons and Fisk is told by Eli Mizrachi in his book *Two Americans Within the Gates*.[28]

Wolff, and others who followed him, decided the only way to overcome opposition of traditional churches and to protect the rights of Protestants under the Ottoman Government would be through establishment of a British consulate in Jerusalem. In 1826, John Nicolayson, a Danish-born, LJS trained missionary, came to Jerusalem to minister to German-speaking Jews in the city. He became the first permanent Protestant missionary to live in Jerusalem. He succeeded, after much difficulty, in purchasing land in front of David's Tower, in 1838, for building a church. The British opened the first European consulate in Jerusalem in 1838/9, on the property of the LJS, where Christ Church would be built.[29]

King Frederick William IV (Kaiser Wilhem) of Prussia envisioned a Protestant alliance in the Holy Land that could gain recognition and privileges for Protestants in the Turkish empire. This corresponded with the desire of British Earl of Shaftesbury to establish a Protestant Bishopric at Jerusalem. Negotiations resulted in consecration of Michael Solomon Alexander on November 11, 1841, at Lamberth Palace, as first Protestant Bishop of Jerusalem. Alexander, a young rabbi of German origin, received Christ in 1825, after listening to a lecture by LJS workers in England.[30] He was to become the first Jewish bishop of the church since the time of the Apostle James. He arrived in Jerusalem in time to lay the first stone in the foundation of Christ Church, on January 28, 1842. After many delays and setbacks, the church was finally consecrated after Alexander's death.[31] His ministry and difficulties are summarized by Lyle Vander Werff:

> First Bishop Michael Solomon Alexander (1841-1845), a convert from Judaism and professor of Hebrew at King's College (London), was given an official ship of the Royal Navy to convey himself to the Holy Land. Arriving there, he found himself bishop of a handful of Jewish converts, unrecognized by local authorities and unprotected by the government, which had appointed him. Soon he was in conflict with Consul Young, attacked by

high church leaders (as an experiment which failed), the subject of debate in British Parliament (1843), and frustrated by Turkish and local authorities. Exasperated, he sought help from diplomats Rose (Beirut) and Canning (Constantinople), threatening to "go and rouse England" (1843). He continued to face cold neutrality of Eastern churches, fearing proselytism, as well as Lutheran and Anglican clergy guarding their independence from his Episcopal control. All these bewildering barriers must have contributed to his early death at age forty-five (d.1845).[32]

Similar in fate to that of the sainted pioneer missionary Henry Martyn of earlier years, Bishop Alexander died unexpectedly in the desert in Egypt on his way to a much needed furlough. He therefore missed the consecration of Christ Church on January 21, 1849.[33]

The King of Prussia nominated Samuel Gobat, a German speaking, Swiss-born Anglican minister who worked with the Church Missionary Society (CMS) as replacement for Alexander. Gobat was an educator and desired to spread the Gospel among all peoples of the Holy Land, through establishment of Christian schools. These he opened in Nablus, Nazareth, Jaffa, Ramle, Bethlehem and Ramallah. He ministered to the Jewish population in the beginning, but quickly turned his attention to Arabs, who were beginning to respond to teaching of the Bible throughout the land, by his predecessors. He soon faced the dilemma of Orthodox believers demanding to be admitted to the Anglican Church. Most were expelled from the Orthodox Church when they became believers. He opened doors of the church to many requesting baptism. Before his death in 1879, members hailed from Greek Orthodox, Jewish, Samaritan and Muslim backgrounds. Congregations formed in Nablus, Salt, Nazareth, Kefr Yasif and Jaffa in addition to St. Paul's Church in Jerusalem.

When Gobat died in 1879 he was replaced by Joseph Barclay, who only lived two more years. The Anglican-Prussian alliance dissolved in 1886-87, since Germans were no longer willing to submit to the veto of the Archbishop of Canterbury. There was also opposition to Gobat's strong evangelical spirit from high-church Anglicans, who sided with Greek Orthodox leadership in the Holy Land in their opposition to conversions.[34]

Into this delicate situation stepped statesman Bishop George Francis Popham Blyth, who served from 1887 until 1914. He sought to soothe the feelings of Greek Orthodox clergy by receiving permission to hold services in the Church of the Holy Sepulcher. At the same time, he took steps to found a church that would not be subject to assumed compromises of the former alliance. He began construction of St. George's Cathedral on Nablus Road in 1892. The church was consecrated in 1898 and served the Arab population.[35]

One cannot help but admire valiant efforts of Anglicans during this century. Numerous schools, churches, bookshops and hospitals opened throughout the land. Their efforts were rewarded. Anglican Church membership in the Holy Land doubled between 1879 and 1910, with a total of 2,323 members, from all religious backgrounds.[36] While their policy of pouring vast sums of money and personnel into institutions would no longer be acceptable or affordable in this day, they laid a foundation for a church in rocky soil. That church still lives today in its Arab, Jewish and international expressions.

Lutherans established congregations in Bethlehem in 1860 and in Bet Jala in 1879. When the Anglican-Lutheran alliance dissolved, they also established a parish in Bet Sahur. Emperor William II made a personal pilgrimage to the Holy Land and inaugurated the Lutheran Church of the Savior on the day of the Feast of the Reformation. They built the church directly across from the Holy Sepulcher, on land donated to the King of Prussia by the Turkish Sultan. His wife, Augusta Victoria, accompanied him on the tour and used her influence to build Augusta Victoria Hospital on the Mount of Olives. It was dedicated in 1910.[37]

An intimate history of Jerusalem and many Protestant missionary groups, during this period and the following, is recorded by Bertha Spafford Vester in her book *Our Jerusalem*. [38] Her father Horatio Spafford, a personal friend of Dwight L. Moody in Chicago, wrote the hymn "It Is Well with My Soul," after loosing his first two daughters in the sinking of the La Havre. Spafford's untiring philanthropic efforts and those of his dedicated family and colleagues led to the establishment of the American Colony and the Spafford Children's Hospital in the Old City of Jerusalem.

A side effect of Protestant activity in the Holy Land during the 19th Century was a renewal of Roman Catholic work. The "Latin" Church, as it is called in the Middle East, was expelled with the Crusaders in the 12th and 13th centuries. Catholics re-instituted the Latin Partiarchate in 1847, the year after Gobat's arrival in Jerusalem.[39] Franciscans established fifty centers throughout the land by 1876, along with dozens of others directly under the Patriarch. Arab Catholics grew from 4,000 to 12,000 in 1840 to 1878, mostly coming from a Greek Orthodox background, as did many Protestants.[40] Their greater numerical success was probably due to the fact it was much less difficult to move from Orthodox tradition to the Catholic Church than to Protestant.

But Protestants and Catholics were not the only competitors for souls of native Christians during this period. Russia had long considered herself protector of Christians in the Ottoman Empire. They especially felt a deep interest in the Orthodox in the Middle, East who were their spiritual kin. They often intervened on behalf of the Church with Ottoman authorities. Their care came to fruition in 1859 with laying of the cornerstone of the Russian Church of the Holy Trinity in Jerusalem, by Grand Duke Constantine. He made pilgrimage to the Holy City in 1881 with two other Russian princes, and the Greek Orthodox patriarch and clergy received him warmly. They established a Holy Land Society upon their return to Russia in 1882, with headquarters in Nazareth, for the purpose of promoting elementary education and free medical services.[41] As C. H. Malik, professor of philosophy at the University of Beirut exclaimed, "But for the Russian Orthodox Church, Orthodoxy in the Middle East would have been an orphan. The Churches of the West come to it as to something alien: they want to change and convert it. Russian Orthodoxy comes to it as to bone of its bones and flesh of its flesh."[42]

Evidence of Russian contributions to education still remain today in the Holy Land, in the form of "Moscobiyas," or Russian buildings, in Jerusalem, Nazareth, and Rama. An earlier generation of leaders in the Greek Orthodox Church spoke Russian. I will never forget being invited in the 1980s to dinner in Nazareth, welcoming Russian Orthodox Patriarch Pimen on his visit to the Holy Land. I was struck by his commanding stature and the beautiful harmony of the Russian Orthodox blessing sung before and after the meal. I noticed his Russian translator spoke fluent Egyptian Arabic also. It left me with the realization, during that cold-war period, that Russia had a religious as well as a political interest in the Middle East.

20th Century Advance

The twentieth century was one of wars, and at the same time, a determined advance in church planting in the Holy Land, even through many setbacks. World War I brought hardship and near starvation to the local population. World War II brought confiscation of German properties, including Ludwig Schneller's orphanage in Nazareth and the Carmel Mission's housing on Mt. Carmel. Russian Orthodox properties were taken after the Russian Revolution.

The present police stations in both Jerusalem and Nazareth, locally know as the "*Moscobiya*," were former Russian church properties. The Communist Party made easy entry into the vacuum left by Russian Orthodox departure and negatively influenced local Arab populations' attitudes toward the West.

Baptists entered the Holy Land in this century of turmoil in the person of Shukry Musa Bishuti, a former Presbyterian from Safad. He became a Baptist in America in 1909, under the influence of George W. Truett, at First Baptist Church in Dallas, Texas. In 1911 he returned to Safad, under sponsorship of Baptists in southern Illinois. There, in a stream that flows through the Valley of Lemun, he baptized his first convert. A year later he moved to Nazareth and taught Bible studies in his home near Mary's Well. He began to gather a flock of believers from the Greek Orthodox community. Illinois Baptists supported the ministry until 1923, when J. Wash Watts and F.B. Pearsons arrived as the first Southern Baptist representatives in the Holy Land. Dr. Truett, along with Dr. Scarborough and others, visited the work in Nazareth in 1925. They were so impressed that, on returning to the USA, Dr. Scarborough influenced Mr. & Mrs. George W. Bottoms of Texarkana, Arkansas, to donate $10,000 toward building a church at Mary's Well in Nazareth. The church was completed in 1928. Pastor Musa died only two years later, and the faithful buried him under the floor of the newly dedicated facility. Rev. Louis Hanna, the pastor's nephew and first believer, returned from college and seminary studies in the States and became the new pastor.

Eventually, Baptist children faced persecution from the Greek Orthodox community, necessitating opening a school for offspring of believers. Then Southern Baptists in the United States built a school in Nazareth in the 1930's and commissioned Baptist Representatives Roswell Owens and Leo Eddleman and their wives to aid in ministry. Leo Eddleman became a living legend among church planters by mastering the Arabic language and preaching it in less than three years! He attributed this to his late night studies throughout curfews imposed during the Palestinian riots of 1936-39.[43]

Southern Baptists built a small chapel in Jerusalem, on Narkis Street, in 1933. It was on the edge of town at that time and near a Catholic institution. Later on, Jewish neighbors moved into the area. A mixture of Jews, internationals and a few Arabs attended services from the early beginnings.

Baptist work, like other evangelical ministries, suffered through World War II, as foreign representatives evacuated. The Holy Land became a bridge for armies fighting in North Africa. Southern Baptists assigned Kate Ellen Gruver at the end of the war, in 1944, to assist in the church and the new George W. Truett Children's Home in Nazareth. Mabel Summers and Anna Cowan joined her in 1947. They worked in the home and reopened Nazareth Primary School. Together, they weathered struggles of the 1948 War of Independence, when Israel declared its statehood. Nineteen children, whose parents either died or fled during the war, were left in their care. These ladies not only kept evangelistic work going in Nazareth and surrounding villages, but opened an orphanage as well!

Settling of hostilities and creation of the State of Israel signaled a new era in the Holy Land. Southern Baptists sent representatives Robert L. Lindsey, Dwight L. Baker, and B. Elmo Scoggins and their wives to build up the work. Dr. Scoggins lived in both Jerusalem and Nazareth, learning fluent Hebrew and some Arabic, and eventually adopted one of the George W. Truett Home children.

Dr. Baker found only five elderly adults left in the Nazareth Baptist Church who could not flee during the fighting in 1948. He developed ministries of the church and outlying villages. Rev. Fuad Sakhnini assumed pastorate of the Nazareth Church, after studies in America and Switzerland. Dr. Baker moved to Haifa, where he developed the Christian Service Training Center (CSTC) in 1965. He also opened a bookstore on property of the al-Jazzar Mosque in Acre. Baker's tireless efforts, alongside Arab leaders he trained, laid a foundation for many Baptist ministries in Galilee. Jim and Betty Smith continued ministries of Nazareth Baptist School and outreach into villages, until they were relieved by Dale and Anita Thorne and Ray and Rose Mary Register in 1966. The Smiths moved to Ashkelon in 1967 to start a home ministry and assist with Gaza Baptist Hospital and church.

Baptists lost their first representative to a tragic death when Henry Hagood suddenly succumbed to spinal meningitis and died in Nazareth, in January, 1946. His widow Julia later married Finlay Graham, a Scottish Baptist who had studied Arabic with her in Jerusalem. They later moved to Beirut for a distinguished career among the people of Lebanon and the Middle East. I am reminded of sacrifices which might be paid every time I pass Henry Hagood's grave in the Church of Scotland Cemetary, on the mountainside overlooking the Sea of Galilee. I am also reminded of life's finality when I hear of the saintly life of Paul Rowden, who served with his wife Marjorie in Nazareth and Haifa, beginning in 1952 until 1959. Paul died of cancer on October 3, 1959, but not before completing his Ph.D. on "A Century of American Protestantism in the Arab Middle East," at Dropsie College. Nazareth Baptist Primary School is named after him. Local people still say, "The Lord takes only the best!" Baptists lost their third representative when Mavis Pate, a nurse at then Baptist Hospital (now Ahli Hospital), was tragically shot in Gaza in 1972. Her life is commemorated in the book *Clothed in White,* and by numerous students she trained as an operating room nurse.[44] The above serve as poignant reminders—church planting may require the ultimate sacrifice.

The orphanage moved from Nazareth in 1955 to a farm outside the Jewish city Petach Tikvah. Milton Murphy and his wife Martha became parents to nineteen Truett Home children, as well as raising five of their own. This orphanage became known as "Baptist Village," as orphans grew and left. It evolved from an industrial boy's school to a camps and conference center used by many of the evangelical communities in the country. The Association of Baptist Churches in Israel was organized at Baptist Village in 1965. Baptist Village International congregation meets there.

Dr. Robert L. Lindsey (d. 1995) returned to the Holy Land after World War II, in November 1945, and reorganized West Jerusalem Baptist congregation in 1962, with only eighteen members. Then the group experienced renewal in the 1970s, and attendance grew to hundreds. Arsons targeted the crowded chapel in which they met and burned it to the ground in 1982. So Lindsey built a temporary tent in the back parking lot, and attendance tripled! The congregation raised over $1,800,000 from Baptists and other supporters around the world for a new sanctuary, seating over 300 regular worshipers. Authorities granted a legal permit verifying the building meets all codes, in July 1996. Lindsey became a living legend in the Holy Land when he lost a leg on a land mine in Jerusalem, while attempting to bring a George W. Truett Home child back from Jordan in 1961. He later became a New Testament scholar of note due to his translation projects and research with Dr. David Flusser of the Hebrew University.

Lindsey also started a bookstore ministry in Tel Aviv named Dugit, the Hebrew word for a little sailing vessel, symbolizing the ship of faith. The first building was destroyed by the local authorities, but a subsequent property on Frishman Street near Dizengoff Circle developed into a quality art gallery, under the leadership of Chandler Lanier. Dugit eventually came under sponsorship of the local Messianic community, upon Lanier's retirement. It is a meeting place for Messianic Jewish believers in Jesus and is the only other Christian institution in Tel Aviv, besides the Bible Society Bookshop.

In 1965, Baptist membership numbered about 120 members, a third of which were expatriate workers. By 1995 the membership grew to over 1,100, in sixteen churches and seven centers. The Nazareth Baptist School enrolls over 1,000 students and rates as a top academic institution in the Arab sector of the country. Theological Institute, formerly the CSTC, trained 25 students in four centers, using decentralized theological education. The Association of Baptist Churches and school are now self-supporting and almost totally directed locally, through a system of advanced subsidy grants and a building/land loan fund. During the thirty-year period from 1960-1990, Southern Baptists sent over twenty career couples as representatives to Israel. Each impacted on the development of churches and institutions in the Holy Land, along with a growing number of dedicated local believers.

Other evangelical groups in the country saw similar growth through many struggles. The Arab Episcopal Church became independent of the CMJ in 1973 and subsequently trained a number of young pastors for its many churches. The British Israel Trust of the Anglican Church (ITAC) continued the original thrust of Anglican ministries to the Jews, with dynamic Jewish messianic congregations in Emmanuel House in Jaffa of Tel Aviv and at Christ Church at Jaffa Gate, in the Old City of Jerusalem. Lutheran congregations in the Arab sector continued ministries through difficulties of the *intifadha* and its aftermath.[45] Their Scandinavian counterparts in the Jewish sector founded Caspari Center to train Messianic Jewish leadership and began a school for Messianic believers' children. The Christian Missionary Alliance continues a long-term ministry in Beersheva, Jerusalem and the West Bank. Pentecostal Churches of Canada conduct a thriving worship service in the YMCA in West Jerusalem and sponsor King of Kings

Colleges for Messianic believers in Jerusalem and Jaffa, which has now become Israel College of the Bible. Assemblies of God operates a training center in Haifa that sends out Arab pastors, planting congregations all over the country. Plymouth Brethren and Churches of Christ are expanding rapidly through home meetings. Messianic Jewish congregations and Russian language congregations are sprouting all around the country. There are now approximately 125 Jewish Messianic house-churches and congregations and 70 Arab congregations and house-churches around the country, in the year 2000. Muslims are also beginning to respond to the Gospel and to unite with local congregations for the first time in a century.

The Sevanto family in Tiberias freely distributed the Bible in Arabic and Hebrew for many years, to churches and centers all over the country and around the world. Mount of Olives Bible Center placed Bibles in thousands of Arab homes through newspaper advertisements. Thousands have been sold in every language by the Bible Society. It truly appears that the Good News has circled the globe and come "back to Jerusalem," despite fierce spiritual opposition.

In Chapter two we will explore challenges that face evangelical Christians and church planters who accept God's call to share the Good News of Christ in the Holy Land today. Is your God able to help you overcome these challenges and turn them into opportunities to advance His kingdom through a church planting movement? To be forewarned is to be forearmed.

chapter two

Challenges Facing Church Planting Movements In the Holy Land

C omplex forces and attitudes challenge the church planter and seek to hinder church planting movements in the Middle East today. The present is bound by the past. Every place you put down a shovel or plow and kick up dust and rocks in the Holy Land, you may find an artifact dating from 100 to 3000 years ago. There are areas where you can feel the presence of spirits inhabiting ruins of pagan temples and tombs of "saints." Separating the present from the past is a venture in futility. People you meet are bound to the past. The past may be your best guide if you plan to venture into the Holy Land to share new ideas, especially about religion or your relationship with God. It helps you understand people's present positions and attitudes.

This is not to deny that a straightforward presentation of the Gospel can produce instant response. The Word of God is still "living and active and sharper than any two-edged sword."[1] You will face local reactions and attitudes when you share the good news of Jesus and try to plant churches in this rocky soil. These reactions may be based, at least in the beginning, on past stereo-types, prejudices and cultural norms. They condition spoken and unspoken responses to our presentation of the Gospel. Each challenge impacts a church planting movement. They can make your work more difficult, or they can be turned to your advantage. The following challenges are shared in the hopes they will aid you in spiritual mapping, to identify Satanic strongholds that have been built up though the centuries against sharing the Gospel in the Holy Land. God will use your informed witness and prayers to attract people of all groups to his anointed one, Jesus, who said, "I, if I be lifted up, will draw all men unto myself."[2]

The Ancient Churches

The Greek Orthodox Church, ancestor to the Byzantines, considers itself successor to the apostles and as the church of the land. Centuries of living as *dhimmi*, or subjugated people under Muslim domination, in religious communities, or *millets*, caused the Orthodox to turn inward. Their traditions have been enshrined in the Holy Places, the priesthood and sacred worship. These provide them with a tenacious capacity for preservation in an often hostile environment. "Orthodoxy" refers to their feeling that they alone believe and practice the true Christian faith. Ex-patriots, persons living in the Holy Land who are not citizens of Israel, and others who come with teachings of personal salvation and the priesthood of the believer, can be looked upon as heretical. They are a threat to the "status quo" of salvation through the covenant community and to the priest as mediator of divine grace through the sacraments.

Evangelicals in the 19th and early 20th Century came to the Holy Land expecting to bring revival to ancient churches through Christian education and hospital work. They soon learned that locals who received Christ though personal salvation were quickly excluded from their ancestral churches, and their children were persecuted as well. This undoubtedly resulted from ignorance of local priests, many of whom were formally uneducated. Arab clergy of ancient churches are still subject to their Greek or Italian leaders, and are encouraged to marry before entering the priesthood, thereby preventing them from ever rising above the rank of local bishop.

This opposition is beginning to mellow, as the local clergy becomes more educated. Competition from evangelical churches and schools encourages innovation. Many Orthodox churches now sponsor their own schools, youth clubs and community centers. Some have Sunday Schools in addition to catechism classes.

It is vital to maintain a respectful and friendly relationship with local clergy of all ancient churches. In many cases, response will be positive. Attendance at weddings, funerals and celebrations of Holy Days in ancient churches shows respect for their leadership and their community. I prefer this to the polemical approach that often antagonizes. Children's Evangelical Fellowship (CEF) takes a non-denominational approach to the ancient churches, finding its ministry accepted by some, because of a non-belligerent stance.

I found many Roman Catholic priests open to dialogue and cooperation in ministry, particularly those of the Franciscans and Salesian order. Nuns of the Sisters of Zion, The Sisters of Charity and many other orders are especially friendly to evangelicals. The Tantur Ecumenical Institute serves as a bridge between evangelical and Catholic communities, as well as between Christians, Jews, and Muslims. I believe the day is soon coming when the Greek Orthodox community, through more enlightened leadership, will be more open to an evangelical message. C.H. Malik offers a positive and candid commentary on contributions of evangelicals in the Holy Land:

> Missionaries had to come from the West. They were most sincere and dedicated. They were as human as the rest of us. Let

no man judge them by their humanity alone, although by this scale, they would still stand above most of us. They can only be fairly judged by their burden and their witness. But they were bursting with something to say. Behind every limitation and ambiguity, what they really were saying was this: Others too had known the Lord Jesus Christ, and drawn by His star, they were coming here, this time from the West, to offer Him in the land of His birth, with passion the gifts of their hearts.

They struggled, they suffered; they fumbled; they served; they were tired; but here they fought the good fight; here it was they witnessed; and above all, here it was where most of them died. And a crown is doubtless reserved for them at the hands of the Just Judge, at the hands of Him who sees all and understands all and in His lovingkindness rewards all way beyond their expectations or merits. They established schools, founded hospitals, tended sick, educated the uncouth and ignorant, trained minds to see in the laboratory and observe in the field, taught youth to gird up their loins like men, imparted to children of the Middle East new dignity and self-reliance, translated the Bible, published books, preached the Gospel, shared the deepest ideas in their heart and in their life. They challenged older churches and roused them from their sleep. If they somewhat misunderstood Mary, Sacraments, Saints, the Eucharist, holy images, liturgy, the hierarchy, the sign of the Cross, holy feasts, monastic life, continuity of the tradition—all authentic marks of Near Eastern spirituality. That was their limitation, no doubt brought about by honest zeal and by that blinding impatience which often attends an effulgence of light. [3]

Greek Orthodox existence today in the Middle East cannot be fully understood apart from the total impact, both direct and indirect, of the great American and European Protestant missionary movement of the past century and a half. Evangelicals differ with Orthodox and Catholic churches regarding the cult of Mary. To the Orthodox, she is regarded as the "Mother of God," and to the Catholics, a co-redemptress, who must be appealed to during every prayer.

Evangelicals see this as belittling of the unique salvation and intercession that Christ alone provides. I sometimes point both evangelicals and traditional Christians to the icon of Mary and Jesus. Jesus does not sit on the lap of Mary, but is suspended above her, as if floating on air.

The icon painters were aware of the unique role of Jesus as Savior. Mary's special role was that of total submission to God's Spirit, as a virgin and for her prophetic words about Jesus, her son, at the wedding feast in Cana of Galilee: "Do whatever he tells you."[4] The words of Malik challenge us in our relation to ancient churches of the Holy Land. If we must disagree with them, let it be done, as he says, for the purpose of: "challenging them and rousing them from their sleep." Let us do it with humility, as to ones who preserved the Christian faith in its Eastern form, in the midst of often stifling oppression. We will also benefit and learn from them a patience and piety that endures hardship, and in times past led to a church planting movement.

Pharisaic Judaism

Another "culture shock" for Christian workers in the Holy Land is to learn that in the minds of a Jewish majority, Pharisees were good guys, not bad guys! Christians from the West grew up with the impression that Pharisees were bad guys who opposed Jesus and Paul. We forget that Paul himself was a Pharisee! Gamaliel, a Pharisee, defended Messianic believers in Jesus during the 1st century and probably saved the early Christian movement from destruction.[5] After all, there were 'good' Pharisees as well as 'bad' Pharisees in the New Testament.

Another surprise comes when we discover that study of Jewish-Christian relations throughout history is a major topic, both in scholarly circles as well as in daily newspapers in the Holy Land. It came as a surprise to me how much time is spent by Jewish scholars on the subject of Jewish-Christian history and interaction. This undoubtedly resulted, in part, from discovery by archaeologists of the close proximity of synagogues and churches in the 2nd Century. An undeniable fact of history is that Jews and Christians are closely linked. Christian workers in the Holy Land are especially obliged to learn about the Jewish roots of their faith.

This is not to deny there is prejudice and anti-Christian polemic in the Holy Land today. Anti-mission groups earn their living by continuing to fan fire under the cauldron of prejudice. They try to make the life of Christian workers and church planters unbearable and actively campaign against their presence. Nevertheless, the number of Messianic Jewish believers continues to increase. The Israeli public has become more informed about the real faith and life of evangelical Christians, making work of the detractors more difficult.

The Holocaust left an undeniable impact on Jewish psyche. Willful and planned destruction of millions of Jews, as well as millions of other opponents to Nazis during World War II, will always weight very heavily on Israeli Jews. The Holocaust was a deciding factor in establishment of the modern State of Israel. I grew up during World War II and knew of atrocities perpetrated against Jewish people in Europe, but I never felt the full impact of it until I visited Yad Vashem, the Holocaust Memorial on Mount Herzl in Jerusalem. My daughter, who married an Israeli Messianic believer, lived across the valley from Yad Vashem. I could stand on her balcony and see railroad box cars that had been used to transport Jews to death camps in Europe. They were poignant reminders that Jews honor the dead and will not forget how they died. They also honor righteous Gentiles who helped shelter hunted Jews. But now life must go on. The most important thing to them now is to live and make sure there is never another Holocaust. Life, not death, is the goal.

It is important for a church planter, in the context of the Holy Land, to know that Judaism in Israel today is not identical to that of the time of Moses and the Prophets. Rather, it is rabbinical Judaism, developed in the period following destruction of the temple in AD 70. It had its origins with the Pharisees. Many opposed Jesus and developed a much stronger polemic as the two branches of Jewish faith separated. The basic argument, centering on the messiahship of Jesus, had to do with keeping the law and the inclusion of Gentiles. Jesus, in opposition to Pharisees, taught that being a member of the kingdom of God took priority over keeping oral laws.

E.P. Sanders explains the difference: "Jesus was a charismatic teacher and healer, not a legal teacher. The contrast between a charismatic, individualistic and populist teacher and a legal expert should be emphasized . . . The great bulk of his teaching, however, is about the kingdom, and the characteristic style is the parable or brief saying . . . We misconceive Jesus if we think of him primarily as a teacher of the law—a rabbi in that sense. Rather, he preached the kingdom and God's love of the lost; he expected the end to come soon; he urged some to give up everything and follow him; he taught love of the neighbor. His message did not have primarily to do with how the law should be obeyed." [6]

Jesus taught about the kingdom of God, how one enters it and lives as a citizen of that kingdom, not how one keeps the laws of men. He warned about the impending disaster coming upon Jewish people because of disobedience to God. Those who heeded the warning were delivered from disaster, as described by Eusebius in his Ecclesiastical History, narrated by Howard C. Kee:

> Eusebius, in the fourth century, describes the flight of Christians from Jerusalem, before Romans attacked the city in 70 A.D. Guided by a revelation that forewarned them of impending doom and destruction of the Temple, Christians left. Significantly, most

went to Pella, one of the Hellenized cities of the Decapolis east of the Jordan River, not to a Jewish community.

The issue is not, "Who are the real Jews?" but, What are the criteria for participation in the life of God's covenant people. A basic issue was whether ethnic and/or ritual links with Jewish tradition were essential requirements. Nearly all early Christians rejected both of these criteria, while insisting that through Jesus and his teaching, death and resurrection, a way was open to share in the new covenant, without respect for ethnic or ritual requirements. There were disagreements among early Christians about the extent to which moral aspects of Jewish law were binding on them, but on the whole, they insisted that Jesus had provided them with the moral essence and living example of God's will for his people, as conveyed through the Scriptures of Israel.[7]

The disagreement over keeping the law and who is really the covenant nation of God led to an eventual split between Jews who believed in Jesus and those who did not. Believers refused to take up arms against the Romans and refrained from declaring Bar Khokhba their messiah, in the Second Jewish Revolt against Rome in 132-135. James Parkes describes the process that led up to a final separation:

> As a result of this dual situation, at some period around about 100 the rabbinical leaders of Jabne drew up a formal indictment of the new sect and its tenets, formally rejected the claims of Jesus of Nazareth to be the Messiah, and sent copies of this letter to all the synagogues of the diaspora. Such a letter would give the local synagogues powers to act in excluding 'Christians' from membership, especially when the Christians in question were identifiable as being of Greek or other non-Jewish origin. Further action, however was required, especially in Palestine, where many of the Christians were Jews who had been life members of their synagogues, and whose adherence to the new heresy may well have been in doubt or wholly unknown to the

fellows in the congregation. *In order to detect these a new bene-diction (or rather malediction) was introduced into the series of benedictions recited thrice daily in the synagogue, which invoked a curse on the Nazarenes as these Judeo-Christians were called.* (Italics mine) A suspected member could be detected by his refusal to say this particular clause. Later, at the time of the second re-volt, the most formal prohibitions of any close intercourse with Christians was published . . .

In the break between the Gentiles and Jewish wings within the Church Palestine was the main victim . . . when these mem-bers were excluded from communion first with the Synagogue, and then with the Gentile Church, an almost fatal blow was struck at the development of Palestinian Christianity. This is the natural explanation of why the original home of the religion so early lost all importance in the affairs of the growing church. The Judeo-Christians excluded from synagogue by the Jews and looked at with suspicion in church by the Gentile Christians, were also excluded from Jerusalem by the Romans.[8]

The institution of a curse against the *minim*, or heretics, inten-sified division between Messianic Judaism and Pharisaic Judaism and exposed the rhetoric of polemic between them, as James H. Charlesworth summarizes:

Minim is the rabbinic term for heretics. It is unclear when a curse on the minim was added to the daily Amidah prayer re-cited in synagogues. Some Jews influenced by Yavneh may have considered Jews who professed Jesus as Christ outside their ac-ceptable boundaries, that is, minim (but certainly not apos-tates) . . .

Might it now be possible to ponder to what degree the per-secution of "Jews" was at least somewhat linked with the claim to be exclusively "God's chosen people," and with the charge that Mary, Jesus' mother, had conceived Jesus through sex with a Roman soldier named Panthera? Some Jews obviously thought that Jesus was a demoniac magician. Some Jews claimed that the disciples had stolen Jesus' corpse (cf. Matthew 27:22-26), denying the resurrection. Understandably, by these polemics, some Jews explained away Christian claims regarding the virgin birth, Jesus' miracles, and the resurrection. By this time in the sixth century Judaism and Christianity had parted.[9]

The persecutions of both Jews in the diaspora and of Messianic Jews in Israel, resulting from the division are regrettable. Also regrettable is the fact that Jews of Israel are still taught to pronounce Jesus' name in Hebrew as *Yeshu* rather than *Yeshuah*. The former is an acronym in Hebrew meaning, "may his name be cursed," whereas *Yeshuah* signifies his real name, "God is salvation." Most Israelis do not know what it means.

Be aware also, the title, "missionary," is a bad word in Israel. The Israeli public is taught that a missionary is a subversive who bribes people to change their religion. A so-called "anti-mission law" was passed years ago, in an attempt to discourage missionary activity. It was basically an anti-bribery law which never stuck, against Christians, since they also abhor bribery as an enticement to conversion. It is ironic that Messianic Jews who believe in Jesus as Messiah are now called "missionaries," as a method of slander or derision. The secular Israeli public recognizes that a greater threat to Israeli society is extreme Orthodox Judaism, which tries to squeeze the country into its mold and restrict religious freedom.

Orthodox Jewish leadership uses all the political clout they can muster to mold Israel into a "Torah State." A rabbi was deputy Minister of Housing and Construction and used this position to aid the Orthodox in planting enclaves of religious Jews in the center of secular neighborhoods all over the country, to impact lifestyle and freedoms of secular Jews in the 1990s. Cities long considered secular strongholds, such as Eilat, were targeted, budgets allotted and Orthodox Jews encouraged to move there. The Orthodox successfully blocked a proposed clause to the Basic Law, which is ultimately designed to form Israel's constitution. The clause secured freedom of movement to all residents of the land. The objection was it could allow for freedom of movement on the Sabbath.[10] The Orthodox also controlled the Ministry of Interior that grants visas and citizenship rights to all who come to Israel, including Christians.

David Dorris was administrator of King of King's College in Jerusalem in the late 1990s. He and his wife Jean witnessed a scene which testifies poignantly to the clash still existing between religious and non-religious persons in Jerusalem:

> We were eating breakfast at the Atari Cafe when we noticed a man setting up a small display on the corner. On it was a sign reading something like "God loves you, and Jesus loves you, too!" He took out a Bible and started reading it outloud in English. We became aware that an Orthodox Jew sitting next to us was becoming very agitated. All of a sudden he got up, went outside and threw his cup of coffee in the face of the Christian and began shouting at him in French! Then a secular store owner came out and began shouting back at the Orthodox, telling him, "Go back to France! We do not do things like this in our country!" The Orthodox then went down the street, got a friend, came back with him and started tearing down the Christian's display. All the time the Christian stood there reading his Bible outloud! An older, bearded rabbi came up and tried to calm the Orthodox man down, to no avail. By the time the police showed up there were Orthodox and secular Jews squared off at each other and the Christian in middle still reading his Bible![11]

You will feel at times the hostility engendered by centuries of polemic and persecution of Christians against Jews. The situation is reversed in Israel. Jews are in the majority, and Christians are now a minority within a minority. Living there requires a great deal of patience and humility. But strongholds of prejudice and bitterness are being broken down as Jews from all walks of life and all nationalities come to believe Jesus is the Messiah of Israel. Many resemble in their experiences and personalities the original disciples of Jesus. His Church is coming "back to Jerusalem."

Fanatical Islam

Ayatollah Khomeini fanned the flames of Muslim renewal with his audio cassette tape-inspired revolution in Iran.[12] Saudi Arabia, fearing Khomeini's Shiite form of Islam, began flooding the Middle East with oil money, to build mosques and encourage a return to fundamentalist orthodox, or Sunni Islam. Mosques began springing up in remote Arab villages all over Galilee and West Bank. Men grew their beards and women dressed in conservative garb. Young Muslims, who formerly rebelled against their parent's religion, began flocking to the mosques for prayer. Islamic universities sprang up in Israel, the West Bank and Gaza.

I asked a Muslim friend who was formerly non-religious, "Why did you return to Islam?"

He told me, "I tried money. I tried sex. I tried Communism. Nothing satisfied the emptiness in my heart. So I knew I needed to return to Islam!"

Many return to fundamentalist Islam in search for meaning in life. They feel the root cause of the pitiful state of the Arabs in the Middle East is that they strayed from the truth of Islam. "Islam is the alternative!" is a slogan that appeals to many seeking identity and victory over life's adversities. Islamic organizations sprang up in Arab villages to deal with social, health and education needs which the Jewish government neglected or under-funded. Islamic parties soon won major victories over Communists in municipal elections. Finally, Arab Muslims regained their pride.

Unfortunately all the gains were not positive. Muslims who were long term friends with Christian neighbors shunned them after returning from the *Hajj*, or pilgrimage to Mecca. Some mosques in the West Bank and Gaza became training grounds for radical militant activity and inflammatory Friday sermons against occupation authorities and the Israeli public. One chilling result was a series of bus bombings and other terrorist acts, designed to stall the Israeli-Palestinian peace process. The Palestinian Authority has retrenched to a position of declaring the Palestinian State an Islamic State under *Shariah*, Islamic law, which declares the death penalty for converts from Islam.[13]

Apocalyptic stories spread about Khomeini's plan to destroy Israel and the West. Muslims began sharing traditions that return of the Jews to the Holy Land was a fulfillment of prophecy. According to these traditions, their return was a necessity, so they could all be slaughtered. One tale widely spread was the tradition that rocks would cry out, "There is a Jew hiding behind me. Come and kill him!"

Anti-Jewish attitudes of the average Muslim originate in verses in the Quran and traditions that are anti-Jewish. Muhammad expected the Jews of Arabia to receive him as a new messiah. When they refused and plotted with his Quraish kinsmen of Mecca to kill Muhammad, he expelled them from their cities or killed them and confiscated their properties.[14] The enmity between Isaac and Ishmael and Jacob and Esau remains. These Biblical opponents represent much of the conflict between Jew and Arab, even to this day. Jealousy and animosity between the unredeemed of both peoples allows a satanic stronghold to be built in the hearts of both, which leads ultimately to violence and bloodshed.

The basis of true peace between Jew and Muslim is love and forgiveness that comes through God, in Jesus Christ. This provides the best motivation for dialogue, understanding and forgiveness. It becomes as some describe it, a "third way," rather than the political extremes of Zionism and Arab Nationalism. The first thing

that happens to a Muslim who comes to Jesus as savior is he begins to lose his hatred for Jews. And a Jew who knows Jesus as
Messiah opens his heart to the need of Muslims for Christ. It is
possible to believe a modern day miracle is taking place as the
Gospel comes back to Jerusalem. Messianic fellowships of Jews
who believe in Jesus help Arabs who have needs or who are un-
fairly treated. Muslim believers join many Jewish Messianic fellowships throughout the land.

I have had the privilege in past years of assisting several fellowships in ministry to Muslims attending their meetings. For example, on one occasion a Muslim family invited us to their home
in the West Bank. They asked us about the message of the Gospel
we shared with Muslims and Jews. The older brother remarked
after listening carefully, "We made peace with the Jews, but we do
not know how to live at peace with them. I believe your message
will give us the way to live with them."

Islam is a religion of power and human pride. Throughout the
expansion of Islam, a religion of submission to God, Muslims
viewed the world in two camps. The "House of Islam," or *Dar al-
Islam,* (Arabic) refers to Muslims who believe in the Quran,
Muhammad and traditions. In Muslims' eyes, these are favored of
God as the "best of nations." The rest of the world is the "House of
War," or *Dar al-Harb* (Arabic), unbelievers who are to be brought
into submission to Islam through persuasion, and that failing,
through "Holy War," or *jihad.*

There is no back door out of Islam. Apostasy is punishable by
death to both Muslims and converts alike, if persuasion to return
to Islam fails. The spirit of Muhammad continues to dominate
millions of Muslims in the Holy Land today, leading to acts of rage
and violence. It is a stronghold that demands concerted prayer
and sacrificial witness to overcome.

When a Muslim comes to Jesus, he can be subjected to systematic ostracism by family and friends. His wife may refuse to sleep with him. The Muslim Brotherhood, or *Hamas* may threaten him with death if he does not come back to Islam. I asked a Muslim believer in Jesus, "Why do the prayers intoned by the sheiks have such a fearful tone?" He said, "Because Islam is a religion that uses power and is based on fear."

Despite the threat of persecution, more Muslims today are coming to faith in Christ in the Holy Land than in any period of recorded history. They tell their family and friends about their new-found faith and many more respond. They find two major themes lacking in the Quran, love and salvation—both provided by Jesus!

Rigid Monotheism

Islam inherited a rigid numerical understanding of "God is one" from Judaism. Rigid monotheism conditions Jews and Muslims to resist the idea of the incarnation. Judaism accepted the triune nature of God until Christians adapted the concept to explain Jesus' relation to God the Father and to the Holy Spirit. The unity of God is an underlying theme of Jesus' and Paul's teachings.[15] To claim that Christians blaspheme in their belief in the Trinity is a distortion of New Testament teachings. Rigid monotheism also limits omnipotence, or the power of God the creator, and compassion of God the redeemer, as revealed in Scripture.

Present day Judaism denies a virgin birth and rejects the resurrection. Islam, however, accepts a virgin birth but denies the cross, despite the fact that the Quran teaches Jesus died.[16] Muhammad, unfortunately, received the impression from Christians of his day that the Trinity consisted of God, Mary and Jesus.[17] Neither Judaism nor Islam provides their followers with certainty of forgiveness of sins, and Islam offers no personal relationship with God as Father. Neither Judaism nor Islam provide the certainty of salvation and eternal life. The best Islam offers is "*insha-allah*," (Arabic for "if God wills.") So their followers hunger for a personal relationship with God.

Jews and Muslims seek this personal contact in Kabala, New Age, Eastern religions, Sufism and the occult. Recent innovations idealize new "messiahs'" in Judaism and the person of Muhammad in Islam, to the degree that they become substitute Christ figures. They remain blind to truths of the Gospel, while chasing after false gods. Rigid monotheism which denies the incarnation limits the power of God and robs man of salvation.

The Trinitarian concept of God can be said to originate in the Old Testament, through the use of names for God such as Elohim, which in Hebrew means a plurality of the Godhead and is a term of majesty or respect. It is also indicated in the theophany, or appearance of the Lord as three Angels to Abraham, at Mamre in Genesis 18. Christian understanding of God as Father, Son and Holy Spirit issues from the New Testament record, and for believers is confirmed by personal experience. Once a person experiences the reality of a living God, revealed through the life, death and resurrection of Jesus, through the power of the Holy Spirit, arguments begin to vanish. A renewal of spiritual life begins for both Jew and Muslim when Jesus is experienced for who he is—the one sent by God to renew the Holy Spirit in the hearts of mankind.

Inherited Religion

Religion in the Middle East is a matter of inheritance, more than a conviction of conscience. A person is born into his religion and is expected to die in it. Religion is a matter of personal status received at birth. One's nationality on an identity card is their religion. Middle Easterners see religion as a matter of birth, whereas

Westerners understand it as a matter of personal choice. You are born a Christian, a Jew, or a Muslim, and you are marked for life by your baptism or your circumcision. It determines your nationality, your marriage, often your occupation, your inheritance and your burial.

Changing one's religion in the Middle East is tantamount to betraying your family, your culture and your country. It is looked upon as a denial of your heritage. To leave your religion is to leave your family, community and nation. A church planter must be aware of these consequences when sharing a message of freedom-of-conscience in such a restrictive environment. A person who receives the message of Jesus and his salvation might be excluded from his family and community forever. He could be kicked out of his home; his wife may leave him, and he may lose his job. At worst, if not protected, he could be killed. The severity of these measures depends upon each person's circumstances. Some traditional Christians have become more open to evangelical teachings. Strict Jews can be severe in their reaction to those in their families who believe in Jesus, whereas secular Jews may be somewhat more accepting. Muslims who receive Jesus as savior can be severely persecuted and may even be killed.

It is necessary for church planters in the Holy Land to study how people to whom they minister make decisions. In the case of religion, a decision appears to be made by birth. Charles Kraft offers anthropological insight into group movements and decision-making processes:

a) In many societies, at least in their traditional state, an ordinary person would expect to have little say in such decisions as those concerning whom he or she would marry, where they would live, and what occupation the husband would engage in. Any thought of an ordinary person changing his/her religious allegiance, then would be completely unheard of. Those of very high prestige are often even more restricted in their ability to make such changes since they are looked upon as the preservers of traditional values. Lower class people, especially the disaffected and marginalized, however, would likely be able to claim much more leeway in many areas of life—either out of rebellion or because they no longer care.

b) A second major consideration with respect to social guidelines for change is the relative importance attached to the choice to be made . . . In many societies, furthermore, their religious allegiance is seen as so integral to their overall identity that they regard religious defection as social treason (e.g., Muslims, Jews). A person who converts to Christianity is, therefore, likely to be treated as dead by his or her society.[18]

Some choose to remain as "secret believers" in such an environment, in hopes that they may influence their families and friends to also put their faith in Jesus. Then they can move in numbers to preserve community and to protect each other. Groups of believing students or professionals provide protection for one another. I counsel believers to understand their families' reaction and to deal with them in love and patience. Unfortunately, unwise and rash actions on the part of believers cause negative reactions from parents and relatives. Many who use wisdom and patience find opportunities to share their witness and to influence others to join them in faith in Jesus.

Minority Status

Jews and Christians lived for centuries in the Muslim controlled Middle East and Holy Land as minorities, or *dhimmi*. These were gathered into religious communities, or millets. Each religious group lives in its separate quarter in the Old City of Jerusalem, to this day. Prior to the Muslim conquest of the area, Jews lived as a minority under the Byzantine and Roman governments. The present day Jewish aversion to change of religion, or conversion, may be in part due to a mechanism of protection developed as a minority, so as not to offend whatever ruling power. Romans were willing to leave the Jews and the Christians (or Messianic Jews) alone, as long as they did not rebel against Rome or take away loyal pagan citizens from the practices required by Roman emperors. Caiphas, the high priest, plotted to turn Jesus over to the Romans so the whole nation should not perish as reprisal from the occupation government.[19]

The *dhimmi* status allows a great deal of freedom, as long as one stays in his birth community. A Jew can practice New Age, yoga, Buddhism, the occult and almost any exotic form of divergence within Judaism and still be considered a Jew in the Holy Land. But if he or she accepts that Jesus is the true Messiah of Israel and decides to follow him, they step over the line and are then considered to have left Judaism. This barrier to faith in Jesus remains a major stronghold of spiritual warfare against the Gospel.

Muslim do not adapt emotionally to minority status in the Holy Land. Muslims are the "best of nations" and should be in charge, from the perspective of the Quran.[20] They are quickly becoming a formidable political force inside Israel through their natural birthrate, which is about twice as fast as that of the Jewish population, with the exception of Orthodox Jews, who also have a high natural birthrate. And a spirit of pride, fostered by Islam, leads to continual conflict with those of other faiths in the area.

Evangelical Christians find themselves a minority among an Arab minority in the Holy Land. Amazingly, Jews who were persecuted around the world through the ages now find themselves in danger of being the persecutors. Many secular Jews and some Orthodox are conscious of this danger and seek to engage Christians in dialogue. The Directory of Organizations and Institutions of the Inter-religious Coordinating Council in Israel lists 60 organizations dedicated wholly or in part to interfaith dialogue.[21]

Minority status need not be a deterrent or a threat to those who know the living God through Jesus Christ. They can be the "salt of the earth" and the "light of the world." Believers are letting their witness be felt in the Holy Land today, and others are taking note.

Religion and Politics

Religion and politics remain inseparable in the Holy Land. This reality requires a difficult adjustment for evangelical Christian workers who come from countries which cherish separation of church and state. Separation of church and state and religious freedom are built into the Constitution and Bill of Rights in our home country. But now we find ourselves, along with other Evangelicals, struggling alongside secular Jews in the Holy Land for inclusion of religious liberty in a document for basic human rights. My particular denomination, for years, led the battle against state interference in church matters, to such an extreme that it united with secular humanists and others to remove Bible teaching from public schools.[22] Not so in the Holy Land! Israel is an avowed Jewish homeland. The Palestinian Authority, while secular by profession, is heavily influenced by a Muslim majority. In the *Knesset*, or Israeli Parliament, numerous religious parties often determine direction and legislation of the coalition government. Thomas Friedman, in *From Beirut to Jerusalem*, interviews representatives of at least four different Jewish groups that hold conflicting views of Zionism and the role of religion in government.[23] Religious parties pressure the government to grant concessions to the religious establishment, in the form of Sabbath restrictions, kosher laws and governmental posts for religious officials. When demands are not met, street demonstrations are common. The assassination of Prime Minister Rabin by a religious Jew in 1995 shocked the nation, but seemed to have little effect on national elections a year later.

Jewish religious schools and seminaries, *yeshivot*, receive subsidies from the government, which subsidizes the education of every qualified pupil. Christian schools receive support from the government Ministry of Education. Nazareth Baptist School, one of the largest Christian schools in the country, with 1,000 Arab students, receives hundreds of thousands of New Israeli Shekels each year in the form of government student grants. These enable it to be financially independent of its Southern Baptist sponsors. The school teaches Bible in class and holds regular chapels for religious inspiration. Obviously, it is the responsibility of schools to teach religion as part of the curriculum, in the eyes of the average citizen in the Holy Land.

The government pays a stipend to religious leaders in Muslim mosques. Priests of Orthodox and Catholic churches teach religion in public schools. Jewish religious schools receive generous government aid. When a local pastor recently asked a government official why Evangelicals do not receive the same benefits he was told, "Because you have not asked!"

So it behooves an expatriate worker to foster good relations with government officials in such a situation. I received invitations, along with other church leaders, to attend presidential receptions every New Year, for the thirty years we lived in Galilee. This provided an opportunity to maintain a witness to government leaders. Good personal relations creates goodwill for visas, for church building permits and for various problems that arise. It is much preferable to have good relations with government officials than to face their wrath! New Testament writers lived in a similar political situation and encouraged us to be subject to governing authorities.[24] I found, in many cases, that face-to-face dealings with government officials yields better results than overt political agitation. It is always best to give local authorities an opportunity to solve problems before engaging outside help. We see from history that Christians sought outside help and protection in the Holy Land, but unfortunately, it often came too late and had negative consequences.

Modern Marcionism

The evangelical church worker and church planter who learns Arabic quickly becomes aware that many clergy and laymen in Orthodox churches, as well as some evangelical Arab leaders, do not believe in the inspiration of the Old Testament. Or, they hold to selective revelation, where some parts, perhaps the Prophets, are inspired and others are not. This view coincides with their political experiences of losing land, home and country to "Zionist invaders." They reject a God who would order the people of Israel to slaughter men, women and children when they occupied the Promised Land. Their view is very similar to Marcion, who was excommunicated by Church Fathers in 144. Latourette summarizes the Marcion heresy:

> Marcion insisted that the Church had obscured the Gospel by seeking to combine it with Judaism. He maintained that the God of the Old Testament and the Jews is an evil God . . . he argued that a world which contains the suffering and cruelty which we see all about us must be the work of some evil being and not of a good God . . . He also noted that the God of the Old Testament commanded bloody sacrifices to him, and, a God of battles, rejoiced in bloodshed and was vindictive. He taught that this God had given a stern and inflexible law for the governance of men, demanded obedience to it, and was rigorous in his enforcement of it, and was arbitrary in his choice of favorites . . . [25]

Marcion held that in contrast with the God of the Jews there is a second God, hidden until he revealed himself in Christ.

I was amazed to find some Christian Arab clergy holding similar views to Marcion about the Old Testament. I was more amazed to find some expatriate workers who acquiesced to this view, even to the point of refusing to read the word "Israel" in the Old Testament during prayers in their churches. They substituted the term, "people of God," or other euphemisms. I learned also that there are Arab Christians among the leaders of radical political resistance movements to the State of Israel.

Canon Naim Ateek, former pastor of Saint George's Cathedral in Jerusalem and director of *Sabeel*, an organization which advocates liberation theology as a solution to conflict in the Holy Land, explains the rationale behind Palestinian rejection of the Old Testament, in his book *Justice, and Only Justice*:

> For most Palestinian Christians, as for many other Arab Christians, their view of the Bible, especially the Hebrew Scriptures, or Old Testament, has been adversely affected by the creation of the State of Israel. Many previously hidden problems suddenly surfaced. The God of the Bible, hitherto the God who saves and liberates, has come to be viewed by Palestinians as partial and discriminating. Before the creation of the State, the Old Testament was considered to be an essential part of Christian Scripture, pointing and witnessing to Jesus. Since the creation of the State, some Jewish and Christian interpreters have read the Old Testament largely as a Zionist text to such an extent that it has become almost repugnant to Palestinian Christians. As a result, the Old Testament has generally fallen into disuse among both clergy and laity, and the Church has been unable to come to terms with its ambiguities, questions, and paradoxes—especially with its direct application to the twentieth-century events in Palestine. The fundamental question of many Christians, whether uttered or not, is: How can the Old Testament be the Word of God in light of the Palestinian Christians' experience with its use to support Zionism? [26]

Ateek's solution to this dilemma is to recommend to Palestinian Christians a: "hermeneutic that will help them to identify the authentic Word of God in the Bible and to discern the true meaning of those biblical texts that Jewish Zionists and Christian fundamentalists cite to substantiate their subjective claims and prejudices."[27] Ateek's recommended hermeneutic is: "the Word of God incarnate in Jesus the Christ interprets for us the word of God in the Bible." [28] This appears at first reading a commendable suggestion, but falls short in that the written word of God in the Bible is our primary valid witness to Jesus, the living Word!

Ateek reveals his bias in interpreting various passages from the Old Testament by remarking: "For the Church in the Middle East, such passages can neither be authoritative nor valid for the Christian's understanding of God."[29] He further reveals a view of selective revelation by explaining: "For what is reported as the words and deeds of God in certain passages of the Bible is not at all the same thing as the authentic Word or the knowledge of God."[30] Ateek, by using a limited view of selective revelation, appears in danger of falling into the same error that he accuses Zionists and fundamentalists of committing. Who decides which passages of Scripture are the "authentic Word or the knowledge of God"? Though Ateek can be commended for trying to find a way to make Scripture relevant for Palestinian people, he must be cautioned against falling into modern Marcionism.

I served the Arab population of Galilee for over thirty years, and I am not unaware of root causes of hostility between Arabs and Jews regarding establishment of the State of Israel. I championed the cause of refugees and intervened in every case where I thought injustice was being done to Arab citizens of the State. Nevertheless, I have difficulty agreeing with a view of Scripture that distorts the nature of God revealed in the Old Testament. The inspiration of the New Testament and frequent quotes by Jesus himself, of Hebrew Scriptures, demands a high view of the inspiration of the Old Testament.

Ateek and others adhering to liberation theology hold a view of the Old Testament that rejects a God who commands destruction of pagan cities. This overlooks the fact that Canaanites, whom the Israelites invaded and destroyed, were offering their first born sons by fire for the pagan god Moloch! The stench of human sacrifice was an affront to the God who created man in his own image. On the other hand, a romantic view of Scriptures, which sees Jews as God's chosen people who can commit no sin, is equally biased and leads some evangelical Christians to a wholesale endorsement of everything Israel does. Both views distort reality. The whole council of Scriptural truth, mediated by love and forgiveness, can alone bring justice and healing to the Holy Land.

Ateek modified and clarified his views about the Old Testament and the land of Israel in a subsequent article in *Mishkan*:

> The land of Palestine/Israel is part of God's world. It belongs to God. God is its creator and owner as God is the maker and owner of the whole world. Today, God has placed on it both Palestinians and Jews. They must share it under God and become good stewards of it. It does not belong to either of them exclusively. They must share it equitably and live as good neighbors with one another. Both nations must do justice, love mercy, and walk humbly with God (Micah 6:8). [31]

It is hard to conceive of a just co-existence when the Palestinian State declares itself under Islamic Law, and the Israeli State considers itself the homeland of all Jews. It will take more than an appeal to justice to bring about the solution Ateek envisions. It will require a radical transformation of both Arabs and Jews, by the Spirit of God, that only Jesus makes possible. This will be assisted by identificational repentance, which recognizes injustices done by both sides in the Middle East conflict and brings the forgiveness of God to bear upon all parties. Many, like Ateek, have been deprived of their homes and suffered the trauma of displacement in the Middle

East conflict. Much spiritual healing is needed to overcome roots of bitterness that have penetrated the hearts of Arabs and Jews, because of the conflict.

Secular Materialism

Despite the overlay of religiosity that pervades the Holy Land and many of its people, secular materialism motivates the majority. Jesus said: "Where your treasure is, there will be your heart also." [32] The goal of an average Israeli and others in the Holy Land is to own a cottage or villa in suburbia, with an ornamental garden in a yard surrounded by a white picket fence. More people realize this dream, since the gross domestic income has risen to $14,700 per capita, which is three times that of the past generation. [33] The "good life" is still the dream of most who live in there. Many acquire middle class status with multiple cars, cable television and higher education, along with, sarcastically, resultant western "blessings" of divorce, abortion and empty lives. Shopping malls abound throughout the land, with a typical American variety of fast foods like McDonalds, Pizza Hut and Kentucky Fried Chicken. Visa cards and other forms of credit spending exert the usual pressures on household budgets of young Israeli couples.

The fast pace of modernization leads inevitably to social and religious conflict, as Orthodox Jewish communities and Muslim fundamentalists seek to lead people back to ethical moorings of the past. These groups oppose abortion and artificial birth control. And they are quickly out-populating secular Jews, as they bear six to twelve children per family.

Closure of the West Bank and Gaza, resulting from terrorist bombings, prevented Arab workers from entering Israel. The economic situation in the Palestinian Authority remains critical. Half of the work force is unemployed, and the gross national product was only $2,800 for the West Bank and $2,400 for Gaza in 1997. [34]

Over 250,000 foreign workers entered Israel from Eastern Europe, Latin America and Southeast Asia due to the closure. Half of these illegally remain in Israel.[35] Their presence has increased existing trade in prostitution to an estimated 25,000 paid sexual transactions every day in the Jewish homeland.[36]

Secular materialism leaves a gapping void in the hearts of many in the Holy Land after the initial attraction wears off, yet bills still have to be paid. While people try to fill their void with every form of music, art, literature and a variety of exotic religions and philosophies, nothing meets the need like Jesus! Many foreign workers and immigrants gravitate toward international congregations throughout the land. Therefore, this is one of the most fertile areas for church planting, not only in Hebrew, Arabic and English, but also in Russian, Rumanian, Spanish, Amharic, Mandarin and other languages. Cable television carries Christian broadcasting into many areas, giving the general public access to the Gospel. Effective outreach takes place in Eilat and other areas of high tourist concentration. Though the spirit of Mammon is still alive in the Holy Land, it can be driven out through strategic level spiritual warfare in prayer that binds the enemy. As in every century and culture, those who are freed from enslavement of secular materialism find that nothing fills the empty heart like Jesus.

Spiritism

It came as a surprise to me that New Age philosophy, Hinduism, Buddhism and gurus are the "in thing" for Israeli intelligentsia. Many Jewish young people leave the country once they serve their mandatory army service. Some travel to the East, to India and Thailand, exploring eastern religions. Those who return to Israel are unaware that these eastern religions contradict the unity of God, proclaimed in Judaism.

Judaism, Islam and even traditional churches have within their religious systems forms of occult practice. Kabala, in Judaism, is replete with numerology and symbolism bordering on the occult. Several Muslim sheiks in Arab villages of Galilee are popular for their *ihjab,* or incantations, and miracle cures, using verses from the Quran. One Catholic priest in Galilee was famous for finding dead bodies and lost objects through visions. The general population accepts these practices but are unable to distinguish if they are from God or from the Devil. Others feel they are foolishness but revert to them when under pressure, in an attempt to gain control over life's misfortunes.

Women in the Middle East, particularly Bedouin, seek the aid of occult practitioners, to supplement treatments of local doctors and hospitals. One Bedouin woman I knew of went to a Sheik for an *ihjab* after a back operation that left her in pain. She and other women paid generously for supposed miracle cures. Yet several became sick in the car on the way home. Their tribe is embroiled in blood revenge, which takes the lives of their sons, husbands and friends on a yearly basis. It is a war between cousins and began over jealousy and grudges of their mothers, all of whom are under a pall of the occult.

The unfortunate payoff for those who follow such practices is sleeplessness, nightmares, suicidal thoughts and murder. A highly educated man from the Middle East, who holds an important position in the area, exclaimed as he watched violence reported on television, "Why do people do such terrible things?" I tried to explain that men often act violently and irrationally because they've surrendered themselves to spirits other than the one true God. The influence of spiritism is subtle, but very real in the Holy Land. It can be overcome by the power of the Holy Spirit, which Jesus gives to those who trust him for salvation and deliverance. Many believers who come into the church need freeing from demonic oppression and unclean habits. Spiritual warfare prayer is a priority in church planting in the Holy Land, due to a high level of demonic activity among the people.

Patriarchal Society

Despite rapid modernization in the Holy Land, with modern highways, new cars, cable television, faxes, the internet and e-mail, the inner psyche of the people still finds its source in a patriarchal society. This is especially true for the Arab population and the Eastern or Sephardic Jews, who come from Arab countries. George Jennings describes how this effects decision making and leadership:

> This form of government is accomplished through the tribal leader and the council of elders from the various clans. The tribal shaykh is not an autocrat, though within the bounds of tribal custom he has considerable power. He must use it, however, in accordance with the tribe's traditional interpretation of its interests, so that he is bound by well-remembered precedents as well as by tribal opinion, expressed through the elders whom he must consult before embarking upon any course of action. Leadership is passed on to the shaykh's son or, if he is not acceptable, to someone else in the shaykh's family. The qualities sought in a tribal leader are courage, tempered by caution and wisdom; wealth, to enable him to be generous; a father attitude toward his people; firm, but just and kind.[37]

The mindset of the patriarch is passed on into modern society through the centuries as people move from nomadic life to the villages and then into the cities. This especially applies to Muslim Arabs in the Holy Land, whom you find building high-rise apartments for the whole family to live in.

> A long-standing view is that the Middle Eastern family is a patrilocal (living in or adjacent to the father's residence) extended group, living in one household or connected dwellings. This

means a man, his wife, their unmarried children, and their married sons with their wives and children.

Also in this typical arrangement is "rule" by the father or eldest male (patriarchy), as well as reckoning a family by the father's name. As to marriage, preference has been for mating within the family. Especially ideal, when possible, is marriage for cousins, through their father's lineage. This structure encapsulates the ideal family relationship pattern; it is what a family should be, even though the reality is seldom present today.[38]

The closeness of a patriarchal family commends itself, compared to the scattering and disunity of western families. But it unfortunately fosters a defect that causes endless strife in homes of Arabs in the Holy Land. Scriptures teach: "at the beginning the Creator 'made them male and female,' and said, 'For this reason a man will leave his father and mother and be united to his wife, and the two will become one flesh'."[39] In Arab homes, the man does not leave father or mother, but instead lives with his parents. His wife often becomes a servant to her mother-in-law. Naturally, this creates strife. The practice of marrying two brothers or sisters with two from another family, or *bedel* (Arabic, "swapping",) means if one couple does not get along and the wife leaves, then the other wife is sent away with her also, even though she wants to stay with her husband.

Rapid transition in Israel today, from village life to urban city-dwelling, or to university study, places great strain on a traditional family, especially for Arabs. Young men gain financial independence through study and work, but young women become acquainted with men of whom the patriarchal family may not approve. If an unmarried young Arab woman becomes sexually involved before marriage, it can bring dishonor to the entire family. And unfortunately, even in this modern age, it may result in her death at the hands of her father or another close relative. The same is true of women who are suspected of being unfaithful to their husbands. George Jennings relates the results of expectations of a patriarchal society on the morals of young women:

> The young woman now poses a significant threat to the good name and the integrity of her family. Should a misstep occur, she may be faced with death at the hand of father or older brother.[40]

Hardly a week passed by during our life in the Holy Land when a newspaper did not report the death of an Arab girl or wife at the hands of her relatives, for cases of "honor." Lovers in the Jewish community, all too frequently, settle arguments with an Uzi submachine gun, and the woman is usually the looser. Women's rights are still a major issue in Israel today, because of so many senseless killings.

Deep psychological damage is perpetrated on Muslim women, since the Quran allows beating of a wife. She is considered property of the husband, and her value is legally worth only half that of a man. She can be divorced readily or be made to submit to the humiliation of a second, third or fourth wife being brought into the home. This humiliation causes bitterness and rivalry among all the wives and their offspring, as they vie for attention and affection of the father, whose loyalties are divided. Unfortunately, this low estimate of women carries over into Christian Arab homes, where I have heard male children cursing their mothers and sisters, while men looked on with amusement.

A significant part of my ministry has been assisting clergy and social welfare workers in finding homes for girls in difficulty with their families. This is an obligation for a Christian worker to take seriously, since to neglect it could mean harm or death to the girl or woman. One evening, many years ago, a social worker appeared at our door with a young girl. She had grown up in an orphanage because her mother was driven to suicide by a jealous husband.

The father refused to accept the daughter and threatened not to give the girl any inheritance. I told him, "Fine. When you die, I will sue your estate and take the money to raise your daughter!" The next day he called the social worker and me to come to his lawyer's office. He signed an amended will to include his daughter, without protest. This is only one of several cases in which we had to intervene to assist girls in dysfunctional family settings.

Rapid transition threatens authority in a patriarchal society. Nevertheless, male dominance still maintains a strong bastion in the Holy Land, in both Arab and Jewish homes. A church planter must know how to pay honor to whom honor is due in approaching families with the Gospel. If the elder male is positively influenced, he can be instrumental in leading the rest of the family to the Lord. If not, he can be a formidable opponent. At a minimum, if treated with respect, he may allow others in the family to listen and respond to the Gospel.

Tribal Loyalties

Loyalty to one's ancestral group, whether based on religion, nationality or language, remains a characteristic of social ties in the Holy Land. Ancient tribal loyalties still run deep, though on the surface communities appear modern and advanced. George Jennings observes wisely: "loyalties to kinship groups which have a common ancestral father, who lived perhaps between three and seven generations before, is common in Middle Eastern groups."[41] There was a time when it appeared the power of the extended family, or the *hamula* (Arabic) or *mishpacha murchedet* (Hebrew), was being broken by political alliances. But the rise of both Muslim and Jewish fanaticism forces people back to group loyalties.

Tribal loyalties affect the make-up of local churches, especially in Arabic speaking areas. Villages and communities are structured around family groups. A pastor usually finds it much easier to attract people from his own family or tribe. When conflicts arise in the church, people instinctively side with their family, regardless of the situation. If a matter is not resolved to someone's liking, the entire family usually leaves in protest. Almost every Arab church I know experienced a split because of family loyalty.

On the positive side, hospitality to strangers and newcomers remains a common characteristic of many Arab and Jewish homes in the Holy Land. A guest customarily receives a cold drink of fruit juice, followed by fruit and sometimes cake. The visit ends with a cup of strong coffee. A guest is made to feel at home and conflict is usually avoided. Such ingratiating treatment makes it difficult for newcomers to ascertain the motivations of his hosts. Jesus admonition: "find someone worthy enough to have you as their guest and stay with them until you leave" is still relevant for church planters in the highly tribal mindset of the Holy Land.[42] If you make the mistake of entering the home of a person of bad reputation, or of a rival clan, you can affect your ministry negatively for years to come. On the other hand, if you choose your first contact wisely and find a "man of peace," your host can attract people to future ministries, which can lead to a church planting movement.

Oral Communicators

It would be natural to assume with a literacy rate of 92% in Israel and 70% in the West Bank and Gaza, the people of the Holy Land would communicate as logical thinkers.[43] Not so! Experience shows that people in the Holy Land communicate orally. When you first see two Arabs or Jews talking with each other, you get the impression they are having a fight! Hand waving, facial expressions and shouting all combine to make the expatriate think combat is imminent. Then, before you know it, they part smiling! Cellular phones quickly became so popular in Israel that it was necessary to pass a law prohibiting their use while driving a car. The tendency for people to speak with their hands made it dangerous to hold a phone and the steering wheel at the same time!

True, the average Jewish home has a large library of books and Israelis are avid readers. But religious thought is often couched in parable or riddle, as it is with oral communicators. Prayers are chanted as the body sways, bringing to mind those who returned from exile riding on camels.

Arabs, though literate, also think and act as oral communicators. Morroe Berger explains:

> The Arab's virtual obsession with oral functions can hardly escape notice; it strikes the observer in Arab reverence for language and oral arts as well as in the Arab attitude toward food.[44]

Ask an Arab religious man, whether a Muslim sheik or a Christian priest, to quote a verse of his sacred scripture. He chants it! Story telling is an obsession for Arabs. I spent many hours listening to Arab fables in my frequent visits to the villages of Galilee. Logical thought often escapes the Arab Muslim, but place a truth in story form and he will grasp it. Those who wish to share the truth about God in Christ in the Holy Land need to learn the art of storytelling the Gospel. This is why Jesus taught in parables and stories with moral content, requiring a decision on the part of the discerning listener.

Semitic Languages

Probably the most formidable obstacle for expatriate evangelicals to overcome in planting a church in the Holy Land is the language. People will tell you it takes two lifetimes to learn Hebrew and three to learn Arabic! Both Semitic languages, they share the same trilateral consonant base, but use different scripts. Hebrew lay almost dormant for 1900 years during the exile from the Holy Land, following the destruction of Jerusalem in AD 70. It was used only for religious purposes and was spoken in small Jewish ghettos in the Diaspora. It revived with the turn of the 20th Century and Zionist movement to resettle the land. Now, modern Hebrew is the spoken language of most Israelis. It relates to ancient Biblical Hebrew but incorporates numerous foreign loan words. Arabic, on the other hand, remained the language of medicine, astronomy, geography and philosophy throughout the Middle Ages. It is said to have around two million words in its vocabulary. Either language is a challenge to Westerners, since it has no equivalents in our Latin based languages.

I am amazed at how the shape and sound of each of these languages affects the mentality and life-style of Jews and Arabs, and how it shapes their reactions to each other. Hebrew script, in its printed form, is written as a series of squares; each letter standing alone. It lends itself to sharp, logical thinking. Hebrew Scriptures, the *Torah*, is composed of teaching and laws which regulate life of Jewish people. Their life is therefore based on law and reciprocity. They tend to say what they think and mean what they say. And they are formidable strategists.

Arabic, on the other hand, is a series of swirls, all interconnected. Arabic calligraphy lines the walls of mosques, impressing upon worshippers the words of their scripture, the Quran, which is *kalaam allah,* or the "speech of God." Muslim religious thought is *ilm al-kalaam,* or the "science of speech." To them, an argument is not won by logic but by the fluency and force of the words with which it is pursued.

Therefore, law and speech clash with each other as Jews and Muslims seek to relate. It is no wonder that outside mediators are necessary to help Jews and Arabs come to terms in political struggles. Evangelicals must continue to play the role of mediators, as they see each culture as estranged children of God, who need to know the peace Jesus gives through the Holy Spirit.

Divisive Spirit

Tension pervades the atmosphere in the Holy Land, due to the above characteristics of its people. You feel it in the aggressive way people drive cars. Road accidents remain the greatest killer there. Merely standing in line at a bank or grocery store can be a challenge to one's patience, as each customer jostles to get ahead of others, and clerks treat you with indifference. Since much of the economy depends on tourist trade, government tour guides and store clerks are beginning to receive special training in relating to visitors in a polite manner. Jews and Arabs simply live like walking time bombs ready to explode at the least provocation. This comes as a surprise when you know that each can be very hospitable under normal situations. George Jennings explains the reasons behind this apparent contradiction:

> . . . In the desert, hospitality comes about as a means of overcoming the individual's helplessness in so harsh an environment. In the villages and cities, it has a different function; it reduces the tendency of the ever-present hostility to burst into violence at every moment. Exaggerated hospitality and politeness are reactions to exaggerated hostility, at least in part.
>
> Most Middle Eastern life is filled with interpersonal rivalry—tribal feuds in the desert, family and village feuds in the settled communities, and inter-group hostility—more controlled, however—in the urban places. Local political writers never tire of stressing not only brotherhood but also contentiousness, which they blame, together with imperialism, for the Middle Eastern failure to achieve total unity. Poverty and frustration—sexual as well as economic and political, as linked with religious beliefs—are so pervasive that there is a great deal of what has been called "free-floating" hostility.
>
> Politeness then, is a means of maintaining enough distance to prevent aggressive tendencies from becoming reality.

Hospitality and generosity are means of demonstrating friend-liness; they ward off expected aggression.

Conflict is ever on the verge of breaking out, so that inter-personal relations seem to be largely directed at avoiding or covering up the slightest tendency toward the expression of difference . . . People seem to sense that the slightest tendency to verbal disagreement may easily lead to unmanageable dis-cord, and must therefore be suppressed or channeled through a mediator. [44]

Through long centuries of being subjected people, under for-eign domination, people of the Holy Land have learned by in-stinct the practice of "divide and conquer." Some have an instinctive ability for planting seeds of discord among brothers. This is par-ticularly common in Muslim families.

Distrust is unfortunately integral to the religion of Islam. The Quran indicates that if man thinks he can deceive God, God will deceive him. It also indicates that God can change verses of the Quran by abrogating one verse and sending down a better one.[45] In the Jewish community, people remain continually suspicious of their own leaders as newspapers weekly describe the latest embezzlement or financial scandal. This spirit of discord spills over into the Arab Christian community also, causing distrust and conflict.

An evangelical Christian and church planter comes into this divisive atmosphere with the message of a God of justice and mercy, revealed in Jesus of Nazareth. Our obligation is to be trusting friends and mediators in an atmosphere ripe with potential disaster. So we must continually be on guard, lest we exacerbate the already divi-sive spirit prevailing in the land. It takes the wisdom of Solomon, the patience of Job and the love of the Lord Jesus Christ to live as mediators in such an explosive atmosphere. Church planters need to be surrounded by a network of spiritual prayer warriors, for protection from the divisiveness that destroys unity.

War

Four times, in the over thirty years we have lived in the Holy Land, the accumulation of the above factors erupted into war. A combination of land, tribal religion and politics certainly makes for a volatile mixture! My unfortunate observation is that if Jews and Arabs did not have each other to fight, they would fight among themselves, as unfortunately Christians have done over the centuries. They share all the weaknesses of sinful humanity. Jennings sums up the factors leading to the failure of peacemakers:

> Regionalism, the existence of established ruling classes in the separate countries, foreign control, the power of traditional loyalties (religious, ethnic, kinship), urban-rural-nomadic differences, and repressive conditions (economic, political, and social) are some of the factors that have frustrated the efforts of nationalists to unify the existing entities within most individual countries, let alone some degree of harmony between nations of the Middle East.[46]

It is easy for an evangelical church planter to be critical of weaknesses of churches in the Holy Land, if he or she forgets the damage and displacement wreaked on the area by periodic wars. We should marvel instead that the church has survived through the centuries and is growing there today.

War remains a likely danger for those who feel led to serve in the Holy Land. People are weary from the loss of loved ones, and they long for peace. But they continue to live and survive in a climate of tension. Every new home in Israel must be equipped with a "sealed room" and bomb shelter. All citizens receive gas masks. Still, life goes on. A businessman once asked me in Nazareth if I thought there was going to be another war soon? He said, "If you can guarantee me five years of peace, I can build a hotel and make a profit!"

While it is true, more people are killed in automobile accidents in any given year in Israel than are killed in war, as pent-up aggression is taken out at the wheel. This fact does not make the pain any less when young soldiers die in border skirmishes, and Arab youth are shot in riots against occupying forces. Every home suffers from the losses of war.

Still, a military spirit dominates the Holy Land. It is especially felt in the spring and summer, when from times past kings went out to war. This spirit all too easily divides Arabs and Jews into camps, as opposing enemies. Evangelical church planters and their prayer supporters must be careful not to allow themselves to be drawn into the opposing camps. The threat and reality of war opens the hearts of many to search for a way to peace. It is our opportunity to share the peace of God through Jesus that comes through the written Word and a personal encounter with the living Word, Jesus, who is Prince of Peace.

Some, claiming to be Christians, have distorted the true meaning of peace through warlike actions in the past, making our work more difficult. It takes those who are strong in heart and compassionate in love to overcome barriers created by war, whose clouds loom over the horizon for the 21st century as more Middle East countries acquire nuclear weapons and lethal gas. Developments in Islamic republics make an Armageddon scenario all too real. We could see the ultimate *jihad*, or Islamic holy war, fought over use of the Temple Mount in Jerusalem, in our time. The days of "rage and wonder" described by George Otis, Jr. in *The Last of the Giants* could become a reality.[47] Strategic level prayer must be focused on the Holy Land to overcome the spirit of Goliath that boasts against the living God and the Prince of Peace.

Refugee Status

Thousands of Arabs and Jews have been displaced from their homes and property as a result of war. More than half the population of Jordan and sizable numbers of inhabitants of Lebanon are refugees from recent wars between Arabs and Jews. Large refugee camps remain in the West Bank and Gaza. They continue to act as breeding grounds for poverty and deep resentment toward Israelis who displaced them. The hopeless situation of youths holed up in these camps contributes to desperation, recently resulting in several suicide bombings inside Israel proper. The plight of Palestinian refugees remains an unhealed sore in the psyche of Arabs. And Jews will never be at peace as long as camps remain. The refugee situation cries out for solution and remains a destabilizing factor in the region, even after a final settlement over Jerusalem is negotiated.

Jews of the Holy Land also suffer from centuries of refugee mentality. Many Jews living in Israel came as refugees from their countries of origin. Some, who formerly lived in Arab countries, were displaced because of the Arab-Israeli conflict. Over time negative experiences hardened some Jews against compassion for Arab refugees.

The irony of refugee status of many Palestinian Arabs in the region is they have become one of the most highly trained peoples in the Middle East, since United Nations schools in refugee camps provided universal education for children of refugees. Palestinians, similar to their Jewish cousins, are highly intelligent and energetic. They became the blue-collar and white-collar workers for Kuwait, Jordan, Lebanon and many other countries in the area. Many students rose to high academic levels and scattered around the world in what has been called the "Palestinian Diaspora."

Another feature of wars and resultant refugees fleeing conflicts is vast property they left behind. The Office of Absentee Properties, or *Amidar* as it is know locally in Israel, and the Government Land Authority, *Mikalkayeh*, remain caretakers of thousands of dunams[48] of land and a vast number of houses and buildings once owned by Arabs, who left as refugees during the 1948 war. Some of these properties are leased to Jews and Arabs who remained or settled in Israel. Sometimes deeds are traded for other lands and properties. The purpose behind these absentee property offices should be to hold lands and properties in the eventuality of a final settlement. But it is left to be seen if final status negotiations will properly compensate both Arabs and Jews for loses in the conflict.

Many Christian organizations labor in refugee camps, seeking to heal wounds of displacement. Every effort to aid both Arabs and Jews who suffer as refugees is to be commended. However, the ultimate solution must be resettlement of those deprived of homes and land. This does not have to entail radical solutions that will displace other people already living in the Holy Land. Prayer and wisdom must accompany all solutions, lest they create bigger problems.

An unusual situation which developed in my ministry touched me. We looked for housing for a Muslim who had received Jesus as Savior. Many Jews were unwilling to rent to him. Finally, one Jew, himself a refugee from Iran, on hearing the story of the Muslim believer, agreed to rent him a house. He said, "Your story touched my heart, since I too am a refugee!" Often, we who come to this war-torn land can act as mediators between the sons of Isaac and Ishmael.

Occupation Mentality

The Holy Land has suffered throughout history, from one foreign occupation to another. Romans, Byzantines, Muslims, Crusaders, Turks, British, and now depending upon your political orientation, Zionists, or Palestinians, have all occupied it! The people have lived under outside authority and power throughout their long history. Jews have experienced statehood for only fifty years, and Palestinians continue struggles to gain theirs. Foreign occupation has stifled local initiative through the centuries. Outside powers taxed people and conscripted youth into their armies.

This led to deception as a way of life, to survive politically and economically. Merchants practiced "four pocket" accounting: One pocket to bribe the official over you, one pocket to bribe the one under you, one pocket for taxes, and finally one pocket for yourself! It is little wonder therefore, that tax systems are often excessive and distrust is rampant. Partly because of these factors, people in the Holy Land did not show their wealth until recently. Yards and entrances to homes were deliberately left dirty and unkempt. Some threw garbage into the streets. Amazingly however, insides of homes would be washed and scrubbed daily!

Political change in the Middle East came usually through death of the conqueror or violent revolution. Foreigners, including church workers, were looked upon as potential spies for foreign powers. In fact, some countries in the past used clergymen and archeologists to "spy out the land" before military invasions. Local security trainees frequently engage people in political conversations and incite youth to illegal acts to open files on them and have leverage in the future.

When I first arrived in the Holy Land I wore a sunglasses case on my belt. I learned later, the elders in a remote village thought I had a radio in the case, to transmit messages to the White House! You convince some people, only with great difficulty, that you are not paid by your government. This makes a verbal witness imperative.

People who live under occupation constantly feel they are pawns of outside powers. They feel helpless to change their way of life. And occupation breeds contempt. Local church leaders hesitate to step out in church planting, fearing failure or loss of control, even after years of living in freedom. They caution expatriates to avoid any political involvement's that would jeopardize the church. We need to share the New Testament as good news for those living under occupation. When Jesus taught: "If any one forces you to go one mile, go with him two,"[49] he was teaching Jewish believers the ethics of dealing with occupying Roman soldiers. Jesus is the truth that sets men free.

On one occasion, the Israeli Occupation Force arrested a Palestinian Arab believer in the West Bank and imprisoned him. He felt alone and deserted, without hope. But one day a Jewish believer, serving in the Israeli army, saw the young Arab reading the Bible. He introduced himself as a believer and eventually gained the Arab's release. Outside the prison, they were able to meet together as believers. This story shows how Jesus can break down barriers between Jew and Arab caused by the occupation.

Two Traumatized People

The Holy Land has been called the "twice promised land." Some British politicians promised the land to the Jews, as a result of their Christian Zionist ideology and political expedients. Others promised the Arabs statehood, in return for support against the Turks during World War I. Both Jews and Arabs see their national and religious aspirations dependent on the same piece of land. The expatriate Evangelical will feel caught in the middle and pulled both ways by felt needs and aspirations of both the Arabs and Jews in this area. Once, while eating lunch in the dining hall of a prosperous kibbutz in Galilee, I innocently asked an older Jewish friend who lived there, "Whose land is the kibbutz built on?"

He exploded, "How dare you ask that question, after what you Americans did to the Indians!" Then I realized the land had belonged to Arabs before 1948, and I had touched a sore spot.

Many Jews and Arabs in the Holy Land today still feel the trauma of displacement and loss of loved ones. Before we judge, we need to admit our own past injustices. We cannot live continually in the past. There is a new desire in the hearts of many Jews and Arabs to settle past differences. The message of the Bible, that God forgives and changes men, needs to be shared continually. He alone heals broken heart of past traumas. This is proven every time a Jew or an Arab confesses Jesus as Savior and lets the peace of God flood his heart. Jesus breaks down the "middle wall of partition."

A Muslim believer in Jesus told me how he had once hated the Jews. But when he began to read the Bible, he felt the hatred leave his heart! His experience rings true to the promise in Ephesians 2:14: "Christ has made peace between Jews and Gentiles, and he has united us by breaking down the wall of hatred that separated us."[50] The miracle of new life in Christ can overcome challenges facing church planters in the Holy Land, if they work purposefully to understand and overcome them. I have watched in wonder and amazement as identificational repentance takes place when Jewish and Arab believers forgive each other for traumas and injustices of the past.

How have the above challenges facing evangelical Christians and church planters influenced church growth in the Holy Land? Has it led to a retreat of the Church, or to its growth? Can we look forward to anything but more violence and frustration in that land? Chapter Three presents positive signs for the 21st Century.

chapter three

Hope on the Horizon
for the 21st Century

Despite many challenges facing church planters in the Holy Land, I see many positive signs that give hope for the 21st Century. The Lord of the Harvest is preparing laborers for the harvest, which is already ripe for gathering. Many faithful workers, both local and expatriate, went before us, clearing the land, piling rocks on the borders, sowing seed and cultivating struggling plants through many difficulties. We are seeing obvious beginnings of notable changes in responsiveness of the people to the Gospel message. We began to see definite growth in churches during the last quarter of the 20th Century. Now, in a new century, church planters and those who support them in spiritual warfare prayer will see a growing harvest in this former spiritual wasteland.

Highly Trained and Motivated Young People

When we arrived in Nazareth in 1966, after a year of Arabic studies in Haifa, I noted the results of a youth revival from the

1950s. Efforts and prayers of expatriate church workers to restore the church, after World War II and 1948, had resulted in a movement of the Lord, motivating local youth to take leadership in church and school ministries. Dr. Dwight L. Baker describes the turning point in these young men's lives, during a summer camp outside Acre in 1952:

> . . . After a full day of activities the boys gathered around a camp fire each evening to participate in an evangelistic service. After each service an opportunity was given to the boys to commit their lives completely to the Lordship of the Master, in order to follow Him effectively in their daily lives. Such a decision was not easy, even though all of the boys were from nominally Christian homes. Their Christianity was traditional and carried no application to a life of sacrifice and service. To them, Jesus was a historical Christ and not a personal Savior. The last Sunday night service was over and the opportunity was extended for the last time before the camp broke up, but still courage was lacking. It was obvious that there was a struggle going on in the hearts and minds of several of the youths. A last challenge was made by the evangelist, in which he presented the possibilities of their lives transformed by the power of Christ and working as a positive force for good in their communities. As he was speaking, deliberately one, two, and then three, until eleven boys joined him in front of the fire indicating their desire to follow Christ regardless of any personal sacrifice it may cost them.[1]

He notes that a prayer meeting of concerned believers, led by Rev. Elmo Scoggins in Nazareth, impacted upon this dramatic turn in lives. These young men became future teachers in the Nazareth Baptist School, as well as evangelist-deacons and pastors of Nazareth Baptist Church and village centers around Galilee. Their children grew up and now lead Fellowship of Christian Students (FCSI), alongside sons and daughters of Jewish Messianic believers. These second-generation believers are leaders in summer camp programs and conduct country-wide student conferences. They formed a youth choir that travels from church to church. They also conduct weekly Bible studies to encourage and train new believers. Together, they participate with Jewish believers in national evangelistic campaigns, sharing literature and testimonies at rock concerts and art festivals in major cities around the country. These activities include students from all local denominations. Most marry other believers and support local congregations. They enter a variety of professions, including architecture, law, teaching, computer programming and counseling. Many enroll in Bible institutes and training programs in the country.

These highly trained young people are one of the brightest hopes on the horizon for the 21st Century in the Holy Land. In the words of Dr. Jack Hodges, former Baptist Representative in Nazareth, "They are running circles around most of the local churches, in mission and ministry activities!"[2]

Middle East Christian Leadership-AWEMA

The formation of Arab World Evangelical Minister's Association (AWEMA) is another hopeful sign on the horizon for the 21st Century. The idea of a fellowship of Arab Evangelical leaders, united for church planting and other causes, first began to take shape in informal meetings in Amsterdam's 1983 and 1986 conferences sponsored by Billy Graham. This led to the formation of Arab World Servants Fellowship (AWSF), which eventually met in Cyprus, in March 1992. AWEMA was formed to encourage fellowship of Christian ministers and for an evangelistic thrust among Arab speaking people worldwide. One of the emphases endorsed at this meeting was "cooperating with existing churches to launch evangelistic programs aimed at church planting in areas unreached by the Gospel."[3]

Arab evangelical leaders have communicated and had fellowship with one another regularly, since the signing of peace treaties between Israel and Egypt in 1979 and with Jordan in 1994. They share a vision for the future and try to deal with common problems. They adopted a statement on "Partnership in the Gospel," emphasizing church planting, after a consultation of leaders in March 1995. Contrary to the typical attitude of Arab Christian leadership in the past, which depended heavily on foreign financial support for churches, these young Arab leaders adopted a resolution to: "recognize financing is not the main problem—but vision and understanding of Church Planting is the main concern."[4]

The Church Planting Working Group presented the following :
PURPOSE
To take advantage of the current opportunities and open doors for church planting and encourage the development of the infrastructure and resources according to the needs of each project.

PRIMARY NEEDS
1. To raise the level of understanding of church planting as an evangelistic and mission strategy.
2. To help the local church formulate and implement their own church planting vision.
3. Research on fruitful and proven ways in which churches are being planted in the Arab world.
4. Identify and promote healthy ways of incorporating converts into churches.
5. We need to implement intensive church planting training seminars to train Christian workers.
6. We need to use creative new ways to strengthen the local church and encourage church planting through locals.
7. We need to make use of already existing and new media on church planting in Arabic and make it known to a wider circle.

Arab evangelical leaders from the West Bank, Jordan and Israel sponsored an area wide conference in July of 1995, on the Mount of Olives in Jerusalem. Bishara Awad, President of the Bethlehem Bible College, chaired the conference. Leaders of AWEMA, the Lausanne Committee, Open Doors and the Billy Graham Evangelistic Association took part.[5] Christian evangelical leaders attended from Egypt, Jordan, the Palestinian Authority and Israel. A spirit of celebration prevailed, despite a threat that the political situation could worsen, with radical Muslim fundamentalist opposition to the peace settlement. The goal of church planting unfortunately took back seat to more current issues, like closure of Palestinian territories and travel restrictions preventing Christians, along with other Arabs, from moving about freely. Leadership also shared anxiety over a large number of Arab Christians leaving territories and immigrating to the West. AWEMA will remain a significant sign of hope for the 21st century, if it keeps church planting as a primary goal and does not get side-tracked with more immediate political problems.

The Jewish Congregations, or "Kehilot"

The drama of beginning the Messianic Believers movement in Israel is a story resembling the Book of Acts. A handful of scattered Jewish believers in Jesus stood up to opposition and persecution from Orthodox Jews in Haifa, Tel Aviv and Jerusalem in 1965. Scandalous attacks in the press depicted these pioneer believers as traitors to their religious community, who used underhanded methods to win converts. A campaign of pressure against these "missionaries" finally succeeded in closing Bethel School in Haifa. Paranoia of the Jewish community would not tolerate Jewish children learning in a Christian school.

An event in the northern Hula valley was to forever change the situation for Jewish believers. Rosh Pina, a Jewish town, nestles at the foot of a mountain on which Safad, the traditional "city set on a hill" stood, high above the Sea of Galilee.[6] Formerly a British check-post and customs station, Rosh Pina housed a few hundred settlers, artists and former yeshiva students, where God worked a miracle in the early 1970s. Some were young immigrants from the USA and England. Others were native Israeli "sabras."[7]

All these students searched Scriptures to find a deeper meaning of life. Suddenly, Jesus began revealing himself through Scriptures as the true Messiah of Israel. In their excitement, these young men began sharing their discovery as "good news" with their family and friends in the area. The response was so enthusiastic and spectacular that people began traveling from around the country to visit the "brothers" in Rosh Pina. It was not long before the Chief Rabbi in a larger settlement town near Nazareth became concerned. He decided to snuff out this fire before it spread by sending a local gang up to Rosh Pina to teach these new believers a lesson. The hired thugs broke into the house where they were meeting, beat up the brothers, and terrorized their families.

One married believer sent his family to live with our neighbors in Nazareth, in the midst of the Arab Christian community, as a result of this persecution. This brother and his family eventually moved to Upper Nazareth, a Jewish settlement town on the hills overlooking the biblical city of Nazareth. He started a home Bible study for Jewish friends and my neighbors Dale and Anita Thorne, discipled these new Jewish Messianic believers and their congregation.

Other Jewish believers from Rosh Pina scattered as a result of persecution, similar to the dispersion in Acts 8, after the martyrdom of Stephen. A group moved to Tiberias and there became the core of a congregation of Jewish and expatriate believers which eventually grew to several hundred. Opponents burned the hotel where they met, so they moved the meeting to a forest above the city. Then a minister in a nearby Arab village offered his church for a meeting place when winter approached. Finally, they were able to meet in a youth hostel.

During this time, Jewish believers encountered employment problems. So a Baptist engineer started an electronics factory, to employ Jewish Messianic believers in the Tiberias area. This factory recently received a Ministry of Commerce award as the largest employer in the region.

A dynamic member of the Tiberias fellowship received blessing from the leadership to pursue a full time prayer and evangelism ministry around the country. This former fisherman from the Sea of Galilee now ministers to Arab and Jew alike, in a powerful prayer ministry. He makes contact with Jewish believers in kibbutzim and towns all over Galilee, where more Jewish Messianic fellowships are springing up.

Other Jewish Messianic believers from Rosh Pina moved to Jerusalem and there became the backbone of an historic ministry of Christ Church, whose congregation grew to several hundred members. The leaders participate in Arab-Jewish believer's conferences around the country and are involved in a nationwide prayer effort.

Altogether, from very humble beginnings after World War II and the establishment of the State of Israel, the number of Jewish Messianic believers in Jesus grew from a handful to about 6,000, meeting in over 100 congregations and house-churches by 1998. Many of these resulted from fuel added to the flames at Rosh Pina in the early 1970s. Little did the rabbi who sent thugs to harass a little group of believers suspect he would play such a vital role in scattering the fire of renewal in the Jewish Messianic movement around the Holy Land!

Leadership of the Jewish congregations established regional groups for fellowship and dealing with common problems. These leaders meet periodically and then gather their congregations together to celebrate Jewish holidays. Groups have grown so large now, it is difficult for them to find facilities in the country big enough for joint meetings! Over 1,000 believers gathered in the Knesset Rose Garden park for a nationwide *Shevuot* (Pentecost) celebration in May 1997. More than 1,500 Jewish believers and their families met for a national day of prayer and fasting at Baptist Village, during the Jewish New Year, in September 1997.[8]

They hesitate to be officially linked to any foreign fellowship, partly because of accusations of anti-mission groups in the country. Today, many Jewish Messianic leaders work for expatriate organizations. Nevertheless, they remain fiercely independent and insistent that the *guf ha Mashiach* (Hebrew: the body of Christ) govern its own affairs and remain basically Israeli. There has been fear in the past of "Judaizing" tendencies in some congregations, which excluded all Christian innovations and tended to be exclusive. In one extreme case, Judaizers required Gentiles to accept the Mosaic law before they could become Messianic believers. Many left congregations in masses, and some eventually converted back to Judaism. There remains a natural tendency of many secular Jewish believers to rediscover their roots in the Old Testament. Despite weaknesses and growing pains, the multiplication of Jewish Messianic congregations remain a sign of hope for the 21st century!

Arab-Jewish Reconciliation

An immediate and welcome by-product of persecution of Rosh Pina Messianic believers in the 1970s was their bonding to Arab Christian believers, who sheltered their families and offered them places to meet. Arab, Jewish and expatriate wives of believers also met during this time and formed the Galilee Women's Fellowship. These women have met monthly for the past twenty-five years, moving from church to church and various Christian homes and institutions in Galilee. Meetings include Bible study, prayer and fellowship. Their offerings support various ministries and institutions.

The Galilee Women's meeting led to joint meetings for their husbands and families at a semi-annual picnic and celebration at a central park in Galilee. These gatherings remind one of fellowship in the book of Acts, when believers of all backgrounds met to break bread. Their common bond in Jesus enables them today to overcome differences between Arab and Jew.

Another ministry of reconciliation between these two cultures is *Musalaha*, directed by Salim J. Munayer. It means "reconciliation" in Arabic. Munayer is an Israeli Arab who grew up in Lod, the biblical Lydda, in a mixed Arab-Jewish community. After Munayer became a believer in Jesus in 1977, he began to realize the basic root cause of conflicts between Jew and Arab as sin and separation from God. He was discipled by a Jewish Messianic believer, who now serves on the board of *Musalaha*.[9] I remember Saleem Munayer as a young man who traveled from church to church with two Jewish believers in Jesus, appealing for reconciliation between Jews and Arabs. Munayer finished his Master degree at Fuller Theological Seminary and returned to Israel to form *Musalaha* with other like-minded Arab and Jewish believers. He built his philosophy on the need of both Jew and Arab to find a higher loyalty to Jesus, "outside the camp" of political and ethnic loyalties which tend to polarize:

> We, the Jewish and Palestinian believers in Israel are under tremendous pressure. One of the strongest influences in our lives is the loyalty to our respective communities. The small communities of Jewish and Palestinian believers have to deal with the crucial issues relating to the loyalty of their people of birth and at the same time their loyalty to their Lord, His commandments and His people . . .
>
> In regard to the loyalty towards our people we desire "to be inside the camp." Nevertheless, we have a higher requirement of loyalties and calling . . .

Today, Arab Palestinians and Israeli Jews are struggling with a golden calf. Both ethnic groups are making their ethnic and political loyalty of a higher level than God and His commandment. We have made our nation and our land a golden calf. If we want to bless our people like Moses did, we will have to go outside the camp to represent God's holiness, interceding for our people to seek Him and to find in Him the true answer to our struggles.

There is a price for this action found in Hebrews 13:13, "Let us, then, go to him outside the camp, bearing the disgrace he bore." If we are true disciples of Jesus we have to go outside the camp to speak about God's holiness, justice and righteousness, to be peacemakers to call for reconciliation between Arabs and Jews. It is our role to confront our people when they are in the wrong, and more than anything else, to intercede for our people that God will have mercy on us. This action is costly for all of us; we need the grace and love of God to do this.[10]

Munayer carries out his Biblical philosophy by directing various activities where Jewish and Arab believers can rub shoulders in practical ways, for a few days together. One such event is a trip to the Negev desert, where Jewish and Arab believers camp together and study Scriptures together, in light of the desert location, their heritage and how to survive. My daughter participated in one of these trips and testifies it brought Muslim, Christian and Jewish believers together in a common bond.

Musalaha recently published a series on differing views of Christian Arab Palestinian, Israeli Messianic Jew and Western Christians concerning theology of the Holy Land. While *The Bible and the Land: An Encounter* admits the lack of inclusion of a Christian Zionist view, it provides an introduction to the delicate subject of the land in the minds of many believers.[11]

The desire of Munayer and many other Jewish and Arab believers for reconciliation is an encouraging sign for the 21st century.

They merit all our prayers and support, in midst of continual turmoil.

The Russian Church

Long before collapse of the Soviet Union, mass immigration, or *aliya,* of Russian Jews back to Israel began to change the face of the Holy Land. Signs in Russian appeared on grocery stores. New suburbs sprouted up, and settlements were built to house the influx of immigrants. Russian was heard on the streets and on television and radio, which broadcast missile attack warnings during the Gulf War in Russian, along with Hebrew, Arabic, English and Spanish. Moscovites, Belarussians, Ukranians, Moldovians and Uzbekis studied Hebrew in *ulpanim,* special language schools set up for new immigrants.

Arabs of Galilee would have out-populated Jews in that region if it had not been for massive immigration of Russians in the 1990s. Housing rental values and property values doubled, placing a strain on the economy. Highly skilled Russians competed on the job market with native Jewish and Arab laborers. Many enterprising Russians, finding jobs limited, began selling souvenirs on the streets or playing classical music to entertain passers-by, in hopes of a small donation.

Russians brought with them not only professional and musical skills, they also brought a thirst to know Jewish heritage and the Bible. Thousands of Bibles and children's story-Bibles, in Russian, were distributed during cultural festivals in the country. Russians who were secret believers in the old country began seeking fellowship with Christians in the Holy Land. Greek Orthodox Churches in Arab cities and villages hosted numerous Russian visitors, who came to light a candle and pray. Russian congregations quickly sprang up alongside Arab and Jewish congregations. Estimates of the number of Christians among Russian immigrants today run as high as 20%. Some Russian Jews, because of seventy years of Communist anti-religious oppression and inter-marriage with Gentiles, were very open to the Gospel. At one point, the number of Russians turning to Christ was so high a Ministry of Religion representative put out a warning to church organizations not to evangelize them. "We are bringing them back here to make them Jews, and you are turning them into Christians!" he exclaimed.

Russian pastors immigrated to lead congregations. They came, not as professionally trained clergymen, but as doctors, engineers, and professors. One congregation in Haifa split over a leadership dispute. Now, two growing congregations share time in the same building! Nationwide, conferences gather hundreds of Russian believers for fellowship and teaching. Several Bible Colleges opened Russian language branches to meet the demand for training. A Russian influx has accounted for much of the growth of the Jewish Messianic church in the past decade. Their growing churches rank as another hopeful sign for the 21st century in the Holy Land.

The Fledgling Muslim Church

The *intifadha*, or Arab uprising on the West Bank against Israeli occupation, caused a shaking in the hearts of many Arabs. They experienced the hopelessness of trying to solve Arab-Jewish conflict by violence. Years of working in Israel and experiencing freedom to associate with Jews and Christians outside restrictions of the Muslim community opened the door to an alternative to radical Islam. The story of formation of one group of believers illustrates how God works through adversity.

When staff at a Christian retreat center decided to clean out their office, in the process they found many Arabic tracts and Gospel portions stored from years ago. I heard they might have to destroy them but asked them to wait. I asked a friend, who lived in a Jewish settlement on the West Bank, to meet me at the center. He drove up with a Jewish friend, in an old Volkswagen "Beetle," and we loaded the front trunk with old tracts. He and his friend proceeded to distribute them in Arab villages all over the West Bank. At one point they were detained by soldiers of the Israel Occupation Forces, who feared they were spreading seditious literature among the Arabs. A Druze officer read one of the pamphlets and said, "Oh, all these talk about is Jesus. Let them go!"

My friend took his old car to the garage one day for repairs and began sharing the message of Christ with a Muslim. He spoke in Hebrew and another Arab standing nearby translated into Arabic. That translator became the first believer, in the process! He then witnessed to his brother, a former terrorist, who also became a believer. So the fledgling Muslim church began to grow.

A young man from another village bought a used car. He found a pamphlet in the glove compartment telling about Jesus, with an address to write for more information. He wrote to receive a Bible and a study program. One day he walked into the office of the organization's representative and told him, "It is not enough for you to send me a Bible and a study course. I have become a Christian. You need to take me to church and teach me how to pray!" Then he returned to his village and shared his new faith with friends. His father and brother received the Lord. A friend who was a Muslim *sheikh*, accepted Christ and came under threats from his family, forcing him to move out of town. A meeting place, set up by Muslim-background believers, was fire-bombed, and the son of one of the leaders was struck by a car on his way to work one morning.

These above stories are being repeated in a number of places in Israel and Palestine, as Muslims decide to break with a past of hatred and violence and embrace the Gospel of love. Most Muslims who become believers in Jesus and begin reading the Bible lose their hatred for Jewish people. Other problems, such as multiple marriages, chain smoking, financial problems, habitual deception, conflict and lying take more time to solve. Radical spiritual formation of Muslim background believers requires intense spiritual warfare and mentoring.

But signs of a church planting movement are beginning to appear, as Muslims baptize each other and disciple their own leadership. This has met with understandable opposition from the Muslim religious establishment. Laws inherited from Islamic countries prevent large gatherings without police permission. These have kept Muslim-background believer's meetings small and mobile, thereby enhancing even more growth. Whole families are now coming to the Lord. Acknowledging these challenges, the fledgling Muslim church appears to be another bright hope for the 21st century in the Holy Land.

Renewal in the Traditional Churches

When Protestant church planters first entered the Holy Land in the nineteenth century, they hoped to inspire renewal in the ancient traditional Christian church. Instead, churches rejected the new believers, forcing them to join Protestant Evangelical churches instead. Today we see a process of slow acceptance of evangelical ideas and practices by a few innovative priests.

Father Elias Chacour, priest of the Melkite, or Greek Catholic Church, in Ibillin village in Galilee, is one of the more notable of these enlightened priests in the Holy Land. Father Chacour grew up in the village of Biram in northern Galilee, on the Lebanese border. The Israeli army evacuated this village after 1948, destroyed it, and prevented villagers from returning, despite a Supreme Court decision supporting their right of return. Father Chacour wrote about his pilgrimage of forgiveness for this tragedy in his book *Blood Brothers*, which became a best-seller. He documented more of his struggles to bring peace and reconciliation between Palestinians and Israelis in his later book *We Belong to the Land*.[12]

Through Chacour's tireless efforts and support of friends in Europe and the United States, he built both a Peace Center and the Prophet Elias High School in Ibillin village. More recently, he developed a junior college, which became the first Christian school of higher learning to receive recognition by the Ministry of Education. Chacour has cooperated with the Center of Religious Pluralism, Protestants and with others, in projects that will advance Bible knowledge among Arab and Jewish people of Galilee.

Another priest who innovates in an effort to revive the ancient church is Father Barnaba Ashkar of the Greek Orthodox Church of the Annunciation, at Mary's Well in Nazareth. Father Barnaba, formerly a Brethren and a Baptist, started a Sunday School for children of his parish, and began preaching sermons in his church. The Orthodox Church Council built a large community center to provide recreational facilities for youth and adults there. The Orthodox Center in Nazareth sponsors a yearly Christmas celebration, featuring Protestant choirs from around the world. Chacour and Ashkar are but two of many innovative priests in traditional churches, who promote renewal. A growing number of Orthodox and Catholic priests have studied with the Academy of Theological Studies, an academic level correspondence institute, and have received diplomas and degrees in Theology and Biblical Studies. Slowly, the atmosphere of reticence and hostility is giving way to a spirit of dialogue. This provides hope for real renewal within ancient churches in the 21st century.

International Congregations

Growth of international congregations in the Holy Land is another encouraging sign of hope on the horizon. Long neglected in strategy for church planting, English language and other language congregations are now on the cutting edge of what God is doing around the world. They have become a platform for ministry to many language groups, including local Jewish and Arab populations. Several international congregations deserve mention now and will be presented in more depth in Appendix B.

Baptist Village Congregation, which meets near Petach Tikvah, ministers in English to internationals in the Central Sharon, coastal plains area. The congregation experienced renewal under innovative leadership of Bob and Barbara Bradley, Southern Baptist Representatives, who transferred from Hong Kong in 1996. The congregation includes Filipinos, Africans, Asians and Israelis, as well as local English speaking embassy and industry personnel. They also hold a weekly Bible study fellowship for Russians. The congregation called Reverend Robert Rogers from the USA as pastor in 1999 and is now fully independent of foreign support. Another congregation made up of foreign embassy personnel meets in Herzlia, under leadership of the Episcopal-Anglican Church.

Two international congregations of note serve hundreds of expatriate English-speaking believers in Jerusalem. The first, Narkis Street Congregation, which was mentioned earlier, ministers to several hundred persons in its new facilities. Narkis Street is Baptist in affiliation but international and interdenominational in focus, under capable leadership of Rev. Charles Kopp and Dr. John Anthony, both veterans in the area. Narkis Street meets on Saturday mornings. Dr. Anthony introduced Sunday worship, due to popular demand from Christians in the area. Rev. Pat Hoaldridge developed a Hebrew language congregation that is now led by a Hebrew-speaking pastor. The Narkis Street building continues to be a target of Jewish extremists for fire-bombings and vandalism, which testifies to its success in outreach to the community.

The second, King of Kings Congregation, is the "Sunday night event" in Jerusalem. Kings of Kings meets in the West Jerusalem YMCA and is a gathering place for hundreds of English-speaking worshippers, some of whom travel from as far away as Tel Aviv to attend. The meeting is one of celebration and praise, oriented with

Bible teaching by Rev. Wayne Hilsden and Chuck Cowen. They expanded to two services to accommodate a large number of worshippers, after they instituted cell groups.

A newcomer to the north, Mount Carmel Congregation, or *Kehilat HaCarmel*, is one of the fastest growing congregations in Galilee. Rev. David Davies and other leaders are active in drug rehabilitation ministries. English speaking residents from around Western Galilee and Haifa attend services. They broke ground in 1996 for a new meeting place, on land behind Stella Carmel Retreat Center. Reverend David Wilkinson, author of *The Cross and the Switchblade* was keynote speaker at the dedication of their building in 1998.

Other language congregations, particularly Spanish, are springing up around the country, to minister to the thousands of workers from South America who came to Israel in the period during closure of the West Bank. Many of these congregations face threat of deportation of members, since their work visas have expired. Despite this possibility, they continue to minister dynamically, in a variety of languages. One large congregation of Spanish-speaking believers in Tel Aviv outgrew their facilities and divided into several Baptist and Pentecostal groups in 1997.

These international congregations set an example for local Arab and Hebrew congregations in innovative ministries. Some join local associations and conventions and provide role models for local Israelis and Arabs, by stewardship of their finances and evangelical fervor.

Active Evangelistic Outreach

The decade coming up to the year 2000 saw an explosion of evangelistic outreach in Israel-Palestine, unparalleled since the 1st century. Jewish and Arab young people formed a nationwide evangelistic outreach, which actively conducts literature distribution and witness campaigns during rock concerts and cultural festivals around the country. They distribute hundreds of thousands of Scripture leaflets and thousands of Bibles and New Testaments yearly, from Eilat to Acre. Amazingly, secular Israelis who attend such events receive this literature willingly, and many engage believers in conversation about spiritual matters. Viewers of Middle East Television (METV) request hundreds of Bibles in Arabic and Hebrew yearly. METV, an affiliate of CBN, airs on cable television around the country.

The Billy Graham Evangelistic Crusade in San Juan, Puerto Rico was broadcast live by satellite in March 1995. A number of churches and denominations, who were members of the United Christian Council in Israel and the West Bank (UCCI), cooperated to record and distribute videos of the live satellite broadcast. Victor Hashweh, international secretary of AWEMA, served as Dr. Graham's Arabic interpreter. Over 3,000 people attended, at six local evangelistic venues, including Jerusalem, Bethlehem and Nazareth. At least 60 made decisions for spiritual birth or rededication to Christ. Middle East Television later carried the programs. Over 300,000 viewed the broadcasts in Egypt, and other thousands watched in Jordan and Lebanon.[13]

One Bible Correspondence Course in Arabic reported over 10,000 persons subscribing to its lessons. 6000 were Muslims. At least ten percent indicated they were believers in Jesus.[14] Another Bible course reported at least 1,000 Muslims who indicated their faith in Jesus. Granted, most of these "secret believers" are not willing to declare their faith publicly, for fear of family or community opposition. They represent a potential harvest for the 21st century.

Global Missions Fellowship (GMF) of Dallas, Texas sponsored the most recent cooperative adventure in evangelism and church planting, in cooperation with the Association of Baptist Churches in Israel. GMF enlists laypersons who spend a week overseas making a religious survey in target communities and sharing the Gospel alongside local believers who act as interpreters. They led a training seminar for local pastors and lay people in preparation for this ministry. GMF and local believers from various churches sent teams into Haifa, Acre and Nazareth, to make door-to-door visits in the Arabic speaking areas. Several hundred persons indicated acceptance of Christ, and two new preaching centers started in 1994 and 1995. One of the challenges in this form of church planting is maintaining enthusiasm and the follow-up necessary after the foreign team leaves. It gives foreign believers an opportunity to share the Gospel in a cross-cultural situation and encourages local believers by helping them see they are not alone in their efforts.

Other organizations, such as Operation Mobilization (OM), carry on a systematic and culturally sensitive visitation program in Arab villages and cities. They find a high level of receptivity to Bible-based literature and occasionally locate Muslims who commit their lives to Christ. They then encourage these isolated believers by follow-up visits. But networking Muslims with other believers is problematic, due to the high level of distrust in a Muslim community.

A countrywide survey conducted by DAWN (Disciple a Whole Nation) in 1993 indicated a total of 104 Evangelical congregations in Israel. Twenty-five of these had started in the past ten years. Surprising results showed that Churches of Christ started nine new congregations, Messianic believers six new congregations and Assemblies of God five new congregations, all in ten years previous to the survey. Altogether, there existed fifty-seven Arabic congregations, thirty-three Hebrew, six English and eight others, for a total of 104.[15] At this writing, the number of Hebrew congregations and house-groups increased to 100, or a 200% increase in the past five years! The total number of all congregations and house-groups combined increased to 200, or an increase of 92%.

House-groups are being opened at such a pace that it is almost impossible to keep up with their numbers. A major difficulty encountered by DAWN was lack of a local person, or a "John Knoxer," willing to take responsibility for follow-up of the survey, which will mobilize resources and personnel to plant churches in unreached areas. Nevertheless, DAWN discovered groups who take church planting seriously. Their methods serve as a model for reaping a harvest in the Holy Land in the 21st century. Some of these models are included in Appendix B.

The most recent survey of Messianic Jewish congregations was compiled in 1998-1999, by the Caspari Center in Jerusalem, and is entitled *Facts and Myths about Messianic Congregations in Israel.* This survey conducted by Kai Kjaer Hansen and Bodil F. Skjott includes information on 82 congregations and house-groups. They indicate that of 57 groups started in the 1990s, most cater to Russian immigrants.[16]

Current opposition by radical religious elements highlights the success of active evangelistic outreach in the Holy Land. Anti-mission groups now claim there are 20,000 Jewish believers in Jesus in Israel! A political and religious leader in the Knesset, or Israeli parliament, proposed a bill in March 1997 to outlaw possession, printing and distribution of literature designed to cause people to change their religion. The legislation was proposed in reaction to a mass mailing from abroad of a Messianic book to Israelis. The bill, if made law, would lead to a one year jail sentence for violators. The "anti-missionary bill" targeted Jewish believers in Jesus, making their non-profit organizations illegal. Public and international outcry against this proposed law caused it to die in committee. Messianic leadership in the land formed the Messianic Action Committee (MAC) to disseminate information to the Israeli public and other countries, to make them aware of the proposed legislation's detrimental affect on religious liberty.

Radical religious and political elements tried to hold the peace process hostage by threatening to withdraw from the government if the bill was not passed. At this writing another bill is being circulated among members of the Knesset that would give a five year prison sentence to anyone convicted of persuading another person to his religion. If such a bill were to become law, which is very unlikely, it could be used against Orthodox Jews as well as against Messianic believers in Jesus. A police inspector who had been investigating charges against believers found there had been twice as many complaints against the Orthodox for aggressive religious persuasion, as against Messianic groups, during the same period of time![17]

I predict these attempted bills will encourage rather than defeat evangelistic activity, similar to what happened when the infamous Abramovich "anti-missionary bill" was passed about twenty years ago. This social welfare law imposed a fine on persons who led a minor to convert to another religion or used material enticement to lead to conversion. The bill was never put into use. I discovered, in a study, that our churches baptized twice as many new believers, in five years following the law, as it did in ten years previous to the law! It is clear such legislation makes believers count the cost and redouble their efforts.

An unexpected result of many attempts to pass anti-missionary legislation has been recognition of the Messianic Action Committee (MAC) as a legal non-profit friendly society, or *Amuta*, by the Israel Minister of Interior, in July 1999. What had been intended to destroy the Messianic movement, in fact resulted instead in the Israel Government officially recognizing the existence of Messianic Judaism.[18]

Theological Education

A number of theological institutes, Bible colleges and discipleship programs offer in-country training for the growing body of believers in the Holy Land. The leading evangelical institution in the Arab sector, particularly in the West Bank, is Bethlehem Bible College (BBC). Evangelical leaders established the college in 1979, to train teachers of religion for public schools there. Baptists, Mennonites and others assisted Dr. Bishara Awad, the president, by providing teachers and curriculum materials in Arabic. The BBC received endorsement from all Protestant Evangelical communities, as well as the goodwill of ancient traditional churches in the area.

They recently raised over one million dollars to purchase a new campus, which had housed the former Helen Keller institution. The BBC enrolled twenty students for the Fall 1996 semester, which is remarkable, considering restrictions placed upon them in the unsettled political climate in the West Bank. In 1999, it enrolled over 130 students in various programs and graduated 21 leaders.

The college serves today as a meeting place for much of the area's evangelical activity. They inaugurated a community library and a Christian center to serve as a Bible distribution center in the region.[19] The BBC also taught extension courses in Haifa and Nazareth. It cooperated with Theological Institute of the Baptist Convention (TI) and the Church of the Nazarene in these efforts. TI (formerly Christian Service Training Center, or CSTC) was established in 1965 by Dr. Dwight L. Baker, to provide off-campus training to Arab believers scattered in towns and villages of Galilee. TI adopted the program of the International Institute of Biblical Studies (IIBS) in 1994.

IIBS was a decentralized, multi-level, programmed study effort developed by Dr. Weldon Viertel, formerly of the Philippine Baptist Seminary. IIBS offers off-campus extension training for groups of 5-15 students on basic discipleship, leadership training and Bible College courses up to a Master of Biblical Studies. Approximately 30 Arab students trained with IIBS, in four centers in Galilee. The program had the advantage of flexibility in curriculum and location. It can meet in homes, churches and other locations where students can gather.

Though it was limited to offering only one or two courses per semester, it did not compete with campus programs, but allowed pastors and laymen to train on location, without leaving their work, families and churches. So it acted as a feeder to campus programs, for students who desire to study full-time. It was a home study program using programmed textbooks and tutor-guided seminars for testing and discussion of lessons. IIBS also cooperated with the Bethlehem Bible College in offering courses in the Theological Institute in Haifa. Present plans are to open a branch of the Bethlehem Bible College in Galilee. The IIBS moved its library and offices to Jerusalem in 1999, to combine efforts with the Academy of Theological Studies and to upgrade curriculum by correspondence in Arabic.

The leading campus program in the Hebrew sector is the Israel College of the Bible, formerly King of Kings Colleges (KOK), with campuses in Jerusalem and Jaffa of Tel Aviv. The program was directed by the late Ilan Zamir, a Messianic Jewish believer in Jesus, who was a second-generation *sabra*, or native Israeli. Zamir, with the encouragement of the King of Kings Congregation and the Pentecostal Churches of Canada and other denominations, gathered a highly qualified faculty and staff and accumulated a sizable library for the college. This effort resulted in the KOK being recognized on first sitting by the Asian Schools of Theology Accreditation Association in 1996. They graduated about 15 students in 1996, many of whom were native Israelis.

Casbari Center in Jerusalem is carrying on another notable Bible training effort. Caspari uses TELEM curriculum in Hebrew. TELEM uses a home study-seminar method similar to the IIBS, but in Hebrew in centers from Eilat to Haifa. They teach at the pre-college level and have expanded into Russian.[20]

Other fine examples are Nativiya Center in Jerusalem, which also conducts a training program, but it is modeled on the Jewish Yeshiva pattern for Messianic Jews. Assemblies of God Bible School in Haifa trained more than ten young Arab pastors who serve in congregations in Israel and the West Bank. Other groups such as MAOZ in Ramat HaSharon sponsors yearly conferences for Jewish and Arab pastors and leaders. A caution must be noted that the multiplicity of training options needs to be coordinated, for the benefit of students, rather than only teaching a certain brand of denominational theology. This is a particular danger in the Arab sector. Nevertheless, these Bible training programs, and others in the Holy Land, offer an encouraging sign of hope for mature leadership in the 21st century.

The Peace Process

Signing a peace treaty between Israel and the Palestinian Liberation Organization (PLO) in May 1994 and between Israel and the Hashemite Kingdom of Jordan in October 1994 sent hopes soaring for most Jews and Arabs in the Holy Land. Unfortunately, the subsequent suicide bus bombings by Islamic radicals inside Israel and the assassination of Prime Minister Yitzhak Rabin by an Orthodox Jew in November 1995 seriously dampened enthusiasm. Violent clashes between Palestinian police and the Israeli Army, in reaction to opening a door to a 2000 year old Hasmonean tunnel alongside the Temple Mount in Jerusalem, placed further strain on cordial relations. Despite these and other setbacks, both sides appear determined to pursue the peace process as Paul Shalom Treat, director of the Center of Religious Pluralism in Nahariya explains:

> The peace process has been shaken to its roots. We are building, block by block, stone by stone, an edifice which will afford peace with security for both Jew and Palestinian . . . The peace must last because it is intrinsic for both sides. Peace will come, with security for all, because there is no alternative. All "publics" know this, be we Palestinians or Jews, be we Israeli Arabs or Jews. I am more hopeful for peace after the so-called Tunnel Incident. Why? Because illusions are being shed by Jews and Palestinians . . . We are tunneling our way toward peace with greater realism on all sides—or so it seems to me. Prudence and progress is the way.[21]

Suicide bombings of Mahaneh Yehuda market and Ben Yehuda pedestrian mall in 1997 brought the reconciliation process to a standstill. These terrorist acts by Hamas Islamic fundamentalists only exacerbated the Israel government's concern for security and increased Palestinian Authorities dilemma over how to control Islamic radicals opposed to the peace process.

Jerusalem's final status remains the greatest hurdle for peace, due to conflicting claims of various religious groups over the Temple Mount. Many Jews and Christians share messianic hopes of rebuilding the Temple at the sight now occupied by the Muslim shrine Dome of the Rock. Jim Sibley, who served 13 years as a Southern Baptist Representative to Messianic groups in Israel, explains the attitude and plans of various Jewish groups regarding the temple:

> There is an important distinction that needs to be made between the rebuilding of the Temple and the re-instituting of the sacrificial system. In general, the Orthodox (Jews) believe in rebuilding the Temple and in the re-institution of the sacrificial system. But the majority believe that Messiah will rebuild it. Some Orthodox believe we must be involved in its rebuilding and therefore, they have *yeshivot* (schools) in Jerusalem that teach temple liturgy to *cohanim* (priests), and they are making implements for

use in the Temple. Some Orthodox believe it is wrong to go on the Temple Mount at all, for fear of inadvertently walking across the Holy of Holies, etc. Others have allowed visits to the area, but only within carefully circumscribed limits.[22]

Some Christians believe the Temple must be rebuilt to prepare for the coming Anti-Christ. Others believe desecration of the temple took place in the time of Antiochus Epiphanies, bringing about the Maccabean revolt in 165 B.C. They see no need to rebuild the temple, in light of Jesus' death, resurrection and sending the Holy Spirit to dwell in the body, or temple, of believers, who constitute the Church. Reinstitution of animal sacrifice would be a step backwards spiritually, according to their view.

Muslim claims also complicate divergent Jewish and Christian theories about the Temple. King Hussein of Jordan (d. 1999), a descendant of the Prophet Muhammad, considered himself guardian of Moslem holy sites in Jerusalem. He paid $6.5 million in 1994 to cover the Dome of the Rock with nearly 180 pounds of 24-karat gold. In 1996 he gave new Turkish carpets, costing $200,000, to replace Iranian ones in the shrine.[23] His successor in the Hashemite Kingdom of Jordan, King Abdullah, will be a major player in the final settlement of Jerusalem, along with Israelis and Palestinians. Election of Ehud Barak in 1999 set the peace process back on course after a number of years of stalemate under the Likud government.

The status of Jerusalem and return of Palestinian refugees to their former homes will both be major issues in a final peace settlement. There is speculation that Abu Dis, a suburb of Jerusalem beyond the Mount of Olives, may serve as an interim location for a Palestinian capital. Some way will be found for Muslim faithful to pray on the Temple Mount, at the Dome of the Rock, without going through Israeli territory. Hopefully, East Jerusalem will update its infrastructure to relieve heavy traffic congestion and the gloomy appearance it received during years of the *intifadha.*

A possible breakthrough in the refugee problem has been proposed by Yossi Katz, Labor government liaison with the Palestinians. He has proposed that 100,000 Palestinians be allowed to return to Israel under the family reunification program. This is in recognition of what he considers Israel's partial responsibility for the refugee situation.[24]

The bumpy and hazardous road of a peace process creates an atmosphere of despair and desperation, mixed with anxious hope, that causes both Arabs and Jews in the Holy Land to search for a deeper spiritual meaning to life. The futility of material prosperity and political solutions becomes apparent. Hopefully, all the gains will not be lost. But whatever happens as we enter the 21st century, evangelical believers will find increasing opportunities to share the message of Christ's love with people of the land who search for real peace.

Already the face of the country has changed, due to the focus on peace. Massive highway construction gives faster access to all parts of the country. Pilgrims, or tourists, are returning in great numbers, despite occasional tension. International Christian Conferences are convening, to usher in the new millennium. It's obvious, the Holy Land is becoming a focal point for outreach into the entire Middle East. The results of church planting here will be felt across the area and around the world.

The Vision

Over thirty years ago, when we first came to the Holy Land, I envisioned a Baptist or Evangelical church or center in every town and village of Galilee. God reminded me of this vision every time I drove home, after meetings and visits in the evening, and gazed on the sparkle of lights from hundreds of villages on mountains and hillsides. Somehow, Baptists were either unable or unwilling to plant churches in all these villages. But the Brethren, Pentecostals and Churches of Christ succeeded in filling many of the gaps. Even in Muslim villages, where one or two Muslim believers struggle to survive, groups like OM nurture their faith through literature ministries. Messianic Jewish fellowships and Bible studies abound in places once thought impossible by human standards. God is fulfilling the vision in Galilee, though much work remains to be done. The results of millions of prayers offered for church planting movements among unreached people groups of the Middle East is being felt.

Could this vision be expanded to include all of Israel-Palestine, the entire Holy Land? Could it include Jordan, Syria, Lebanon, Iraq, Egypt and even Saudi Arabia? The vision is only limited by our ability to see what God desires for these countries. God brings the harvest. Today He is doing a "new thing" in the Holy Land and in the Middle East. A strong vision is required to give us insight and courage as we encounter critical issues that face us in the attempt to pray for and encourage church planting movements. Chapter Four will examine some of these critical issues.

chapter four

Critical Issues Examined—
Danger! Land Mines!

W hen touring the West Bank and the Golan Heights, you may see little triangular signs hanging on barbed wire strung alongside the highway. Many of these have faded and rusted over the years, but they issue a warning that must be heeded; Danger! Land Mines! Some wander into these forbidden areas to hunt artifacts or wild boar. A neighbor of mine lost his leg on one such vain excursion! Sharing the Gospel and planting churches in the Holy Land occasionally makes one feel he is also walking in a minefield.

You never know when you may overstep a boundary created by the history, culture or religion of the area and step into a minefield of explosive issues! Or, you find yourself caught in the crossfire of conflicting ideas and attitudes. The Holy Land is a minefield of church planting policy and strategy, and there have been many casualties. Perhaps, by mapping some of the critical issues, we can better wind our way through these danger zones. You will want to refer back to Chapter Two, Challenges Facing

Church Planters in the Holy Land, for background to understand many of these problems.

One of the most critical issues facing a prospective church planter is that of long-term dependency on foreign support and leadership. In recent years, some have adopted the phrase, "co-dependency" to describe this abnormal relationship between foreign workers and local churches. It basically means doing for others what they can or should do for themselves. Co-dependency is a symptom of a dysfunctional family, where some members cover for an immature or sick member. By this, neither grows to maturity or health, and the abnormal relationship continues without healing.

Most expatriate church workers and local leaders desire to see a vital expression of the New Testament church re-planted in the Holy Land. Some expatriate church workers come bearing guilt feelings for affluence of the western church. They hope to create an "ideal" New Testament church here, only to be disappointed. They harbor unrealistic expectations and find the locals are as materialistic as they are! What are some of the critical issues facing church planters in the Holy Land?

Expatriate vs. Local Idea of "Indigenization"

It comes as a great surprise to an expatriate church planter to find that "indigenous" means foreign support! In recent years, a well-meaning foreign church organization took steps to turn an institution over to local people in a large Jewish city. They appointed eight Jewish believers to serve on the board of the institution. But to their amazement, they found seven of the eight Jewish Messianic believers received support from foreign organizations! Ever since Paul raised a gift among New Testament churches, to send to the poor in Jerusalem, a pattern of foreign support has been indigenous to the Holy Land.

Foreign church planters often bring unrealistic expectations, and they are incapable of modeling what they expect the locals to perform, as indicated by David J. Bosch, in *Transforming Mission,* in his chapter "The Vicissitudes of Accommodation and Indigenization":

> The Christian faith never exists except as "translated" into a culture . . . After Constantine, when the erstwhile *religio illicita* became the religion of the establishment, the church became the bearer of culture . . . Thus Christian mission, as a matter of course, presupposed the disintegration of the cultures into which it penetrated . . . In the Western church, indigenization had for many centuries been a fait accompli; the gospel was perfectly at home in the West but still foreign elsewhere . . . Last, often the initiative, in respect to indigenization, did not come from the newly converted but from missionaries with a sentimental interest in exotic cultures, who insisted on the "otherness" of the young churches and treated them as something that had to be preserved in their pristine form.[1]

I found, in my short experience of working with Muslim believers, they do not want to pattern their new faith after mosque and Muslim customs. They prefer to learn new forms of prayer and family life that will better fit their new-found faith. Perhaps Jesus' admonition: "new wine is put into fresh wineskins"[2] applies in the cases of new churches. We should allow the Gospel to transform the culture of Jews and Arabs, rather than force "indigenization" on the churches, as indicated by Sherwood Lingenfelter in *Transforming Culture:*

> The old system of Jewish beliefs was not erased on the Day of Pentecost, but rather was reformulated and reinterpreted in terms of the new gospel message the people received. Likewise, the cultural system of Greek believers was not eliminated, but

reformulated in terms of the new information and beliefs provided in the gospel. As people reflect upon and receive this new information, they must rethink to achieve a new logical consistency in their knowledge, eliminating those things that they perceive as contradictory and retaining that which they see as complementary to their new beliefs . . .This process is one in which people learn and incorporate the truths of the gospel, the theology of Christ, into their cultural system.[3]

Perhaps "inculturation" is more suitable and natural than "indigenization." David Bosch clarifies how inculturation differs:

Inculturation does not mean that culture is to be destroyed and something new built up on its ruins; neither, however, does it suggest that a particular culture is merely to be endorsed in its present form . . . The West has often domesticated the gospel in its own culture while making it unnecessarily foreign to other cultures. In a very real sense, however, the gospel is foreign to every culture. It will always be a sign of contradiction . . . On the one hand there is the "indigenizing" principle, which affirms that the gospel is at home in every culture and every culture is at home with the gospel. But then there is the "pilgrim" principle, which warns us that the gospel will put us out of step with society . . . The focus, then, is on the transformation of the old, on the plant which, having flowered from its seed, is at the same time something fundamentally new when compared with that seed.[4]

You find, in the process of planting churches in the Holy Land, that Arabs and Jews possess an unusual store of Biblical knowledge and tradition which helps an expatriate worker better understand the Bible. Muslims still practice many Bible customs regarding marriage, such as the long marriage feast, with the uncertainty of when the bridegroom will arrive to take his bride. Jews still observe Passover that gives setting to the Last Supper of Jesus and his disciples.

Would it not be more appropriate for an expatriate church planter to come to the Holy Land as a learner? Is it not possible we have much to learn from local people of the Holy Land, rather than seeking to impose our view of indigenization on them? The shape of the future church should be determined by the sharing of the best in both cultures, and acknowledging the limitations of both. Church planting movements begin when locals take up the challenge to disciple their own people, without continual support and control from outside.

"3-Selves" Formula vs. Local "Shared Purse"

No other issue causes as much "weeping and gnashing of teeth" in the Holy Land, for church planters and local leadership alike, as the "3-Selves" formula for church development. Rufus Anderson, foreign secretary of the American Board of Commissioners for Foreign Missions, first promoted the idea of planting "self-governing, self-supporting, and self-propagating" local churches, in 1866 in a series of retirement lectures at Andover Seminary:

> ...The mission of the Apostle Paul... embraced the following things:
> When he formed local churches, he did not hesitate to ordain presbyters over them, the best he could find; and then throw upon the churches, thus officered, the responsibilities of self-government, self-support, and self-propagation. His "presbyters in every church," whatever their number and other duties, had doubtless the pastoral care of the churches.
> ...The grand object is to plant and multiply self-reliant, efficient churches, composed wholly of native converts, each church complete, with its pastors of the same race with the people.[5]

It must be noted that Anderson never served overseas. And his own missionaries encountered difficulties in following his ideals. Church planting strategists in the Holy Land often use the

"3-Selves" formula to justify cutting all financial aid to pastors and young churches.

John Livingston Nevius served as a church planter and theological educator in China in the late 1800s. The "3-Selves" formula is ascribed to him as the "Nevius Plan." His wife, in her biography of Nevius, quotes him as being in favor of financial support of qualified lay pastors:

About this time Dr. Nevius replied to a letter which had been addressed to him asking his opinion as to the advisability of employing laymen in missionary work. He wrote:

> I say, if earnest, devoted, practical, able-bodied, efficient laymen apply, accept them, and send them out by all means . . . I hope you will encourage suitable persons to come, on a salary of five hundred, or two hundred, or entirely self-supporting, if they can do so . . . I think our church has made a mistake in shutting out from the ministry all who have not had a full classical and scientific training, although they may have other qualifications just as important, and may be specially gifted for some positions of influence.[6]

Nevius began to modify his view about hiring local Chinese to teach and preach, after he determined that this practice tended to cut the believer off from his native countrymen. It also inspired financial motivation in new believers, which proved unhealthy for their spiritual life, as he explained:

> The Employment System tends to excite a mercenary spirit, and to increase the number of mercenary Christians . . . The mercenary preacher, whether paid or hoping to be paid, as naturally draws to himself others of like affinities as a magnet attracts iron fillings.[7]

He came then to advocate Paul's teaching in I Corinthians 7:20: "Let each man abide in that calling wherein he was called." He felt the negatives of paying local pastors and evangelists far outweighed the positive. Encountering strong opposition from other church planters in China, he had difficulty implementing the "3-Selves" formula there, due to the established practice of financial aid. He was invited in 1890 to share his views in Korea. The "3-Selves" formula, applied in this virgin territory, met with great success.

We must note that Anderson, Nevius, and their predecessor Roland Allen, who popularized the "3-Selves" formula for church planting and development in his famous book *Missionary Methods: St. Paul's or Ours?*[8] placed emphasis not on "self support" but on "self-governing." Both Nevius and Allen were more practical and lenient in their application of "self-support," because they were working on the field, and not from an academic or administrative position. They provided financial aid to deserving and qualified local workers, at least for an initial period, with an emphasis on biblical and practical training.

Perhaps a major fallacy of imposing the "3-Selves" formula rigidly over every culture and every age is a failure to realize the Apostle Paul worked within Jewish and Greek cultures. Each had established leadership and giving patterns, with which he was intimately familiar. He had difficulties encouraging early churches to give generously, as indicated in his second letter to the Corinthians. And knowing his culture, he insisted on earning his own living by tent-making, so as not to be a financial burden to others, or to give others control over his church planting efforts.

The "3-Selves" formula has been criticized by Bosch for imposing a western model on third-world cultures:

> Protestant missions only appeared to be different . . . This could even be seen in cases where they deliberately set out to encourage indigenization, as in the celebrated case of the "3-Selves" as the aim of mission (self-government, self-support, and self-propagation), formulated classically by Rufus Anderson and

Henry Venn, almost a century and a half ago . . . In both Catholicism and Protestantism, then, the prevailing image was a pedagogical one—over an extended period of time and along a laborious route the younger churches were to be educated and trained in order to reach selfhood or "maturity," measured in terms of the "3-Selves." In practice, however, the younger churches, like Peter Pan, never "grew up," at least not in the eyes of the older ones. Most of them could only survive, and thereby also please their founders, if they resolutely segregated themselves from their surrounding culture and existed as foreign bodies.[9]

In a more local application, Lyle Vander Verff points out that Temple Gairdner, who worked as an evangelist and church planter among Muslims, for the Anglican Church in Jerusalem and Cairo in the early 1900s, echoes this concern for the "3-Selves" formula:

Gairdner stresses that overseas workers have a continuing task of offering mutual encouragement to the national churches in mission. If the "3-Selves" principle is pressed to the ultimate, it leaves the new church in isolation, cut off from its truly catholic life. At this point Gairdner envisaged a church in which national and foreigner work together in true brotherhood, in a spirit of genuine equality.[10]

Vander Verff ironically points out how Communists in China used the "3-selves Movement" to isolate the national church.[11] Those who insist on strict application of the "3-Selves" formula to church planting in the Holy Land tend to overlook that history. Also, they fail to recognize the multiplicity of cultures in which a church planter works in Israel-Palestine. Each culture responds differently to the ideals of indigenization.

The Christian Arab culture, with heavy influence of the Byzantine Church, presents many problems. They join Protestant evangelical churches, bearing with them a two thousand year tradition of expectations of clergy, church buildings, cemeteries and foreign protection. Dr. Cal Guy calls this the "edifice complex."[12] So naturally, they take very slowly and reluctantly to the "3-Selves" formula.

Jews on the other hand, model the synagogue and a spirit of independence from external authority, combined with a business acumen. They simply by-pass, if you are not willing to offer them financial support, and find other donors!

Muslims are perhaps easier to work with, since they have no model of former church life and tend to support each other as family. Their biggest problem is they are always borrowing from one another and therefore always in debt!

Filipinos, Chinese, South Americans and other language groups appear to expect less than local Arabs and Jews and are generally resourceful.

Russians tend to attach themselves to already existing church facilities, but exhibit capabilities of developing self-support.

The "3-Selves" formula is correct in theory, but very difficult to implement in an area where financial support is already an established practice. In fact, older, local leadership of Arab churches in the Holy Land takes to its imposition with an attitude of dressing in "sackcloth and ashes!" One foreign church planting organization decided to wean Arab churches from financial support after establishment of the State of Israel in 1948. They decided to cut financial aid by 20% a year. After the second year, pastors who found themselves starving began looking for other denominations to support them. That organization lost many Arab churches in the country.

Another larger organization introduced a different plan to cut their subsidy by 10% a year. The senior pastor over their churches literally ground his teeth down in his sleep, worrying about the impending financial crisis, and often reflected bitterly on its imposition. At the same time, his church began banking tourist offerings for the inevitable day they would be "self-supporting." In addition, his church ceased all financial assistance to other churches. Consequently, surrounding village churches and centers nearly caved in due to the lack of financial support, while his church survived. Field personnel and local leaders spent endless hours, days, months and years negotiating and strategizing how to implement these policies. Church planting was an uphill battle during this long period, and the resultant church has not reproduced itself, except by division.

Foreign church planting organizations usually react with exasperation to the negative response of local leaders in the Holy Land to the imposition of the "3-Selves" indigenization formula. The administrators of one denomination in many Middle East countries met in Cyprus and decided the best way to encourage local churches to multiply was to cease all funding for church planting! The reasoning behind this drastic measure was that all new church plants would now be funded by local churches in these countries. It is worth noting that few of these administrators were directly involved in church planting. The response of local leadership was dismay and disbelief, largely due to the fact that neither they nor the foreign church planters who worked with them were consulted in the process of making the decision. Would it not have been better to include people actually involved in planting and development in this decision? Melvin L. Hodges, a former field secretary for the Assemblies of God, though a strong advocate of the "3-Selves" Formula and indigenization, cautions against unilateral imposition:

> Some missionaries have themselves reached the decision that
> the work should become indigenous, and have tried to make it

so by simply announcing that from that time on, the work was to be self-supporting. They have then precipitately cut off support of workers. But there is much more to the problem than merely cutting a worker off from financial support. Initiative for evangelism and leadership must spring from within a national's own spirit, which takes time to develop.[13]

Would not a better approach to the whole subject of indigenization be a partnership, advocated years ago by Gairdner? Rather than imposing our western "self" emphasis, which is another form of applied humanism, on our Holy Land brothers, why not see them as partners of equal value to ourselves? In the words of my retired mentor Dr. Finley Graham, former Field Representative in the Middle East of the International Mission Board of the Southern Baptist Convention: "The local people believe in a shared purse. We share and they share!" Local believers in the Holy Land respond in kind when we exhibit a generous spirit. The question then becomes, "How, when, and how much do we share in the 'purse'?" It has been my experience through the years that the people of the Holy Land respond generously to causes they see as challenging, especially when we, as partners, also share willingly. Nevius, himself modeled this spirit of the "shared purse" by contributing ten percent of the cost of new buildings and sharing in the expenses of theological students.[14]

Some church planting strategists now add another "self" to the "3-Selves" formula, that of "self-theologizing." [15] It is when local people of the Holy Land create their own theology of church planting, in keeping with the teachings of Scripture, which they will implement with their own cultural nuances. These are the ideals of the "3-Selves" formula.

Some groups try to handle the transition to self-support through establishment of loan funds for churches. Southern Baptists granted the local Association in Israel a lump sum to fulfill their obligation toward a church subsidy program. Local leadership now administers funds as they see fit. Interestingly, the local Association cut the time period of aid to churches from ten years to three, indicating they desire to see a new church self-supporting as soon as possible.

Hope is on the horizon, as we see by the stated church planting goals of AWEMA, and the dynamic examples of a few local pastors and leaders who inspire their flocks to practice biblical stewardship and actively engage in church planting. The bigger issue is how to move from church planting to a church planting movement? Only when this is done can we overcome the "edifice complex" that has plagued churches in the Holy Land and worldwide, since the time of Constantine.

Institutions vs. Western Disenfranchisement

The dominant place of institutions in the life of people in the Holy Land continues to be another critical issue in church planting. A traditional church, convent, or monastery of various Orthodox or Catholic denominations mark the site of many biblical events. In the eyes of local people, a building establishes permanence and credibility. Early Protestant evangelical pioneers realized the importance of a building to establish "presence" in a Muslim dominated area. Therefore, they struggled in the nineteenth century to build Christ Church, St. George's Cathedral, The Lutheran Church of the Redeemer and other churches around the land. Institutions such as Gobat's School, The Nazareth Hospital and Saint Margaret's Orphanage met educational and health needs. Baptists followed in the twentieth century with the Narkis Street Church, Nazareth Baptist Church and School, Baptist Village and numerous churches and chapels. Institutions were not only important in the eyes of local people, but also in the eyes of the government. The Israeli government grants visas to foreign church workers on the basis of the number of institutions they operate in the country.

Local people view institutions as essential and also use them for income making purposes. Going back centuries, Moslems built the local mosque above shops, which provided income to maintain the property. Churches followed suit, reflecting a common practice in Arab villages of building houses of at least two floors. They used the ground floor for as a barn, shop, garage or a variety of family businesses to provide income.

Several factors change Western churches' attitude toward the value of institutions for church planting. First, once a "presence" has been established through a viable local church, the need of an institution diminishes. Second, the cost of running institutions, particularly hospitals, becomes prohibitive. And third, national local churches progress and assume control and financial responsibility for institutions.

We saw earlier that difficulties experienced in planting churches among local Muslim and Jewish populations led foreign churches to concentrate efforts on the traditional Christian population instead. Persecution of new believers led to a necessity of also establishing schools and other basic institutions for their families. A majority of students in Christian schools came from more well-to-do families, as the economy of the country improved. These schools provided "social lift" for the community. Unfortunately, local churches did not always keep up with development of the schools. Many church members came from lower economic classes in the cities and villages. Their children did not have the academic qualifications nor finances to gain entrance into better quality Christian schools. When time came to turn these schools over to local leadership, the churches could not come up with trained personnel. School boards also resisted the more conservative leadership of pastors and church leaders. David Hesselgrave, in his insightful book *Planting Churches Cross-Culturally*, explains some reasons behind the spirit of competitiveness between institutions and local churches:

> One reason for this tension is service enterprises, such as hospitals and educational institutions, have a way of preempting finances and energies. Therefore evangelism and witness tend to get crowded out. Another reason is some of those in service enterprises have downgraded verbal witness and insisted that acts of compassion are the only witness needed. Still another reason is some specialist organizations have majored in certain types of Christian service, and others in evangelism—a fact that tends to foster competitiveness within the Church.[16]

It is my impression that most evangelical institutions in the Holy Land struggle to maintain a balance between witness and service. Many home-boards purposely scale-down financial involvement in institutions and try to assist local leadership in assuming responsibility. Some simply cease financial support and appeal to other church and government agencies to assume responsibility instead.

Efforts on the part of foreign church organizations run into unexpected difficulties trying to turn properties over to local, national leadership. Land transfer fees and improvement taxes may also make legal transfer of property prohibitive. Neither a local church nor the foreign owner benefits. The only winner is the government land authority and tax offices! Some local leaders hesitate to turn church properties over to the control of the local people, especially in the Arab communities. They fear factions in the churches will take over the properties and the former leadership will lose control. A hidden fear on the part of foreign church administrators is that once local peoples have full ownership and control of properties, they will turn them into money-making businesses. This is highly likely, especially on the part of pastors who find their support cut by decreasing subsidies.

Somehow a compromise must be found between Western idealism and local pragmatism. A long-range solution for schools may be found in joint school boards representing a wide segment of church leadership and the local community. In the case of transferring ownership of churches and institutions to local churches, it may be necessary for foreign organizations to incorporate local church bodies into their legal structure, for the sake of property ownership. In these cases, foreign leadership will have to be willing to relinquish control over how church properties are used by the local leadership.

In the end, we must all agree; the local church is the most basic institution. Only what a local church can sustain on its own power, with God's help, will endure. Our purpose as church planters should be to contact the unreached peoples, not to prop up long term denominational structures. As someone has said, "Our goal is presence with purpose, without perpetuity!"

Decision Making—Centralized or Decentralized

Who makes decisions and how they are made remains a critical issue of church planting in the Holy Land. The western attitude is simple: "Who holds the purse strings?" Decisions in the West are usually made by executive administrators and carried out by subordinates, through a chain of command somewhat reminiscent of the military. This appears effective and cost efficient. If one objects to such decisions, he has usually two alternatives, either to hunker under and carry out the decision or to leave.

Unfortunately, decisions made abroad, without adequate input, are sometimes imposed with disastrous results in the Holy Land. The worse case scenario I remember happened after the 1967 war. A church organization abroad followed suggestions of a local pastor to combine both Arab and Jewish work in Jerusalem. At his advice, church property on the other side of the city was sold and a veteran foreign church planter was sent home. To make matters worse, the pastor whose advice they took left the country when he succeeded in getting his way! This same organization later hired a new local pastor who proceeded to undermine the authority of the foreign pastor, just as his predecessor had done. But the situation backfired on him, once the foreign organization became wise. They ended up in a protracted court case which the local man lost. No one really won, due to years of energy and money spent in resolving the dispute.

Another church organization acquired prime business property in Jerusalem, which in its better days had generated hundreds of thousands of dollars in income for local churches and institutions in the Middle East. Some Westerners in the organization objected to the philosophy of the local church generating income from a business. Their ideal was local churches should operate only from tithes and offerings of believers. They leveled continual criticism at the business because it did not operate according to western standards. So, a local board of pastors and businessmen took measures to rectify business practices to bring them into compliance with western demands, but to no avail. Despite their efforts, the western oriented group voted to close the business, over objections of local leadership. Ironically, the western group opened a similar business across town, only to find themselves in financial problems also and with threat of closure within a few years after they had succeeded in closing the same type local-led operation!

The above two "worse-case scenarios" emphasize the necessity of both local and foreign church workers making prayerful, informed decisions together. Neither local nor foreign leadership is without bias and weakness. But together, with patience and much prayer, they can come to informed decisions. Many times decisions have to be made which are painful, but necessary. But every effort should be made to allow both local and foreign leadership to "buy into" decisions. I discovered that local leaders rejected suggestions offered by expatriates at first, but later adopted some of them as their own, after periods of reflection and experience. Those decisions which were made hastily, or imposed from outside, often left unresolved bitterness, which took years to overcome.

Church Planting—Who Funds and Leads Out?

It should be the dream of an expatriate church planter to someday finish their work in the Holy Land, transfer to another unreached area, or return home, unless by remote chance they decide to immigrate. Our task is evangelism or sharing the Gospel with a goal of establishing local church planting movements. We train and encourage local leadership for the task of fulfilling the Great Commission. Who funds and leads out in the enterprise depends a great deal on each immediate situation. The ideal is for an expatriate church planter to link up with local pastors and evangelists, if these are available and willing to work with him.

A church planting organization has as its goal evangelism which results in churches that multiply other churches. As much as possible, this should be done in concert with local leadership. Occasionally, local church authorities demand cooperation and submission of expatriate church planters to their leadership, even though they do not have church planting as a major goal. Before expatriate planters relinquish their prerogative, they would do well to heed the advice of David Hesselgrave:

> The responsibility and opportunity to do so should not be forfeited in order to integrate with receiving churches which do not have a vision for that God-given task. (With this caution he adds the insight:) Full partnership has the most potential for planting new congregations as long as the mission recognizes that it exists to strengthen and add to the national church.[17]

A high level of maintenance motive prevails in traditional Arab churches where most Evangelical Protestants originate. Local pastors tend to become highly involved in maintaining and developing their own congregations. They have little time or energy to expend in starting new congregations. An expatriate church planter could offer real assistance to local pastors with a vision for outreach. I found it refreshing to take an Arab pastor-trainee along on visits to prospective members. His advice encouraged me, and later he trained others in ministry.

Funding can come from local associations of churches, a local church, or others interested in church planting. Little financial help is needed in beginning a work, if it is kept simple. Most new work begins in homes of interested prospects, but soon outgrows the space available. I believe local and expatriate church planting organizations should have a "head-start fund" for new work. This limited fund could provide assistance for transportation, literature and rental of meeting space, for a limited period of time. The idea is to encourage church starts without leaving a situation that local people cannot finance on their own efforts.

Some church planting organizations institute loan funds for purchase of land and buildings for congregations. While these are effective in assisting already developed congregations, they have limited value for church planting, since a new group has no collateral to guarantee repayment of loans. Ideally, when local churches receive adequate vision to lead out in church planting, they will provide the money to assist new church starts. But until that day comes, expatriate church planters need head-start funding, assuming that local believers share in the cost. I always insisted that operating expenses of new meetings be financed by local offerings. That way the local group could maintain itself, after I would leave.

Church planting in the Hebrew sector is carried out today almost entirely by local Israeli believers. Some move to new areas of the country, gather other local Hebrew speaking believers, and begin a meeting in their home or rented space. The high level of networking between these believers enables them to keep up with who lives in their new area. Many earn their living through secular work or employment in Messianic institutions. There is one small community in the country where as many as one third of the inhabitants are now believers. A few expatriates attempt to plant churches in Hebrew sectors, but come upon stiff opposition when the anti-mission organizations discover them. Hebrew speaking congregations multiplied significantly in recent years, despite opposition, due to their high motivation and mobility.

The outcome of church planting among Muslims in the Holy Land is yet to be seen. Early indicators show that Muslim believers take the initiative themselves to introduce their relatives and friends to their newfound faith. They continue to call upon expatriate planters to train them in personal visitation, teaching the Bible and sharing their faith with their relatives and friends. The depressed situation of many Muslims in the Palestinian sector leaves them hungering for friendship and a good word from God. One Muslim believer celebrated his fourth birthday in the Lord by inviting 25 friends to hear his testimony of what God had done for him. Another Muslim believer responded to threats from the political and religious authorities by winning another Muslim to faith in Jesus! This is good technique, because each Muslim believer has a network of ten to twenty family members and friends whom he or she impacts.

When God works and the Holy Spirit moves in men's hearts, the spirit of competition and selfishness gives way to enthusiasm. This is the prevailing atmosphere in the Holy Land today, for those who know the hope that is in Christ. Some local groups are reaching "critical mass" and multiplying rapidly, bringing a welcome shift in the role of the expatriate church planter from that of having to take the initiative to that of partner with local leadership. An expatriate, from the beginning, must be careful to avoid dependence on outside funding and leadership, which can stifle or impede a church planting movement. When a real church planting movement takes off, resources will be found in the harvest.

Tentmaker vs. Salaried Church Planter

Is starting new churches dependent on having a paid church planter? Certainly not! As we see above, Jewish and Arab believers start churches without being paid. Plymouth Brethren in Galilee start churches without paid preachers or church planters. Admittedly, each has some way of raising funds locally and abroad. The point is; if the local people do the fundraising, it is much healthier for them than to have a foreign organization to do it. The idea is to encourage local "ownership" of planting projects. This does not mean we discourage local organizations from supporting gifted church planters. Evangelism which results in churches planting other churches is the goal, and not the promotion of one particular method of financing the work.

Reality must be faced if you or your organization chooses to support a local church planter financially. His salary is only one part of the pay package. Highly structured labor laws in Israel enforce payment or compensation of a thirteenth month's salary, social security, income tax, health insurance, and vacation pay. Therefore, you must budget at least one-half more than salary costs to cover all benefits. All of the above is cumulative and must be paid. Church workers whom you retire or terminate will not hesitate to ask for all or more than is legally theirs. I know of one local non-profit organization that was forced to declare bankruptcy due to their inability to pay employee retirement benefits ruled by a labor court! Foreign church organizations often choose to let local organized church bodies deal with local workers for this reason.

Our problem, as expatriate church planters, is we cannot model the tentmaker image we advocate among local churches. Many of us receive salary, housing and travel expenses in our support package. Therefore, we can dedicate a major portion of our time to visitation, study and prayer, which is essential to our task. Local believers who work for a living find themselves exhausted and unable to put all their efforts into church planting and developing. Nevius struggled with this dilemma a hundred years ago in China, and he came to the conclusion that an expatriate church planter was justified in receiving financial support:

> Our circumstances . . . are different from those of the Apostle Paul in almost every particular. He was a Roman citizen in the Roman empire. He labored in his native climate; was master of Greek and Hebrew, the two languages required for prosecuting his work; and his physical and intellectual training had been the same as those with whom and for whom he labored. We...are obliged from the first to undertake the work of acquiring a spoken and a written language, both very difficult, taxing mind and body to the utmost, and demanding all our time and energies. We have to submit to the drudgery of learning in comparatively advanced life—as far as we are able to do it—what Paul learned, in childhood and early manhood. Besides, for a foreigner to support himself...in competition with natives in any department of manual labor is manifestly impracticable, and one attempting to do so would diminish rather than increase his influence . . . Is it not obvious that the only persons who can furnish...the much needed example of propagating Christianity while they labor with their hands, are not Europeans, but natives laboring for and among their own people?[18]

Nevius' point is well taken for most expatriates. The Israel government grants clergy visas only on the guarantee of a foreign organization maintaining support of expatriate workers and paying for return to their home country at the end of their service. Work permits are granted only with the added endorsement of the Ministry of Labor. The government is interested in protecting the domain of the local labor force and is not too willing to grant visas to foreign expatriates who would compete with local employees.

All of the above considered, it behooves an expatriate to make his presence useful to local churches and leaders. Even though we cannot model financial independence, we can be examples of evangelism which result in churches, by being good stewards of our time, talents and money. The old example stands: teaching a man how to fish is much better than giving him a fish every day.

Opposition to Church Planting

You may expect to receive opposition to church planting from unbelieving Jews and Arabs. After all, you appear as a threat their social solidarity and religious traditions. Sadly, unexpected opposition sometimes comes from local evangelical ministers. They may feel threatened about losing members to the new church. They fail to recognize the truth discovered by an African pastor during a survey of five hundred Baptist churches in his area: If a church does not multiply itself within seven years, it will split! Despite this fact, some local pastors oppose church planting in their area because they feel we need to strengthen the existing churches. They feel new churches will lead to fragmentation of the body of Christ. Dr. Bill Wagner, consultant for church planting in Europe and the Middle East, found similar objections in a study of churches in Europe:

> There are obstacles for the church planting strategy, the largest of which is opposition by the leaders of the existing church, both free and state related. It is not surprising that a ground swell of doubt is voiced about this activity which is gaining momentum. The reasoning begins with the fact that so many Protestant churches which own nice, well-located buildings are dying. They stand as monuments of the past. Those opposing new churches feel that more resources should be put into resurrecting the older ones. They also point to the

fact that modern evangelical missionary work in Europe has followed a pattern whereby a mission begins a church, and before it is self-supporting it is turned over to nationals who must then take on the responsibility for the "child they did not want." The mission then is free to "beget" again, thus following the same pattern . . . Dr. McGavran warned of the danger of such cooperation with national churches, that the result is a dead church dictating to a living mission . . . Evangelicals will applaud success, while those from the other side will view each new "planting" as a further fragmentation of the church.[19]

Interestingly Wagner notes that most of the members of new congregations are people in transition, those who recently moved to an area. They are either new arrivals or foreigners, which means they were not members of local established churches anyway. A similar situation can be found in larger cities of Israel-Palestine where people have moved in from villages and kibbutzim. New fellowships may attract these newcomers better than existing fellowships. We have an obligation to share the Gospel with them and to gather them into believer's congregations, despite the opposition. Of course, every effort should be made to encourage local churches to reach out and plant new work, but we must not give up our mandate even if they fail in theirs.

One serious omission characterizes arguments of those who oppose planting congregations near other evangelical work. They fail to recognize people join groups that are closer to their age and social class. Therefore, one type or denomination of evangelical church cannot appeal to all people in an area. I have often thought that each area needs at least a Baptist, a Brethren and a Pentecostal type church, to reach all classes, ages and dispositions of people. I would probably have to add, some will chose an Episcopal, Lutheran or one of the traditional churches. The body of Christ is bigger than any one denomination. In Israel-Palestine we see growth of Messianic and Muslim fellowships which may and may not resemble any of the above, except for core doctrine.

Hesslegrave shares relevant research into "homogenous units" which is basic to church planting and growth theory:

> . . . It includes groupings and segments of society which tend to persist: class, caste, age-sets, secret societies, and kinship groups. When Donald McGavran refers to "homogeneous units" in society his primary reference is to these groups. (Of course, more is involved than that. Ties of language, ways of thinking, value systems, and cultural preferences also tend to bind groups together.) As McGavran notes, people like to become Christians without having to cross the major boundaries that distinguish these groups from one another . . . There is no getting away from the fact that though there are numerous instances of multi-class, multi-ethnic, multilingual churches. Most churches tend to be class, caste, ethnic or tribal churches in addition to being Christian churches![20]

When Donald McGavran published his book *Understanding Church Growth* in 1970 I knew his "homogenous units" theory perfectly described the Arab community in Israel-Palestine. It also has direct application to the Jewish community in its many varieties. I found there were at least three social groups in each Arab village, one ruling, one in opposition and one neutral. To appeal to one group automatically excluded the other. So those who limit their horizons to only one church in a community limit the number of people who will find a church home. Opposition is more often a matter of control than of spiritual concern for one's flock. How to deal with or avoid the "gatekeepers" is an essential ingredient in a church planting movement. The barrier of opposition is a critical issue to be faced with courage, patience and prayer.

Religious Community vs. Spiritual Conversion

One of the greatest challenges to church planting in the Holy Land is opposition to spiritual conversion to Jesus Christ as Savior, Lord and Messiah. The new birth, more than anything else, threatens the fabric of Jewish, Muslim and traditional Christian ideas of religious community. A church planter here needs to realize from the outset that he or she enters a territory of tremendous spiritual conflict. In the words of a leading Muslim: "The patient is sick, and knows he is dying. But he does not know the cure!" Satan blinds hearts and causes people to believe that the cure will kill them.

There is strong resistance to spiritual conversion to Christ on the part of leaders in all religious circles in the Holy Land. What they fail to admit is that both Judaism and Islam have a history of missionary activity. Today, one of the most active missionary enterprises in Israel is Orthodox Judaism in its many forms. One can see colorfully painted recreational vehicles or "Torah Tanks" circling the country, seeking to draw all Jews into Orthodox Judaism. Admittedly, one must admire the zeal and tact of many of the advocates for a return to Orthodox Judaism. Concealed behind frequent attacks on the evangelical Christian endeavor is the fact that people from a Christian background convert to Judaism every year in Israel and abroad. Their story is told in daily newspapers. Some undoubtedly convert because of genuine religious desire, but financial benefits given to Jews by the state of Israel provide other less spiritual incentives

I lived for 25 years close to a kibbutz in Galilee which served as a conversion center for Judaism. A Christian young person could not spend the night on that kibbutz for fear they might influence other young people who were in the process of conversion. Christians could only stay in the guesthouse as tourists on an organized tour. This procedure was known in the kibbutzim in the area. When a young person showed any interest in Judaism, they were sent to this kibbutz to go through the process of conversion.

Islam practices *da'wah,* or "invitation," for backsliding Muslims to return to prayers in the mosque, and for others to embrace Islam as a religion. Islam is an active missionary faith. Groups of roving sheiks move from village to village in the West Bank and Israel on *da'wah* visiting from house to house and encouraging Muslims to attend mosque for daily prayer.

I met one such group in a West Bank village. Each dressed in a white robe. They acted graciously. One young sheik repeated a canned message about faithfulness to God and to prayer, which all present listened to patiently. One day I was on the main street of a Christian village in Galilee when I saw a strange group approaching. A bearded sheik dressed in a turban and blue Arab *ghalabiya,* or flowing gown, led the group. He carried a large walking stick in his hand, which he tapped as he took great determined strides. Alongside him and behind him were his followers, trying to keep up. He reminded me of what Jesus and his disciples might have looked like as they went from village to village in Galilee! These groups of enthusiasts try to maintain the momentum of Islamic renewal in the area. Their leaders do not hide their desire to convert all people to Islam.

Christians of evangelical persuasion maintain the New Testament teaches that every believer should "go into all the world and preach the gospel to the whole creation."[21] The Great Commission of Jesus in Matthew 28:19 tells us to: "Go therefore and make disciples of all nations, baptizing them in the name of the Father and of the Son and of the Holy Spirit." Jewish leaders in Israel now admit that Christians obey what their religion commands when they share their faith with others.

K. McKim focuses on what most evangelicals believe about conversion in the *Handbook on Religious Conversion:*

Christian conversion is focused on Jesus Christ. God's work in Christ makes conversion possible. Those who are "converted" are "turned around" and released from the bondage of sin and by the grace of God are enabled to live a new life of joyful obedience to God in Jesus Christ through the power of the Holy Spirit. The entire Trinity is involved in the work of conversion. But the focus of the "new life" is on obedience to God's will as God is known in Jesus Christ. Thus conversion is focused in soteriology and involves a complete reorientation of the human being and a restoration of the image of God (Eph. 4:23-24) in Jesus Christ who is himself, "the image of the invisible God" (Col. 1:15). [22]

The act of conversion to Christ is called in popular terms, being "born again." Jews and Muslims, as well as traditional Christians who experience this new spiritual birth, find their lives radically changed. Some receive new power to break old destructive negative lifestyles of drugs, homosexuality and prostitution. Many feel their attitudes toward former enemies changes as they study the Bible. They find fellowship in congregations of believers that encourage them in their new relationship with God. They also find, in many cases, their marriages are strengthened.

Questions naturally arise as to the need for Jews and traditional Christians to experience conversion to a new life in Christ. Liberal theologians created a "double covenant" theology that advocated that Jews are brought into God's kingdom through the Old Covenant and Christians through the New Covenant. The conclusion from this theology would naturally be there is no need to evangelize among Jews. Such teaching lures Jews into a false sense of security and discourages Christian evangelism. It denies the New Testament, which clearly teaches the Gospel is for the Jew first and then for Gentiles. A great outcry of protest arose from Jewish organizations in 1996 over a resolution passed by the Southern Baptist Convention. It declared God's love for Jewish people and the Christian responsibility to share Christ with them. The resolution said nothing new. It only reminded Christians of what the New Testament teaches clearly, that there is salvation only in Jesus, for everyone, including the Jews.[23]

As for the question of whether traditional Christians should be a target for evangelism, the New Testament clearly teaches that any man or woman without a personal faith in Jesus Christ as Messiah, Savior and Lord will not enter the kingdom of God. A traditional Christian without a personal faith in Christ is just as lost spiritually as a Jew or Muslim without a personal faith in Christ. This in no way lessens the importance of a covenant community nurturing the Christian faith. It simply means a person enters the covenant community through personal faith in Christ as Messiah, not through natural birth, as is clearly taught in the first three chapters of the Gospel of John.

The matter of how a person relates to his former birth community after coming to believe in Jesus depends largely on each situation. A Jew still remains a Jew, even if he believes in Jesus, because there is continuity between the two covenants. Muslims become Muslims in the true spiritual sense, in that belief in Jesus is true Islam, or surrender to God. But there is discontinuity in that Islam rejects the historicity and spirit of the Bible and replaces it with the history of Islam and the spirit of Muhammad. Traditional Christians who experience the new birth can find new meaning from prayers of their ancient churches, but they will also find emphasis on saint and Mary worship to be a departure from the Scriptural norms. Most evangelical Christians in the Holy Land still maintain their legal identity in the ancient Christian churches. Truly, ways must be found for born-again Jews, Muslims and Christians to remain a part of their culture and heritage, to bear witness to their family and friends.

Contextualization, or "Reverse Contextualization"?

"Contextualization" is sharing of gospel in such a way as to make it understandable and meaningful in the context, culture and language of the people we are trying to reach as church planters. The term itself is a modern one, while the concept is as old as the incarnation and Paul's attempts to "please all men in all things . . . that they might be saved."[24] Hesselgrave and Rommen note two hazards involved in attempts to contextualize the gospel:

1) The perception of the communicator's own cultural heritage as an integral element of the gospel, and
2) A syncretistic inclusion of the receptor , which would alter or eliminate the message upon which the integrity of the gospel depends.[25]

Attempts to contextualize the gospel run into unique problems in the Holy Land. We are attempting to bring the gospel back to its origins! It was lived and written here. Therefore the problem is often "decontextualization," or "reverse" contextualization. The church planter finds himself or herself, as a student in the Holy Land, learning the original context of the Bible, with its Hebrew, Arabic and many of the ancient customs still being practiced. I found, on arriving over thirty years ago, most of my Bible commentaries received little use, since the land and people were the best commentary to the meaning of the Bible! Warnings of the hazards of attempting to contextualize, nevertheless, need to be heeded in church planting there.

It is too easy to detect the imprint of Americans, English, Germans and Scots on worship and organization of "indigenous" churches in the Holy Land. Ancient churches also betray their Egyptian, Greek, Latin, Lebanese and Syriac origins. Little is left of what could be called "original" Gospel forms. Local believers often adapt "foreign" innovations and freeze them in time, while churches that sent a planter move on to other forms of worship and organizations in their countries of origin. It is somewhat like finding old and unused "rare" coins from many countries in the drawers of merchants in the Old City of Jerusalem, where they were deposited by pilgrims, for souvenirs in days past. Lest we become too critical of the worship forms and organization of local churches and congregations, we need to recognize that the New Testament milieu was one of Hebrew, Aramaic and Greek cultures. Paul's desire to become all things to all men was and is still the only valid approach to sharing the gospel in the Holy Land today. Various attempts by church planters to return to the original forms meet with mixed response.

The two areas where contextualized forms have been used with some success are Bible translations and music for worship. A culturally sensitive translation of the life of Christ in Arabic was written by David Owens and Adnan Baidoon in the 1980s. *Sirat al-Masiah* attempted to appeal to religious Muslims using Quranic terms, which could be chanted in Arabic, similar to the Quran. It met with negative reaction from a few Christians in the Holy Land, but had some success with Muslims in the Gulf States. A later translation of the four Gospels into Arabic, by the late Baidoon, *al-Injeel*, was widely distributed to the Arabic community in the West Bank, in the 1990s.[26] Saleem Munayer and Phil Goble wrote *The New Creation Book for Muslims* to adapt to prayer forms of religious Muslims. Though current political situations at that time limited distribution of its Arabic version, the book received approval from religious Muslims who read it.[27] Arabic literature and audio cassettes of Call of Hope and The Youth Center in Switzerland and Germany have wide appeal to Muslims in the area, due to their quality and scholarship.

The Jesus film is probably the most successful attempt at contextualization, since it was filmed on location in the Holy Land and uses local Arab and Jewish actors. It is available in Arabic, Amharic, English, Hebrew and Russian, which covers most of the languages spoken in the Holy Land.

The New Testament for the Hebrew sector underwent a new translation to remove archaic and misleading expressions, in 1991.[28]

Then the Israeli believing community published the entire Bible in parallel Hebrew and Russian for a large influx of Russian Jews, also in 1991.[29]

A return to more Biblical music and worship forms has revived churches and congregations all over the area. Psalms and Scripture in Arabic, written by Arab pastors and musicians in the Arab countries surrounding the Holy Land, paved the way for renewal in churches in the 1970s. The *oud* (Arabic mandolin), *derbeki* (Arab drum), and tambourine soon became common in house meetings and conferences. Hebrew congregations returned to using stringed instruments, horns and tambourines, along with dancing to express feelings of the Psalms and various praise hymns. Jewish festivals and holy days received new messianic meaning. All this has led to contextualization of worship in the Holy Land.

Scriptures of the Torah, Prophets and Writings remain the best contextualized source for witness to modern Jews in the land. Attempts to bar use of the New Testament would be of no avail, since the "older Testament" is full of prophecies of the Messiah, which only Jesus fulfills. Revering the Virgin Mary for her purity and obedience to God, and appealing for believers' baptism as a type of confirmation, both enhance witness to Arab Christians from traditional churches.

Muslims understand the gospel better when Quranic terms are used to describe Biblical truths. The "great sacrifice" referred to in God's substitution of an animal for Abraham's son in the Quran takes on real meaning when Jesus' death for the sins of mankind is emphasized. As one can see, contextualization is an ongoing process in church planting in the Holy Land.

New Paradigms vs. Old Wineskins

We live in a day when church planting concepts are changing as rapidly as the speed of e-mail and the Internet. Church planters in the Holy Land are experiencing these changes as home offices race into the 21st Century way of doing business. Old terminology and concepts are being put aside at a mind boggling pace. This new century race can leave veteran planters feeling they will soon be obsolete, as they see entire structures of leadership changing.

One new paradigm or way of thinking is "church planting movements" as opposed to the older concept of single church planting. Movements have the advantage of being self-reproducing and are more in keeping with the model of rapid expansion of the Church in the 1st Century. It is a concept I can affirm as I see Muslim believers winning other Muslims to the Lord and gathering them together for fellowship and discipling. The problem with the old concept is it took too much foreign involvement, and the church which resulted tended to be inward looking, rather than outward focused, in multiplying other churches. It is an old wineskin that must be discarded if we are to see an ingathering of the magnitude needed to reach all those who do not know salvation that is in Jesus alone.

Jerry Rankin, President of the International Mission Board of the SBC, explains rationale for restructuring and adopting the "new directions:"

> We must move away from the time-consuming processes that limited strategic decisions to the annual mission meeting and required large-group consensus before anyone could launch innovative initiatives. Cooperating in smaller team configurations focused on a specific people group or geographic entity provides more ownership of strategic planning and results in more effective mutual accountability. It creates an efficient and flexible process and liberates everyone to contribute their gifts and assignments in implementing the strategy.[30]

A companion concept is that of "unreached people groups." Jim Montgomery of DAWN pointed out in his book *Dawn 2000* that there are about 9,000 such groups in the world, if you use the definition of the biblical term "nation" to describe them. Depending on your definition, whether cultural, language, or ethnic, you could find up to 100,000 people groups in the world.[31] It is a mistake to paint with too broad of strokes in the Holy Land and Middle East to define a people group.

When the 10/40 Window was first introduced, over 100 million Muslims in the Holy Land, which included Lebanon, Syria, Jordan, Israel, West Bank, Gaza and Egypt, were excluded as an unreached people group. This was due to assumptions that the Bible had been translated into their language and all these countries had evangelical churches. This broad definition has been corrected, and it is now recognized that Palestinian Muslims, Druze, Bedouin, Circassians, and a vast variety of Jewish peoples are part of the unreached groups who deserve our prayers and attention. The main point of the new paradigm of unreached peoples is our efforts in church planting need to be focused for maximum effect among these groups, rather than on the already churched evangelical communities. The ultimate survival of these beleaguered Evangelical churches will be dependent on their living witness to larger unreached Muslim community.

What is a "Church"?

This simple question takes up an inordinate amount of time in strategy discussions for church planters. Views differ from: "...two or more gathered together in my name..." to a *minyan*, or quorum, of ten adult males, to thirty. Charles Brock, who served as church planter among Christians and Muslims in the Philippines, found that six families committed to Christ makes a good foundation for a new church.[32] He uses the following definition for a local church:

> A group of people who have turned from their sins to place
> full trust in Jesus as Savior and Lord. They are then baptized by

immersion. These individuals continue to meet on a regular basis as members of the family of God. They will fellowship in prayer, praise, and Bible study for the definite purpose of glorifying Christ and expanding His kingdom on earth. This is a church.[33]

The International Board of the Southern Baptist Convention, USA defines the local church as "a group of baptized believers drawn together into a visible fellowship by the Holy Spirit for the purpose of worship, fellowship, witness, nurture and ministry."[34] I would personally add to this definition observance of the Lord's supper or communion. Some of Mennonite persuasion would also add foot washing!

As mentioned earlier, I consider two or more believers meeting together in the name and spirit of Jesus an "embryo church." Our problem really boils down to differences between the spiritual and practical definition of what a church is. The "edifice complex" of many Arab believers in the Holy Land complicates the matter further. They consider a church a body of believers who worship in a building, under leadership of an ordained priest or minister, because of their Byzantine background.

It is interesting that the word for "church" in Arabic is *kaneesa*, which is obviously related to the Hebrew word *kenis*, or a gathered group. The Arabic word for a synagogue is also *kanees*. The New Testament Greek word *ekklesia* means basically "a called out people." Peter calls the church: "...a chosen race, a royal priesthood, a holy nation, God's own people..." in obvious reference to the Children of Israel in Exodus 19:6.[35] Messianic Jews prefer not to use the Gentile word "church" and instead call their groups a "congregation," or *kehila* in Hebrew. Muslims call their place of prayer a mosque, which is derived from the Arabic word *masjid*, which means a place of kneeling or prayer. The other Muslim title for a mosque is *jami'a,* which means a place of gathering, similar to the word for church or synagogue. Their word *ummah*, or "nation of people," and *mu'miniin*, or "believers" comes closest to the concept of "church." The term, *hizballah*, or "party of God," could represent a group of believers, but is tainted by current radical, political connotations.

Whatever the name of the group, a church is a group of people committed to Jesus as Savior, Messiah, and Lord. They do not have to meet in a building to be called a church, nor must they be led by an ordained clergyman. The more we can be freed from these added ecclesiastical trappings, the easier it will be to plant churches in the Holy Land.

The concept of a "cell church" is an exciting development in church planting, particularly among people from a Muslim background. Basically it is where two or three meet together in Jesus' name. It is especially adaptable to people under persecution from family or authorities. A cell church can meet in a house, a car, under a tree, in a construction shed or wherever believers can be alone to share and study the Bible. They can also gather with other larger congregations, as the situation permits. Early churches were ones which met regularly, as believers gathered. It had mobility and reached the known world. We see the same happening today as the Gospel comes back to Jerusalem.

We dealt in this chapter with some major, critical issues facing church planters in the Holy Land. There are other issues, such as the place of Israel in God's plan for history, the practice of multiple marriages among Muslims, and the status of churches in the newly forming state of Palestine. These concerns will wait for others more qualified than myself to deal with them. I share the above to encourage church planters, both expatriate and local, to devise ways of allowing and encouraging new churches to grow into mature bodies of believers who impact positively all the peoples of the Holy Land. Jews, Arabs and internationals alike desperately need the *shalom*, *salaam*, and peace that Jesus gives through the Holy Spirit of God. Planting churches which multiply other churches, among a specific people group, remains the most effective way of sharing Christ with the most people and of making a long-term impact for God in the Holy Land. Section II will suggest methods to encourage church planting movements. Are you aware that you can begin at home to prepare for the harvest?

Methodology for a Church Planting Movement in the Holy Land

chapter five

Preparing Laborers
for the Harvest

A ll signs point to the fact that God is doing a new thing in the Middle East, and especially in the Holy Land. Both Arabs and Jews are turning to Jesus as Messiah and Lord in record numbers, despite the obstacles described in earlier chapters. Parallel to this new receptivity to the Gospel, and inspired by the prayers of millions of Christians for Muslims and Jews living in the "10/40 Window," a growing number of young people and adults in praying countries feel God's call into this harvest field. The Middle East, once seen as unfruitful for evangelical Christian missions, has become a field of potential harvest for church planting movements.

Many questions come to those who feel the burden to pray and go: "What can I do to prepare myself to gather this harvest? How can I be sure that I am called and capable of partnering with Arab and Jewish believers in the Holy Land as a church planter?" "How can I pray intelligently for those called to go?"

Begin at Home

The first and most obvious step to take is to get involved with Arab and Jewish people who live in your home country. An estimated four million Muslims live in the United States. Many of these are Palestinians. Other millions live in Australia, Central and South America, England, France, Germany and Scandinavia. Mosques spring up all around the world as Muslims travel for study and business. Large communities of Jews also live around us. If you feel called to witness and minister to Arabs or Jews in the Holy Land, an obvious test of your sincerity will be to befriend those who live near you, send their children to school with your children and run businesses in your neighborhood. It is highly likely that a church in your area has an Arabic speaking congregation meeting in its facilities. New mosques are being built to accommodate Muslim worshippers, and Messianic Jewish synagogues and meetings are developing many places in the West.

Take a trip to the mall or local shopping center and begin counting the people who look like they are from the Middle East. You will find in many areas that one out of ten persons are from one of the Middle Eastern countries. Many are lonely and would like a friend in their host country. Some will appreciate your friendship and even accept invitations to special church events.

Social and business contacts made with Arabs and Jews in your home countries can impact decisively on your future. As a first year student at the University of Virginia, I met a Muslim from Damascus at a reception for new students at the YMCA. He invited me up to his room, and I admired the tapestry hanging on his wall. He explained, "This is my prayer rug. I take it down and pray on it five times a day." I knew as a Christian that I did not practice as regular a prayer life. This Muslim challenged me to begin one!

Later, while serving as an officer on a Navy destroyer, I met a young Jewish midshipman. We began to discuss our religious beliefs. He came to my stateroom one day and asked, "Do you really believe the Bible?"

I said, "Yes, of course!"

He then asked, "Do you tithe?"

I replied, "I do now!"

So, I began a regular prayer life through the influence of a Muslim, and started tithing through the challenge of a Jew! These events happened years before I felt called to serve in the Middle East.

Getting acquainted with Middle Easterners in your home country provides an excellent cross-cultural experience if God leads you to serve as a church planter or prayer partner in the Holy Land, or other areas of the Middle East. True, many left the Middle East to get away from problems described in Chapter Two. They are now "upward mobile," seeking higher education, a better standard of living, and may be materialistically motivated. Nevertheless, they serve as valuable contacts with their relatives in the Middle East. Some of them accept the Lord and receive a burden for people in their home countries. Getting to know them on your home territory gives you the advantage of knowing their customs and language before traveling abroad.

I served as pastor to Palestinian Arabs for two years, while on home assignment in the USA, from 1974-1976. A distant relative of mine married a Muslim from the Holy Land. She told me, "If you want to minister to Muslims, here we are!" and invited me to her home. Sitting in her kitchen with her Arab Muslim husband she remarked, "I used to remember a verse that they taught me in Sunday school as a little girl. It was John 3:16. Could you explain to my husband what it means in Arabic?" Knowingly or unknowingly, she gave me the opportunity to share God's love in Christ with her Muslim husband. They then proceeded to introduce me to hundreds of Arab Muslims from Israel-Palestine, scattered across North Carolina. These, in turn, introduced me to the Arab Club at

North Carolina State University, which had a membership of one Christian and ninety-nine Muslims! From there I was introduced to leaders of the Muslim Student Association. I spent two years introducing Muslims to Christian friends in churches in the area. I had found one of the greatest locations for witness and dialogue with Muslims right in my own homeland. The same can be true across the United States, Europe, South Africa, Australia, and other countries, where millions of Muslims now live.[1]

You have the same opportunity to meet Jewish people in your own home territory. Many Jews visit Israel, and some eventually immigrate to live there. Israel, for them, is the fulfillment of 1,900 years of longing for a Jewish national homeland, and they feel obligated to support it. Understand, they can be suspicious of our desire to "convert" them, because they harbor fears of past centuries of persecution and inquisition which forced Jews to convert to Christianity.

The year 1492 refers to more than the year Columbus discovered America; it is also when the Spanish Inquisition began on the Jews! Thousands were forced to convert to Christianity or suffer death or expulsion from their homes. But today, Jews become people of genuine and lasting friendship through sincere dialogue and the assurance that we respect their right not to believe as we do. Through their friendship, we come to appreciate the Jewishness of Jesus and his disciples. Some come to see Jesus as a true Jew and the Messiah for their people. We do not have to be "up tight" about giving witness to Jesus. Thousands of Messianic Jews carry on an active witness for Him themselves, both in Israel and around the world. Most likely, you can find a Messianic Synagogue or Jewish believer's congregation in your area.

Training Opportunities

Another excellent place to prepare for service as a church planter in the Holy Land is in a Bible college or seminary that has a program for overseas service. A few seminaries offer a Master's program in church planting. They usually require two years of study and two years service abroad, in preparation for full-time overseas service. Several institutes and Bible Colleges also provide excellent courses on witness to Muslims in the United States, Great Britain and other countries. Numerous colleges and universities offer courses in Arabic, Islamics and Judaics. It is entirely possible for you to become better informed about Islam and Judaism than many Muslims and Jews! Be aware, you are entering a field of spiritual warfare. A thorough experiential knowledge of the Bible is prerequisite to study of Islam and Judaism. Prayer covering and fellowship with a trusted body of believers is also a must. The International Board of the SBC is now requiring that each church planter sent out from the USA recruit at least 200 prayer partners for their ministry.

The Internet also offers a unique opportunity to learn about Muslims and Jews. Many organizations sponsor a number of web pages designed to influence public opinion, to nourish the faith of Muslims in foreign countries or to try to convert Christians and others to Islam. Other web sites devote their energies to the Jewish people, Israel, the Middle East conflict and related topics. Some secured sites offer information to Christians interested in witnessing to Muslims or Jews. Be aware that some verbiage on Muslim sites can be offensive to Christian sensitivities and border on libel. Web sites offer an opportunity to dialogue and debate Muslims and others about many issues. You can get a taste of what you will face in overseas ministries through this unique and growing method of communication.

Another help is to save up enough money to take a tour of the Holy Land, or other countries of the Middle East, to check out opportunities of ministry first hand. Some tours offer college or seminary credit and are led by competent experts on the area. The only disadvantage of such short-term tours, usually ten days to two weeks, is they leave you bewildered with an overload of information. It is easy to get a romantic view of the Holy Land, which can be deflated when reality sets in.

Perhaps an even better way to get acquainted with the area is through short-term volunteer service. Southern Baptists and Operation Mobilization offers opportunities of between two months and two years voluntary service in the Holy Land, and in other Middle Eastern countries. The Anglican Church in the Middle East offers similar short-term service. It is possible to volunteer for work on a kibbutz, or communal farm, in Israel. You need to be cautious about loose morals and isolation from Christian fellowship, which can take a heavy toll on your spiritual life.

Global Missions Fellowship coordinates short-term evangelism and church planting experiences with local churches in Israel and the West Bank. They provide a short orientation in the USA, with churches that minister to Arabs and Jews. Southeastern Baptist Theological Seminary sponsors a Master of Divinity with Church Planting. This program offers two years practical experience overseas as a prerequisite to appointment by the International Mission Board (IMB). The IMB also now offers a three-year apprentice program, which allows you to get to the field faster and to learn the language at a younger age, before career appointment as a church planter. Columbia Biblical Seminary & Graduate School of Missions in South Carolina and London Bible College now offer a Master degree in Islamic studies.

However you choose to prepare yourself to be a better church planter, or a better prayer warrior for the Holy Land and the Middle East, you owe it to yourself and to the people whom you plan to serve to learn as much as you can about Islam and Judaism. A basic knowledge of Church history and ancient Christian churches will enable you to appreciate traditional Christians of the Holy Land.

The better your preparation, the more rewarding your life will be, and the deeper your understanding will become of the people of the area.

The Holy Land and Middle East impact our lives through continual turmoil in the area. The only long-term answer is for Jews and Arabs to know about Jesus and his love, and to be discipled by life-style mentoring. Church planting movements are beginning in the area, as local people take hold of the vision God has for an ingathering of unreached peoples. If God lays this burden on you, you owe it to yourself and to the people of the land to prepare well before you come.

Catalyzing a Church Planting Movement

What can you do to become a catalyst for a church planting movement in the Holy Land, from your home base? Church planters use these approaches, which are adapted from those proposed by Erich Bridges. You and your church can do the same, but be ready when you do, to answer with your life and your resources:

1. Ask God to give your church a vision for reaching a particular people or group.
2. Develop a passion. Ask God, "What is it going to take to reach these people? Be ready to act when He answers.
3. Recruit a committed prayer network in your church and beyond, for your targeted people.
4. Network with church planters and others committed to reaching your target people.
5. Mobilize volunteers, teams and resources to help share the Gospel with your people.
   Remember: whatever it takes![2]

Chapter six and following will provide practical steps toward your involvement in church planting movements on the ground in the Holy Land.

Down in the Trenches and Enjoying It!

C hurch planting in the Holy Land is a spiritual battle. Satan invaded the hearts of men, from the first encounter in the Garden of Eden. God used the children of Israel to model this battle. The Prophet Jeremiah records the rebellion which separated them from God and made them captives of sin. He said: "This people has a stubborn and rebellious heart; they have turned aside and departed."[1] Jesus, a true Jew, paid the price for their rebellion. The Prophet Isaiah said: "He was wounded for our transgressions, he was bruised for our iniquities. The chastisement of our peace was upon him, and with his stripes we are healed. All we like sheep have gone astray; we have turned every one to his own way, and the Lord hath laid on him the iniquity of us all."[2] Jesus defeated sin by death on the cross and rose victorious from the grave. Church planting basically takes back territory in human hearts falsely claimed by Satan and his demon angels. This includes Arabs, Jews and expatriates in the Middle East. Much of what we saw in the earlier chapters gives evidence of this battle. There are victories and there are casualties. Every church planted in the Holy Land is evidence of God's victory in the hearts of men and women, through faith in Jesus as Savior, Lord and Messiah. I would like to share some tried advice for church planters and for those who pray for them in this chapter. The goal is to enable you to stay on the battle-field, to be productive and to avoid becoming a casualty.

Most Critical Issue—Survival of the Church Planter

Survival of the church planter remains a critical issue in the Holy Land and Middle East. Whether a church planter is an expatriate from abroad or a local who attempts to live in a new area of the land, each faces unique challenges. The "honeymoon" fades after a few months on the field. Cultural and spiritual props unconsciously leaned upon in the home country fall away, leaving you feeling naked, stranded and empty emotionally, spiritually and physically. This is a common experience for church planters in cross-cultural situations worldwide.

Somehow, we expect things to be different in the Holy Land, but to the contrary, the situation is usually more intense! A crisis of calling sets in. "Culture shock" intensifies as family members each go through their own crisis and offer little or negative support. The church planter can find himself or herself with different or opposing views to those of members of their support organization, if he or she chooses to bond with the local culture and people.

I can well remember nights during my first years in Israel, when my wife stayed awake nights, retching from an intestinal disorder. My children cried and asked, "Why did you take us away from Grandmother?" My support organization made what I considered unreasonable demands in the midst of Arabic language study. A dysfunctional family background cropped up to haunt me and plague my relationships with others. I found myself in the middle of a spiritual battlefield for which I had not been adequately prepared. I could have become a casualty, had God not been patient He provided a German Jewish doctor and patient friends and coworkers to encourage us during this initial period of adjustment.

Be aware, Satan is not at all happy you are trying to plant churches! Added to all the above, he is unloading his arsenal on you. What can you do to insure longevity and productivity as a church planter?

Be Sure of Your Calling Before You Come!

You will fall back upon your calling from God time and time again. It will keep you going in times of crisis. This is as true for local church planters as for expatriates. Jewish believers who leave another country and return to Israel suffer the same crisis as do Arabs who leave home in Haifa or Nazareth and move to a Galilean village to plant a church. Trials are sure to come, and when they do, do not blame God! Local people will ask, if you leave prematurely in the midst of a struggle, "When did you hear the call of God? When you came or when you left?" There comes a time when God plants the church and your task finishes. Then it is time to move on. To stay longer could stunt the growth of the church and cause needless dependency.

Remember! Getting to the "field" is only part of the calling. Where and how to serve once you arrive becomes an application of that calling. Sometimes you have to decide whether to go where the fish are biting and the harvest is ripe. Other times you must be willing to clear away rocks so seeds can be planted. Church planting in the Holy Land usually involves both! Our calling to go to a particular place to plant a church must be reshaped by realities that face us when we arrive. Allow the Lord to clarify your calling once you get oriented, and to give you a local vision of churches planted all over His land. He often does this in very practical and unexpected ways.

Take Language and Cultural Acquisition Seriously!

Learning local languages is a lifetime process at which one never becomes perfect. It is hard work, but the end result is worth the effort. As Charles Brock exclaims: "Nothing will capture the attention of a group of unbelievers like a foreigner speaking clearly in their native tongue . . . There is no better way to communicate love than to speak to people in a language they can understand."[3]

Jim Slack puts it in other words:

> How tragic to traverse 10,000 miles at great expense to the family and the faithful, only to stop one "tongue" short of making the journey complete . . . Contextualization does not mean compromising the Gospel…but rather communicating the gospel correctly in the appropriate language of a culture, so that nothing is lost when the message is brought over by means of life, lip and language.[4]

The time, effort, pain and pleasure you put into acquiring a basic use of Arabic, Hebrew, or Russian, and in understanding the respective cultures, represents a wise investment for the future. So, think big. Think long term.

I had the advantage of studying Islamics, Jewish life, Classical Arabic and linguistics at Hartford Seminary Foundation before arriving in Israel in 1965. Learning spoken Arabic was a challenge. I studied it for a year, intensively, in Haifa, with the late Issam Nureddin Abbasi, an Arab Muslim poet. I determined to absorb the language and culture day and night and restricted my exposure to English speaking people, including worship services. But after a year and a half in Nazareth I felt as though I was drying up spiritually!

One Thursday night at Bible study in the Nazareth Baptist Church my ears supernaturally opened to Arabic. I was being fed spiritually in Arabic for the first time! The passage of scripture being explained was Acts 1:8, on the coming of the Holy Spirit. Overwhelmed, I ran outside and wept for joy! Continuing to grow in the use of Arabic after this experience, I later learned that other church planters, such as Hudson Taylor in China, had similar breakthrough experiences in language acquisition.

The spiritual keys to incarnational language and cultural learning are found in Jesus' saying to "become as a child to enter the Kingdom," and Paul's willingness to be a "fool for Christ's sake."

Arabs worship their language and often can be severe in criticism if it is not pronounced correctly. You must learn to laugh at yourself and to be laughed at to learn Arabic. Early-on in language learning I was driving an elderly matron of the Nazareth Church, along with church leaders, to a meeting. In my best classical Arabic I asked the lady, "Would you like to fasten your safety belt?" She looked at me with a shocked expression on her face. The pastor and deacons roared with laughter. What I had said to her was, "Would you like to get yourself pregnant?" I am grateful to those saints who overlooked my stumbling.

Learning Hebrew is said to be a little easier now, because of the large number of Israelis who are new immigrants. Special schools for language learning, called "ulpans," are set up to take them through the various levels of Hebrew language learning. An expatriate church planter can join Russians, Argentineans and others in their struggles to learn Hebrew. I have been able to carry on limited Hebrew conversations with Russian and Uzbeki neighbors, who themselves are still learning the language.

Perhaps the most humiliating aspect of language learning is how fast your children learn the language, especially if they go to local schools. My children used to joke with each other in Arabic. Their favorite after-meal entertainment was to sit around the table and mimic my Southern accent when I spoke Arabic. Their accent was so good, I have seen Arabs look around behind my children to see where a real Arab was hiding!

Southern Baptists developed a cost-efficient program of language and culture acquisition, with the assistance of linguist Don Larson. It accelerates the learning process by involving a church planter in the Arabic and Hebrew speaking community from the beginning. This community-based approach promotes development of "cross-culture communicative competence" (CCCC). The student depends on local community members for language learning, cultural knowledge and lifestyle development. A more experienced Entry Orientation Coordinator (ENOC) advises new learners in this process. I assisted Larson and others in initial development of the Arabic learning tool and saw the genius of this method, when it is utilized as Dr. Larson intended. Knowledge of each student's Myers-Briggs Personality Inventory (MBPI) profile helps him or her maximize the effectiveness of this method. A church planter can then embark upon more advanced Hebrew or Arabic studies as needed, to polish literacy-related skills which he or she will use in the church planting process.[5]

For those who need a more structured language study environment for Arabic, the Kelsey School in Amman, Jordan is recommended. Students live in homes of Arabs while studying the language intensively. Those who come from Kelsey School acquire an Arabic accent and learn to pray and read Scripture in Arabic. Another possibility for Arabic study is at Beir Zeit University, north of Ramallah in the West Bank. Beir Zeit offers a three-level Arabic studies program, in an academic environment.

Local friends are your keys to language and culture. Arabs teach you how to sit without showing the sole of your shoe or foot, which offends those around you. They cover the legs of your wife with a towel or blanket to protect her modesty. They teach you how to peel an orange and eat it in sections to get the most out of it. They tell you never to place your Bible on the floor or carry it below your waist, to give due honor to God's Word. They caution you to use your right hand in greetings, as the left is used for unclean purposes. You observe that they do not talk while eating, and in some rural settings are allowed a hearty belch after the meal!

Local friends remind you of the "red flag items" that Jim Slack cautions will make people resistant to the Gospel.[6] Christians may be offended at your lack of reverence for the Virgin Mary. Muslims usually object to hearing you call Jesus God's son, or references to the Trinity and crucifixion. The Holocaust and inquisition are very sore points for Jews. Each of these red flags, if unavoidable, can be turned into bridges, to share a clearer picture of what you as a born-again Christian believe about these issues. It may be the first time they have heard about them in a biblical perspective from a believer.

Language and cultural acquisition in the Holy Land can be fun, in the midst of much work and occasional humiliation. The payoff comes when you can share the simple Gospel message in Arabic or Hebrew and see people responding. An ideal is to have a year or two set aside for nothing but language and culture acquisition, though this is not always possible for volunteers and persons assigned to English language work. Mothers with growing children have limited time and energy with which to study. Long term effectiveness as a church planter is often determined by the ability to both speak the language and understand the culture, which endear you to locals and cause other expatriates envy. It is worth the effort, especially when you see God's Word coming alive, renewing yourself and planting His church in the Holy Land.

Add a Big Dose of Patience to Your Calling

God called you to one of the most difficult places in the world to be a church planter. Church planting strategists of the International

Board, SBC once met to discuss potential around the world. One stated: "In Africa a church starts under every tree."

Dale Thorne, Area Director for the Middle East and North Africa (MENA) responded: "In the Middle East it is hard to find the trees!" Patience is the name of the game in the Holy Land.

Plan to spend long evenings over charcoal fires in Muslim homes, listening to endless fables of Jesus and the three thieves, drinking cups of sweet, thick tea, eating exotic food, and then sharing the Gospel in a way they have never heard before. You will be challenged by questions like: "Why do you not honor the Virgin Mary?" and "What do you mean by 'being born-again'?" in Christian homes. You will face the haunting ghost of the Holocaust and Christian complicity, along with fears of the Arab's on-going war of attrition, when sharing with Jews. Many are cynical toward all religion, including yours. When hearts open to the love of God in Jesus you know it is God at work, because only He can do it in such a spiritual wasteland.

Accomplishing basic chores of everyday life takes longer in the Holy Land. Inherited and imported business practices from Turks, British, Germans, Russians and many other cultures complicate the simplest transaction. When I first arrived in Israel, I needed a signature from a specific customs official. He sent me from office to office until I finally returned to his office. Exasperated, I pounded on his desk and demanded the signature. He quietly signed the paper, smiled and said, "Now you have learned how to get things done in Israel!" Few things are done without a hassle and an argument, which is very disarming for Americans and Europeans, who are used to "service with a smile." Shahar and Kurz explain in their book *Border Crossing* that Israelis smile only when they want to and consider Americans superficial in friendships because they smile too much![7] *Border Crossings* is a helpful tool in understanding different social norms, expectations and behavior patterns in Israeli society.

Men usually do much of the shopping, in the Arab culture, which is ordinarily assigned to women in western culture. You also are expected to engage in conversation during the daily rounds of business. I used to say I spent one third of my time doing Muslim work, one third doing church work and one third doing donkey work!

A trip to downtown Jerusalem, Tel Aviv or Haifa at high traffic time is a challenge to the patience of any normal person. Nazareth is impassable due to one-lane traffic during peak hours, or drivers making U-turns in the middle of the highway. Wisdom dictates avoiding any downtown at rush hours, or using a cassette player to listen to sermon tapes, music or language lessons. A slogan in many Arab shops says in Arabic, "Help me Lord, to add patience to my patience!" Time in the Middle East is measured from event to event, not according to the clock and the calendar. History is when God decides to make it happen. So, after many frustrating failures to keep a schedule, you learn to head home a half-hour early and enjoy the customary afternoon nap, letting your nerves settle and your body refresh from the dry heat.

Bond to Local Christian, Jewish and Muslim Friends

When you become known as a person trying to learn Arabic, Hebrew or the language of your target culture, the Lord will bring friends of that language and culture. They will be your long-term advisors on how the church or congregation can be planted in their culture. They know how their own people think and how to "scratch where it itches." I had several Christian Arab friends and two special Muslim friends who helped me understand the people I was seeking to reach. They advised me before making plans and debriefed me about what people were saying about me and the Gospel after I left. This advice never cost me a penny, but it was worth millions! They were key ingredients to a network of Christian churches and a few Muslim believers, all over Galilee.

A word of caution for those who are new in the land. Some local persons, gifted in "bending the ear of a foreigner," will make a beeline for a new church planter, to fill his ears with their ideas. They are usually people with a hidden agenda, wanting to get you to fall in line with their objectives, usually in opposition to other people. You can waste much precious time listening to the latest version of on-going sagas of personal gripes. It is best to learn the Middle Eastern custom of "testing the waters" by gaining a consensus of opinions before launching prematurely into time-wasting adventures. Words that are whispered in secret and confidence about another person most likely end up in that persons ear before the sun goes down anyway. So, be warned.

All of the above considered, many Arab and Jewish friends are like those who stick closer than a brother. If you keep their confidence and do not betray their secret thoughts to others, they will love you for a lifetime. They are part of the "hundred-fold" the Lord promises for those who leave friends and brothers back home. The same goes for other church planters with whom you partner. Seek the advice of veterans who matched their walk with their talk. Some idealists have great plans that do not work, in the practical sense. Partner with people who give you balance. Like your local friends, they should be willing to tell you when you are wrong, and be patient and wise enough to show you a better way. I had many people give me advice, but few who knew how to model so I could follow their example. Treasure and honor those who model what they say.

Give Your Wife and Children Quality Time

An ever present tendency and danger in the life of a church planter is to be so absorbed in his "work" that he forgets his family. After all, he or she might reason that Jesus said: "He who loves son or daughter more than me is not worthy of me," and "Every one who left houses or bothers or sisters or father or mother or children or lands, for my name's sake, will receive a hundredfold, and inherit eternal life."[8]

While these verses challenge us to total discipleship and to keep our priorities straight, they do not excuse us to neglect husbands, wives and children who chose to follow us and live with us in the Holy Land. We must be balanced by the clear admonition of Paul: "If any one does not provide for his relatives, and especially for his own family, he has disowned the faith and is worse than an unbeliever."[9]

Your family's survival may determine your longevity in church planting. That does not mean you have to give them full time, but it does mean to give them quality time. There is a balance to be maintained between ministry and family. Your mate and your children will be one of your greatest assets in meeting people the Lord wants reached. Make your home and family an integral part of your ministry. Give them the privilege of sharing in your work, both its successes and setbacks. Let it be their work, also. But remember, they are to be loved and cared for, not only because of their contribution to your ministry, but because they are a special gift and responsibility of the Lord to you. It is often a difference in the quality of caring within a church planter's family which shines as a bright light in Jewish and Muslim communities in the Holy Land. Hospitality shown in your home, by a wife and family who feel supported, are a great asset to your ministry. Friends made by your children in the neighborhood and at school often lead to more positive encounters for church planting.

Be patient with your wife. Do not expect her to spend the same amount of time in language study and ministry as you do, especially if she has the burden of caring for a home and raising children. Appreciate her for staying with you in a strange culture, far from home! At a minimum, make it possible for her to learn enough of the language and culture during her first two years to be a hostess who can serve graciously and talk intelligently with the average person, in Arabic or Hebrew. She is co-ministering with you, though this ministry during child-raising years will be primarily through your home. She will become more proficient than you in certain areas of language and culture, so you can help each other. My wife found the Arabic she learned in these earliest years was used even more effectively in later years, when the children were grown and gone.

Remember the advice of Solomon, who had perhaps thousands of wives: "Rejoice in the wife of your youth, a lovely hind, a graceful doe. Let her affection fill you at all times with delight, be infatuated always with her love." [10] Do not let Satan deceive you by distraction of an occasional Israeli or Arab woman's beauty. Be careful! Others watch your eyes, to see how you look at their women! The Jewish and Muslim culture is very earthy, and it is all too easy to fall into deceptive fantasy which could lead to destructive action. We knew only a few who fell for this deception in our long career. But the ripple effect of divorce and broken homes is long remembered by believer and unbeliever alike. Marriages of church planters need to be mutually renegotiated as they pass through the rites of passage of life. Relationships of husband and wife get more satisfying physically, emotionally and spiritually as years pass and you share the trials and victories of ministry together.

There will never be total agreement concerning the education of church planter's children, in a cross-culture situation like the Holy Land. There are those who maintain that children should always go to local schools in Hebrew and Arabic. While this has advantages, it is not always possible or feasible. Others maintain that children should study in English language schools or home school, to better prepare them for re-entry into western schools and universities in their home countries. Certainly this has merit, but it could have the disadvantage of cutting them off from benefits of learning local languages and culture. Our experience is that every situation and every child is different. A blend of the two extremes may be best, adapted to the special gifts and needs of each child. We used both, and our children survived. Each had problems unique to their personality and situation, but each also excelled in special areas.

I certainly concur with Charles Brock in that values of a Christian home should be maintained, and the child's values to his home country must be taught and reinforced also.[11] I do believe it is impossible to avoid all tension between a host culture and one's home country. Our experience is that children seem to adapt and survive much better than parents! Long experience reveals many church planter's children, or "third-culture kids" as they are sometimes called, end up as high achievers academically and professionally. (One of ours became a Doctor of Chiropractic, another a research scientist, and a third became an artist.) There is no substitute for being fluent in several languages and for being knowledgeable to the cultures in the Middle East. Advantages far outweigh the disadvantages, from our perspective. Besides, who said raising children in America or Europe or any other western country is safe and without peril? The United States has the highest rate of teen suicide and murder of any industrialized nation.[12] We need to keep things in perspective and realize God loves our children as much or more than we love them. Taking them overseas may be the best thing we ever did for them.

Quality time with family means, at a minimum, a day or evening a week for fun and fellowship as a family, away from ministry. It means, in the Holy Land, camping trips and hikes to a multitude of parks and archeological sites. It means eating in Arab restaurants and swimming in warm spring pools, once dammed by King Herod. It means huddling together in time of war, peril and personal family emergency. It means celebrating the Fourth of July and Israel Independence Day, or Land Day in the Arab sector. It means swimming in pure waters of the Sea of Galilee or in the surf of the Mediterranean. It means growing up together, learning Arabic or Hebrew together, parent-teacher meetings and all. It means fighting and overcoming drugs and perversions which pervade Israeli and Palestinian society, together. It means a date, at least once a month with your spouse, without the children, to renew and refresh your relationship. It is worth it, and it insures longevity.

What About Singles? Do They Have a Role?

The answer is a resounding "Yes!" Life as a single church planter in the Holy Land has advantages and disadvantages, like any other place in the world. There is a unique role for women to minister to Muslim and Christian Arab women, since Arab society limits the contact a man can have with women to whom he is not related by blood or marriage. One of the most effective church planters I know among Arab women is a single woman. Another is a divorcee who has instant rapport with Muslim women, who are in constant fear of divorce from their husbands. Single women served as pioneers, church planting in Israel and Palestine in the days following the turmoil of World War II. They laid the foundation for married couples who followed.

Single men have been effective in teams of door-to-door book sales and witnessing, through various para-church organizations. They find the experience of living in an Arab or Jewish communities excellent preparation for future ministry. Many come as students, serve as volunteers on a kibbutz, work with youth in churches and have other volunteer positions. One single male now leads a large organization of others, following the affirmation of his peers who are mostly married couples! Another leads a vital prayer ministry that has been effective in networking church planting in Arabic and Hebrew sectors throughout the country.

Any single must accept constant pressure, within Arab communities, to find a marriage partner. Why not accept this as a positive indication of the Arab's caring, and not be offended by their persistence? They are concerned because of perceptions of loneliness and temptations that are real in both an Arab and Jewish society. For this reason, single church planters, male or female, need the "covering" of a family to whom they can relate on a fairly regular basis. This can be a local Arab or Jewish family, or an expatriate family. Also, they must find a church home for fellowship and spiritual support. Certainly, single church planters do have a major role, following the model of both Jesus and Paul!

Enlist Prayer Partners, Local and Abroad

Find prayer partners who can keep your needs before God's throne. One of the best ways to build long term relationships with local pastors is to spend time in prayer with them. All cultural and language differences, and your personal weaknesses, may be overlooked if they know you share their burdens in prayer. Every church planter needs at least one local person who can pray for him. My privilege was to have a great man lift me and my family before God in prayer every day. Only eternity will tell the work those prayers accomplished.

Be sure to also keep faithful prayer partners in your home country informed of your personal and ministry needs. You benefit from their prayers, and your requests makes overseas ministries more real to them. It is easy and instantaneous to communicate by e-mail and relay prayer concerns, as well as the answers God brings in his perfect timing. Be sure to protect the identity of Muslim and Jewish friends when corresponding, since all electronic communication can be considered public.

Church planting in the Holy Land is a spiritual battle. Those who engage in it must have special preparation to stay alive spiritually and not to become a casualty emotionally. Those who fall in the battle should be restored by caring nurture, rest, encouragement, and if necessary, forgiveness and restoration. Of all people, believers in the Lord Jesus should not shoot their wounded! My hope is the preceding information will help you be productive and fruitful. Enjoy being a soldier for the Lord Jesus Christ, the Messiah and the only hope for Israel and Arabs. It can be fun, amid the real struggles and pain of life in the Holy Land.

Your relationships in your family and with fellow church planters and local believers are the front-line of defense in the spiritual warfare of church planting. Along with a personal relationship with the Lord, which needs daily nourishing, the important "others" in your personal life can help you succeed in your planting career. Be sensitive to their needs and feelings and aware of your own. Let the "joy of the Lord" be your strength and learn how precious it is for brothers to dwell in unity. Learn to practice identificational repentance, to keep lines of communication open. Enjoy the challenges and privileges of serving in the Holy Land.

Now you ask, "Fine. But I cannot spend all my time nurturing myself, my family and friends! How do I go about getting a handle on church planting?" Chapter Seven will attempt to get you started.

chapter seven

Practical Suggestions for Church Planting Movements

The Lord of the Harvest is the best church planter in the Holy Land and all of the Middle East. After all, He knows the soil best. He knows the hearts of the men, women, boys and girls He created. Jesus told Peter: "On this rock I will build my church, and the gates of Hell will not prevail against it!" (Matthew 16:18) You and I, as believers, have the keys of the Kingdom to unlock the hearts of people with the good news. These keys may be a special approach to a particular peoples group, or a village or city. Different keys open different locks. Use of these keys, along with the power of prayer and sharing the Gospel, brings a response from traditional Christian Arabs, Muslims and Jews. History and experience proves that the Church can be planted in the Holy Land. It is never easy, but God, the Lord of the Harvest is able!

The following information is not intended to be a comprehensive, exhaustive or technical approach to church planting and church growth. Many excellent books are available on the subject.

Classics like Roland Allen's *Missionary Methods, St. Paul's or Ours;* Robert Coleman's *The Master Plan of Evangelism* and Donald McGavran's *Understanding Church Growth* shaped my thinking for years, as I struggled to get a handle on church planting in the Holy Land. Other excellent books are available on the subject, but few deal specifically with this area in the Middle East, with the exception of George Jenning's *Welcome to the Middle East* and Greg Livingstone's *Planting Churches in Muslim Cities.* I share the following, in hope it will help you find ways to "get a handle" on the work of church planting in this crucial area of the world.

I concur wholeheartedly with Gene Mims, when he reminds us in *Kingdom Principles for Church Growth:* "Always place divine process ahead of methods . . . Methods are not the answer to ongoing church growth, because methods are not the problem . . . God uses all kinds of circumstances, especially failure and crisis, to melt the hearts of people who are separated from him."[1] I believe we are in a time of kingdom growth in the Holy Land and the Middle East. God is working in hearts and lives like never before. He uses some of the following methods.

Pray in All Seasons

Church planting must be bathed in prayer. A church planter can do nothing more, nor nothing less than pray, pray, pray! Prayer resembles the aerial sowing of storm clouds, which turns them into showers of blessing. Prayer alone can break the spiritual bondage over people's hearts in the Holy Land—and around the world. Many believe worldwide revival cannot come until it comes here first. Only the power of prayer overcomes spiritual oppression which looms over Jerusalem and Nazareth. It alone breaks the bondage of drugs and prostitution that binds Acre, Haifa, and Tel Aviv. Much work in "spiritual mapping" needs to be done in the Holy Land to identify areas of spiritual bondage carried over from

Baal worship, the oppressive use of witchcraft and subtle worship of the dead through the centuries. When these forbidden areas are identified, they can be prayed through until God releases his power to free thousands enslaved by them.[2]

Jesus prayed all night before choosing and sending out disciples. He told them to pray for the Lord of the harvest to send forth laborers into it. They begged him to teach them how to pray. He spent the night in agonizing prayer, before bearing the cross for mankind. But God restored him to life on the third day, a prayer answered. And the Spirit fell on the group huddled in prayer at Pentecost.

Prayer not only prepares the soil, it also enables the sower to sow wisely. Concerned Jewish believers from around the country gathered on the banks of the Yarkon River in Tel Aviv, after the signing of the Oslo Peace Agreement. Over 600 believers from 16 congregations divided into smaller groups to petition God for their nation, in focused prayer and fasting. At the end of the time of corporate prayer, evangelism teams witnessed to young people gathering for a heavy metal rock concert that evening. The young people were so hungry for literature that every team ran out of Bibles, books, and tracts. God opens hearts, through prayer, to receive the seed of the Gospel.[3]

A champion church planter in Galilee uses prayer walks as his first strategy for new plants. Before entering a city or a kibbutz, he gathers concerned believers there to pray. God reveals the potential of the harvest and breaks spiritual bondages, so the planter does not have to waste time on barren soil. God gives the release for ministry or turns him to a more fruitful place. Often believers' groups spring up in every city, town and kibbutz. Prayer is not only pious, it is practical. We put feet to our prayers because the harvest season does not last forever.

I always find prayer an effective and practical tool in church planting. Muslims, Christians and Jews all respect the power of prayer in the Holy Land. I have experienced direct answers to prayers in Jesus' name for healing, discerning the thoughts of the heart, and for casting out demons. The ways God chooses to answer prayer continues to amaze me and challenge my weak faith.

I have found several books helpful in understanding the role of prayer and spiritual warfare in church planting. Though they are written from a western perspective, they are based on the Bible that is native to the soil of the Holy Land. *Breaking Strongholds: How Spiritual Warfare Sets Captives Free,* by Tom White from Corvalis, Oregon is such a book.[4] Tom attends a united prayer conference in Jerusalem every year. *Confronting the Powers: How the New Testament Church Experienced the Power of Strategic Level Warfare* is another powerful book, by Peter Wagner.[5] He shares his own spiritual pilgrimage to a new awareness of the power of God over Satan, which causes me to identify with new realities we experienced during renewal in the Holy Land in the 1970s. *Healing America's Wounds* is a classic book on identificational repentance, by John Dawson.[6] Dawson is international director of urban missions for YWAM, who spent 23 years in overseas service before immigrating to the United States from New Zealand. I have witnessed reconciliation between Jew and Arab using the principles he advocates in this very readable book.

A regular prayer and devotional life enables church planters to recover from the low times of "burn-out" in ministry. Spiritual, emotional and physical attacks encountered in church planting in the Holy Land can quickly result in broken sleep patterns, feelings of malaise and loss of temper. These symptoms require us to take spiritual, emotional and physical inventory. When we cry out to God in prayer, he sends caring friends and counselors who can advise us to gain rest, recreation, proper diet and if needed, professional help. I see in myself, and in other church planters, a tendency toward perfection and achievement, which can lead to discouragement. We need simply to trust God and wait on His timing to accomplish the task that, humanly speaking, we cannot do alone.

Analyze the Soil

Finding people responsive to the Gospel enables you to concentrate time and effort most effectively. Israel is a small country, even if you include the West Bank and Gaza, or Palestinian territory. It is a very complex country with hundreds of "homogenous units" and people groups. Each responds to the Gospel with a different level of receptivity. Some remain resistant, and others open up unexpectedly. I conducted a church growth survey of the Galilee or northern region, in 1991. I inquired about correspondence course response results and the proximity of evangelical Christian witness and known believers to various peoples groups. Results indicated there were at least three possible responsive target groups among the population of 1,400,000 people. These were students, Bedouins, and Druze. I also discovered several Russian congregations made up of recent immigrants. I found evangelicals had a witness in only 22 of 60 cities and towns of over 5,000 in population, leaving at least two-thirds unreached. These findings were shared with various evangelical churches through the United Christian Council and personal contact. (See Appendix A)

But this was only a preliminary study. More research could reveal pockets of responsive people in the various villages and towns of Galilee. How did I get my figures? I purchased a copy of the latest *Statistical Abstract of Israel,* published by the Central Bureau of Statistics, from Steimatsky Book Store! Using maps printed by the Survey of Israel I made a large map of Galilee, pinpointing all evangelical Christian ministries in the region.[7] Interviews with church leaders and institutions determined membership. They confirmed observations made through visits to many of the towns and cities, as well as interviews with local believers. I also found helpful information from willing school principals, social welfare workers and local town officials.

The DAWN survey of 1993 indicated eight new churches started by different evangelical churches in Galilee, between 1991 and 1993. This means the Lord sent laborers into the harvest during a responsive period. But were the harvesters sufficient for such a large work? Most of the churches planted were among traditional Christians, not among unreached non-Christians.

A wealth of information on a potential harvest is available from directors of Bible correspondence courses, Operation Mobilization teams, Children's Evangelical Fellowship and others. The Coastal Plains area, Jerusalem, the Negev and Eilat need similar surveys, to find potential receptive groups. Cold figures on paper become living people when God opens hearts by prayer-walks through possible areas of harvest. Claylan Coursey emphasizes: "Church growth is not just a matter of finding people . . . Rather, church growth is a matter of finding those people who are ready to receive the gospel."[8] Testing the soil by a general survey is one way to find out.

Another way of analyzing soil for response is to visit believers who have moved to new areas. They are usually lonely and need fellowship. Some welcome a Bible study to which they can invite neighbors and new friends. This can be the beginning of a cell group, which could develop into a church. In one northern Galilean village, into which a believer from Nazareth married, we found four families open to the Bible. All it takes is a person willing to follow through with a home or community study.

One way congregations form in the Hebrew sector is through "hiving off." After checking the compatibility of the area to Jewish believers, or at least the ambivalence of the community, a group of believers will move to a new settlement and other believers join them. They start Bible studies, where receptive local people begin attending. Soon a congregation forms. The number of Hebrew-speaking congregations increased 50% in a period of ten years, from 1983-1993, partly through using this method. They know where the soil is good for church planting.

Sow the Word

Scripture distribution in any form proves effective in opening hearts and minds to the Gospel. The Word of God in written or spoken form convicts hearts of sin, brings the peace of salvation and causes a hunger for fellowship with other believers. Sowing of the written and spoken Word for years is bringing fruit in the Holy Land. Newspapers advertise correspondence courses. Thousands request Bibles and New Testaments in various languages, including Hebrew, Arabic, Russian, Amharic and many East European languages. I once received a request from an Islamic University for a Bible for each professor and student. The director felt his students should know the Bible as well as the Quran. Reading it enables Muslims to better understand their Quran, and to inquire about the differences.

Mass distribution of the Bible, New Testament and scripture portions creates an awareness and hunger in the hearts of people of the Holy Land and Middle East. One Bible distributor cannot keep a supply of Arabic Bibles, due to a steady demand from around the world. We see a ripe harvest in homes, at repair garages, on beaches, in parks, in cars and buses. Recently, every Palestinian soldier and policeman guarding Manger Square in Bethlehem willingly received a New Testament. People open their hearts and hunger for a new word from God, in times of change and uncertainty.

The Jesus Film, basically a verbatim presentation of the Life of Christ from the Gospel of Luke, continues to be one of the most popular films on Middle East Television and in video stores. It is available in Hebrew, Arabic, Russian, Amharic, as well as in

English. Along with Billy Graham's recent satellite films, believers present them as house gifts to those who want to watch and hear the Gospel with interested neighbors. This exposure to the message of salvation creates a potential for future response.

Coordinated follow-up of people who indicate interest and response from sowing the word can bring results. Groups that canvass the country from door-to-door need to keep records and share discreetly those names of persons who request personal follow-up and encouragement. We discovered many people who receive Bible literature do not want exposure to pressure and opposition of family, friends and neighbors, until they mature spiritually. They often prefer to be met away from home.

Bible correspondence courses remain a major untapped resource for follow-up and church planting in the Holy Land. Tens of thousands of Arabs and Jews have subscribed to these courses in the past. A good percentage indicated decisions for Christ in the process of their studies. The desire for privacy and confidentiality prevents sharing their names. Directors of correspondence courses need to work out a way for correspondents to indicate a desire to meet with trusted church planters for counsel and direction in their new found faith. Some courses sponsor conferences for interested students, where they can gather to meet other students and study with visiting lecturers in greater depth. Church planters who know the language and cultural sensitivities could utilize these courses to plant churches.

Story the Bible

The majority of people of the Holy Land communicate orally, despite their education and literacy. They think and act as oral communicators. Tales, fables and storytelling still provide the evening entertainment in the Muslim world. The Friday evening Arabic language TV film from Egypt is a national institution in

Israel-Palestine! Muslims memorize the Quran through rhyme and musical chant. Ask a Christian priest to quote a Bible verse and he will sing or chant it to you! They in turn learned it from the Jewish Psalms of David. Opera, theater drama, art and classical music fill the evenings of sophisticated Jews.

Chronological Bible storytelling, repeating proverbs and parables, remains an effective method of reaching children and adults. Because a majority of Arab women over the age of forty are functionally illiterate, they need an oral Bible. Child Evangelism classes, using flannel graphs with pictures and scripture songs, remains popular in the Arab sector. Traditional churches readily accept this form of Bible teaching, with its emphasis on memorizing scriptures and songs by group oral repetition.

The first thing a church planter should learn is how to give his or her own personal testimony, and how to present simple Bible stories in the Arabic or Hebrew language. This activity will never wear out or get old, and will remain an effective way of storytelling the Bible for years to come. Start simple and build step-by-step. Become as a little child to enter the kingdom. God will reward your efforts.

Team Up!

Harvest season for olives usually comes in October, in Galilee. Everyone goes out to the olive groves to harvest. Each family works on the trees it owns, beating branches and catching the ripe olives which fall on blankets spread on the ground. The harvest requires a team effort, because the season only lasts a few weeks. One person alone cannot do it. Church planters need to see the wisdom of team effort, to reap the harvest of winnable people to Christ.

But team effort in evangelism and church planting is not new. Jesus sent out his twelve disciples two-by-two, after intensive training and empowering. Then he sent the seventy out in teams also.[9]

They carried specific instructions and marching orders and reported back to him about what they achieved. Robert Coleman describes Jesus as the Master Teacher who poured his life's mission into a select group, concentrating on three choice men.[10] Hesselgrave points out that Paul seldom worked alone, but worked in teams with Timothy, Luke, and Titus.[11] Chaney recommends using a team drawn from people in the community who know the local situation. He feels five to eight families are ideal. They become the "movers and shakers" of the new congregation.[12] Stuart Christine points out that a team should have a unified vision and be compatible on spiritual and practical matters of church planting. He feels the leader must live in the community and team members should be actively involved in the community survey, to adapt their ministry and philosophy to local needs.[13] Jim Slack describes church planting as an overall team effort, which requires cooperation of all ministries of an organization, which should have church planting as their main thrust.[14]

Greg Livingstone uses examples from the Book of Acts which involve several people working together to enter a city. They become significant trusted residents or sponsored guests, and proclaim the good news of Christ as change agents. They make disciples, enabling others to assemble themselves together, representing Christ in that area, as his ambassadors. This endorses the homogenous unit principle, which understands new believers want to fellowship and worship with their own kind. He believes church planting teams need members with a variety of gifts and experiences, to be fruitful.[15] But one should proceed with caution in Muslim areas, since too high a profile will inevitably lead to expulsion of the church planters and possibly the whole team.

All of the above considered, it is obvious a church planter does not work alone. His task is to train, encourage and model for others.

This cannot be done in strategy and prayer meetings alone. The task must be performed on the ground, with others of like mind and commitment. Most planting skills are caught, not taught. Jesus and Paul used this method. Sufi Muslim leaders and Jewish sages still use it. Find a man or woman of peace, lead them to Christ, disciple them and encourage them to win and disciple others of their people group. This is the way to a church planting movement.

The individualistic mindset of many Westerners does not yield easily to the team approach. Independent-minded church planters find it difficult to submit to discipline and cooperation necessary for a team approach. Teams are conceived of as being made up only of expatriates. But this is really only a "strategy team." The real church planting team should be made up mostly of local people who fit naturally into the culture and know the language. If you will bless local believers to win and baptize others, you will find your church planting efforts multiplied a hundred-fold.

The Holy Land will become churched when committed Christians and believers from local churches and congregations team up and move into areas ripe for harvest. They support one another and share spiritual gifts, while gathering persons in the area for Bible study fellowships that eventually become local churches. This happens naturally, as believers marry and settle in cities and villages, open businesses or teach school. We need to be alert to what God is doing in the lives and hearts of others and team up with them for the harvest!

Teamwork in church planting allows you to encourage others and allows them to encourage you. Also it gives opportunity to review, evaluate, and if necessary, change approaches to maximize fruitfulness. No church planter is perfect. Few are experts. We need each other. Getting together to review and evaluate provides time for fellowship, as well as for strategy and prayer.

Network Believers

Years ago the late Dr. Elmer Douglas, former Methodist church planter in North Africa and professor at Hartford Seminary, told me: "God will give you Muslim believers. The big problem will be, What to do with them?" He knew the difficulties Muslim believers experience trying to fit into the normal Christian congregation in the Middle East. Muslims and Jews come to the Lord in the Holy Land and the Middle East and think they are the only one like themselves in the country! They may go years before making contact with another believer. Where do they turn in an environment hostile to the Gospel? Whom can they trust? Their life often depends on it. A discreet phone call or letter can put them in touch with other believers in their area for fellowship. These form cells of two or three believers, who encourage one another, and in turn, win others within their sphere of influence to the Lord.

Cell groups of believers spring up all over the country when they know about each other and gain confidence they will not be betrayed. Sometimes it is better for new believers and inquirers to travel outside their home area for worship and fellowship. Caution is advisable, so they will not be exposed to possible hostility from family or community elements, until they are strong enough spiritually and able to share their faith openly with their family and friends. It may be advisable for a church planter not to visit often in the home, unless there is assurance that the family approves, or at least allows freedom to believe.

Years ago, in my enthusiasm to encourage Druze young people, who attended services in a village church, I visited them in their home. They never came back. I unwittingly exposed them to parental and community pressure. Each situation and person is different, and we must be wise. A church planter in the Holy Land must be aware of security needs of new believers and not expose them through open contact, until they have their own faith network. A survey of

150 Muslim-background believers in a Muslim country revealed only four survived, after a period of a few years. Most had been killed or left the country. The main reason for their persecution was not their belief in the Gospel, but their relationship to foreigners and foreign organizations!

Networking takes place along family lines in the Arab community. The extended patriarchal family offers a scripturally compatible avenue for sharing the Gospel, person to person. If a church planter gains the respect and approval of the senior member of the family, often the father or grandfather, he has a golden opportunity to share with the rest of the family.

The Lord works in Muslim families through multi-individual, mutually interdependent conversions.[16] They accept the Lord one by one or in pairs. Then they gain confidence to network with each other, and the whole family then accepts the faith through consensus. One Muslim-background church planter I know will not introduce new believers to other believers for a period of time, sometimes up to half a year or more, until they are certain of their motivations.

The rapid moral decay in Jewish communities, and the constant pressure of political situations, causes young people to seek alternatives to traditional Jewish orthodoxy. Some go east to study Buddhism and Hinduism. Others go west, in search of material gain. A growing number are finding their hopes fulfilled through faith in Jesus as Messiah. They network with other believers, to find victory over drugs, promiscuity and the downward pull of society around them. Formerly only handfuls met together. They now demand space to house meetings of hundreds. Jewish believers network through conferences, camps, holiday celebrations and many other events. Whereas, the best networking among Muslims is in small cell groups who meet for fellowship and study of the Bible, even if they have to move from place to place for security.

Preserve Family Integrity

Accepting the Lord, especially in Jewish and Muslim families, often brings an instant negative reaction. The new believer is expelled from home and may lose his job, in at least one third of the Muslim situations. It may be necessary to find alternate shelter until tempers cool. Reaction in traditional Christian homes is usually less hostile. There may be others in the home who are also searching and open to the Lord. It is best to advise patience rather than cause unnecessary reaction.

Be careful not to encourage normal teenage rebellion. Build character into the new believers. Encourage respectful relations with family, relatives and friends, unless these drag the new believer back into sin. Challenge new believers to keep the scriptural command: "Honor thy father and mother," and not to forget: "Have no other God before me." When the Lord frees drug addicts, prevents suicides, reconciles marriages, heals the sick, and in some rare cases raises the dead, families usually rejoice.[17] Or, at least they respect the fact that something unusual happened which they cannot explain. They may also secretly admire the new believer.

Due to rapid economic and political changes in the Holy Land, there is an increasing generation gap between teenagers and adults. Divorce, infidelity, prostitution and abortion plague secular Jewish society. The same problems threaten Arabs who move to big cities from villages. One of the best contributions a church planter can make to Jewish or Arab society is to teach family values and be a reconciler of marriages.

Celebration of holidays is especially important for Middle Eastern families, whether they be Christians, Jews or Muslims. A church planter who wants to enjoy life in the Holy Land needs to affirm these family gatherings. Occasions such as Christmas, Passover and the Muslim Feast of the Sacrifice, or *eid al-adha,* provide unique opportunities to share the scriptural meaning of these events. Also, rights of passage such as births, baptisms, circumcisions, weddings and funerals bring the family together and offer unique opportunities for affirming relationships.

Meet in Respected Homes

Most churches in the Holy Land and Middle East begin as home Bible studies. The advice of Jesus: "And whatever town or village you enter, find out who is worthy in it and stay with him until you depart," still remains a viable strategy. [18] The attitude of the community toward a family or persons in whose home you meet sets the tone for future ministry. If the family leader is dishonest, he will eventually trick you and you will be the laughing stock of the town! Local people know each other's histories, motivations and track record. Find a respected local person, a "man or woman of peace," who can give you references before making permanent arrangements for meetings. Better still, let local people decide these matters from the beginning, and let them take responsibility for furnishing the meeting place.

Our experience in Arab villages led to a conclusion that there are at least three factions in each village. One is the leading family, second is the opposition, and the third is neutral. Which family you start with will determine who will attend meetings in the future. There may be a need to start two churches rather than one! Hesselgrave advises against beginning with the first people who approach you, unless you know they represent a broad segment of your target population.[19]

Brock, who worked in the Philippines, cautions against starting in homes because of limited space and restrictions of the people who will attend. He recommends homes as a "feeder" to a larger community meeting. He also advises inviting community leaders to the first meeting as a matter of courtesy, rather than asking their permission, which may be refused.[20] His advice, while well taken, may need to be modified in potentially hostile Muslim and Jewish areas. So you may need to start multiple home meetings until a larger and more neutral place can be found.

I personally believe the home Bible study, or "cell group," needs to be a continuing element in church planting, even after a permanent meeting place is established. It is not necessary to have an ordained church planter to lead a home meeting. With proper training, encouragement and resources in local languages, laymen can lead multiple home Bible studies, which meet an ongoing need in the local church. In Muslim areas it may be better that meetings remain mobile, due to security considerations. A definite meeting place can quickly bring violent reaction from opposing religious elements.

Create Space

A given in church planting in the Holy Land, as well as in other places in the world is space limitations. To have "church-growth eyes" means not only to find responsive homogenous groups of people to disciple. It also means to envision the extent of the growth of the group. One of the greatest disadvantages of home meetings in the Arab sector is that an average living room will only hold the members of an immediate family. A home meeting usually fills to capacity within a month or less. So people who could be reached will stop coming, simply because there is no place to sit, or stand for that matter.

Charles Brock encourages "community Bible study" as a better concept than "home Bible study," if your goal is to start a self-supporting church. Those families which bond within the group, from the beginning, become the core leadership of the future church. The more people reached from the beginning, the more viable a church in the future. He lists at least fifteen possibilities for locations of a community Bible study, including a park, a restaurant, an office, a garage or carport, a day care center, a hotel and a store front.[21] The main thing is that local people become involved from the beginning, in providing the place to meet. This encourages local initiative and self-support.

We assisted a local believing Arab family to start a house church in a suburb of Nazareth, after the 1967 war. Their living room filled immediately with family members and a few friends. We then moved to an unfinished part of the house for more space. Then, so many children showed up for Vacation Bible School that neighbors complained of the noise. The group began immediately saving a building fund and eventually partnered with our organization to build a multi-purpose building. It housed a day-care center and the church. We learned many lessons though those years of trial in creating adequate space and involving local initiative from the beginning.

Sometimes persecution is a hidden blessing. A Jewish fellowship grew so rapidly that the group rented a local hotel. But pressure from rabbis and hostile elements forced the hotel owner to evict the group, only to have his hotel burned anyway! The group found itself meeting in the forest, overlooking the city. Yet the congregation continued to grow. When winter came, a local Arab village pastor offered his church for the meetings. Finally the group rented a remote youth hostel. The group continued to grow until the youth hostel manager doubled his facility. Now the congregation numbers in the hundreds.

While home meetings provide intimacy and personal discipling, a larger community meeting is necessary for long-range church planting. Overcrowding in home facilities could create problems with neighbors and violate city ordinances. Space requirements will often necessitate finding a larger, more public place for congregational worship. This may mean meeting in the great outdoors or in a more remote location, but it can be good for the health and long life of a congregation. In some Palestinian areas, laws may prevent more than five people meeting without police permission.

This, in fact, encourages church growth, since it keeps believers groups small and mobile.

Wolgang Simson, in his provocative book *Houses that Change the World,* sees the house church as a wave of the future, particularly in rural areas as he has experienced in India. Multiplication of believers groups, regardless of available space, is a necessary ingredient for a church planting movement. A congregation of believers must not settle into the "edifice complex" or as Simson indicates, a return to the Byzantine professionalizing of the church.[22] If a group becomes turned in on its own needs, church multiplication is stifled. When this happens, the Lord allows internal strife or external persecution, to encourage church multiplication. This often happens after a church builds a new building. Several examples of this are found in Appendix B.

Cooperative Funding

When the harvest comes, everyone shares in the work. Reaping before rains come and spoil a harvest remains the immediate issue. The optimum is for all new churches to be started by local people and funded the same. Long-term dependency, described earlier, makes this problematic, particularly in the traditional Christian Arab community. Therefore, a church planter, from the beginning, must present himself as a teacher of the Word. His main role is to equip others to teach, especially if he is an expatriate. The church cannot be reproducible if it is dependent on expatriate funding and leadership. Though he can share both, along with the locals.

Brock wisely points out that a church planter should allow locals to provide all necessities for the meetings, except the first Gospel portion and song sheets. In that way, they get used to doing it and learn more quickly. He feels local people will provide if we expect them to do so.[23] But this may be easier said than done in areas where other church planters and organizations have provided financial help to new groups in the past. And as we learned earlier, this was often the case in the history of the Holy Land.

I came to the place where I had to decide if my goal was evangelism, resulting in churches, or financial self-support. Ideally, both should be our goal. If we get so hung-up on "self-support" and fail to understand the local custom of a "shared purse," we may only frustrate ourselves and demoralize the locals. The time will come when they will thank you (or maybe not!) and tell you they do not need you or your funding, but prefer to do it themselves.

Give priority to witnessing, teaching, discipling core leadership and modeling a generous, but wise spirit. Do not spoil people. Do not stifle local initiative. If others want to provide funding, there is really no polite way to stop it. We need to remember vision, not funding, is the real issue. When locals receive the vision, funding will be forthcoming, from their own sources and from God's bounty. The resources are in the harvest. A church planting movement spreads from person to person, family to family, village to village and throughout neighborhoods and apartments of large cities as believers share the Gospel with family and friends and acquaintances. It cannot be contained in present church and denominational structures. The lower the profile of expatriates and their money, the better, as this often impedes spontaneous growth of the church.

Find a Sponsor

The best sponsor for a new church start in the Holy Land, as elsewhere, is another church or congregation which shares a vision for church planting. Chaney found from experience that a parent-child concept of church planting is the primary method of church extension.[24] We do need partners in church planting. Sponsors, or advocates, back us up with prayer, advice, ordination and recommend resources for needed funding. Church planters need local advisors and partners who know the people in the area of the new church. Blessed is the planter who finds a good mother for his churches, so they do not grow up as orphans!

The real frustration comes when you face resistance from local church leaders. Some do not want new fellowships or congregations started in their area. Fear of losing members, funding, and power may motivate them. Others may fear persecution if you target the non-Christian population. They forget that a church which does not multiply dies from within. A church that is on fire for the Lord will split on the inside if not allowed to multiply from the outside. The irony comes when they claim their resistance comes from concern for the church. In fact, it often comes from concern for their position and status. If all Christian churches in the Holy Land were filled on any given day of worship, ninety-nine percent of the population would be left outside, because the churches are too small! Few church leaders have church-growth eyes. The church which shares in planting other congregations experiences new vitality and often increases its own membership in the process.

Resistance of established leadership to church planting makes it very tempting for the church planter to ride lines of division in local established congregations. This usually proves an exercise in futility. It is better simply to find another church, even a smaller one, willing to sponsor a new work. As a last resort, try the local association of churches or a church planting group more open to new work. Try to find ways of affirming local leadership. At the same time, share the vision for church planting with those who are open to it. They will learn the law of the harvest—those who sow bountifully will reap bountifully.

Share the Burden

Report back to your sponsoring group regularly. Even the most callused local church or sponsoring group softens when they hear about Jews and Arabs coming to the Lord. Share the struggles of a new fellowship with your home church. Ask for their prayers for specific persons and issues, without betraying confidences. Let them know how God answered. I found that the most disinterested congregations come alive to specific prayer requests for Muslims and Jews. And national associations often become willing to receive new churches for fellowship as the Lord burdens their hearts. Remember, it takes time for churches to break out of a self-centered edifice-complex and get the vision for outreach to unreached peoples groups. You may be the one who will help get them started.

The above are only a few suggestions for ways to share in planting the church in the Holy Land. Many more could be added. I refer you to the writings of Brock, Chaney and Hesselgrave for clear guidelines and proven step-by-step methods that worked other places in the world. Church planting and church development are a continuum and cannot be separated. You naturally ask, "After I help start a cell church or a house church, how do I lead it to be a strong, self-producing church which multiplies other churches?" Chapter Eight deals with this crucial question.

chapter eight

Developing Strong Churches

C hurches in the Holy Land acquire their personality and vision largely from the church planter who initiates them, as well as from the people who join them. Paul told the Corinthians: "I became your father in Christ Jesus through the Gospel. I urge you then, be imitators of me." He challenged them: "Be imitators of me, as I am of Christ."[1] He did not speak from spiritual pride, but from the fact that his goal was sharing Christ, his model. Good Muslims model their life after Muhammad and his teachings. Orthodox Jews model their lives after their favorite rabbi and his teachings. We follow suit by telling others to model their lives after us, as we follow Jesus, our Messiah and Lord.

Sharing our vision comes foremost as we start new congregations and lead them to spiritual maturity and fruitfulness. My support organization adopted the following vision statement several years ago: "We envision strong local congregations multiplying all across Israel, which are effectively proclaiming the gospel and equipping believers for ministry." Their mission statement is: "To join God in planting and developing indigenous congregations throughout Israel, and with them, to share the gospel with every person and then disciple all who believe."[2] Our home organization defines a church or congregation as "a group of baptized believers drawn together into a visible fellowship by the Holy Spirit, for the purpose of worship, fellowship, witness, nurture and ministry."[3] With clear vision and mission statements like these, little should prevent us from establishing strong congregations.

I shared my vision for Galilee with my support group about ten years ago. This came after a period of discouragement, when I almost gave up on the vision, but God renewed it. As I look back, I see things might have been easier if I had adopted a simpler church planting model from the beginning. The "edifice complex" of traditional Christian Arabs among whom I ministered caused church planting to take years. It included acquiring land and a building, which at a minimum usually took five to seven years after the church formed. The end result left heavy dependency on foreign support. While our average ratio of baptisms to membership was about 10.5%, we lost 42% of our members by the back door. It is impossible to encourage a church planting movement among all the responsive peoples of the Holy Land using such a slow, inefficient and laborious method. The following proposes a less complicated and hopefully more fruitful approach.

Let us assume your church planting team formed around a common vision, and you now have a responsive group of people among your target population. They became interested in the gospel message because of the testimony of family and friends, or in a variety of other ways. They gather week by week in homes for Bible study. Several receive the Lord and request baptism. Then who does the baptizing? I always prefer to baptize with a local pastor or dedicated lay leader, if the work is in the beginning stages.

Why? I want them ultimately discipled by and bonded to local leaders. They will be here long after I am gone. Most of what I do as a church planter, I do with or through local leaders. The greatest growth took place in my ministry when I blessed, trained and released Muslims to baptize other Muslims.

Later, who disciples the new believers? I, the church planter, am responsible for beginning the discipling process. If I do it wisely, using transferable or reproducible concepts and methods, others gifted in teaching can take over the process. Chaney wisely observed: "the resources are in the harvest."[4] Every believer is gifted by God to complete the body of Christ, which is the church, in some way. Charles Brock's theme "Everybody is somebody" is well applied in the small group. Use a method of discipling which gives everyone a chance to have input and encourages local initiative that can be passed on from person to person, without you having to be present.

The following consists of highlights gleaned from our years of ministry in church planting in the Holy Land. Again, they are not exhaustive. There are many ways to plant churches and many methods of growing strong churches. Those who want more comprehensive ideas for developing strong churches can read *Planting Churches Cross Culturally*, by David Hesselgrave; *Indigenous Church Planting*, by Charles Brock; *The Purpose Driven Church*, by Rick Warren, and *Planting House Churches in Networks*, by the Fellowship of Church Planters.

Cell Groups

Multiple programmed home Bible studies, or cell groups, prove a flexible method of church development. Cell groups have definite advantages for fellowship and discipling. The disadvantage is a limitation of size and space. An optimum cell group is the biblical 12, divided into four to six groups of twos or threes.

You train a cell leader and an intern to head each group. Their ability depends on their available time, training and resources. When a group gets to 25-30 members, it is best to divide into two or three cell groups.[5]

Several studies show that cell groups or small groups presents the best approach to reach transitional communities. Tim Matheny, in *Reaching the Arabs, A felt need approach,* notes eighteen felt needs of Arabs who move from villages to cities, for education and employment.[6] *TAFTEE,* in India, determined the compact world of rural man is splintered when he moves to an urban community.[7] Bible study groups provide needed fellowship and spiritual growth for these transitional peoples, and are an excellent tool for church planting.

It needs to be clear in the beginning whether the cell is a house group under the sponsorship and authority of a local church, or is it, from the beginning, to become a house church that is to eventually become an independent group under its own leadership. There are many names for cell groups, such as a "house group," "Bible study," "fellowship," or "meeting." It will be helpful, for relations with church leadership in the area, to be clear in your objective for forming the new group.

There is a basic difference between a cell church and a house church. Most groups of Muslim believers are cell churches. They consist of two or three believers, who meet at different places and different times, for fellowship, prayer, study of the Bible, sharing and solving problems, and exchanging information for networking with other believers and inquirers. A cell group of two or three believers, including their wives, makes six. Each of these has their network of family and friends with whom they share the Gospel.

One church planter can supervise up to five cell groups, perhaps from different towns and villages. Each group needs a leader and an intern, who can then become a leader when the cell multiplies. Ralph

Neighbors designed a system where every five cells has a zone supervisor and one intern, and every 25 cells has a zone pastor and one intern. A whole church, made up of many cells, can be led by a team of coordinating leaders. Cell churches are ideal for Muslim and Orthodox Jewish communities, where security is an issue and persecution of a more visible church of new believers is highly likely.

An excellent study of the cell church concept is New Wine-Cell Church Seminar. While successful in England and Europe, it is also highly adaptable to realities of the Holy Land.[8] Cell group meetings can take place in an apartment, under trees, in parks, in cars, in a cafe, an office, or wherever two or three believers can meet securely. The main thing to remember is a cell group is an embryo church, with the Lord in its midst. They are leaven, which can permeate all of society. The Church of Samaria is one example of a cell church in Appendix B.

A house church that meets regularly in the home of a member, and is usually related to a local Christian church for leadership, is better suited to the traditional Christian Arab community. This type of regular meeting attracts family members and neighbors who are nominal Christians, and it gives them an opportunity to be personally involved in Bible Study in a non-threatening environment. But the house church is most likely too high a profile for a Muslim or Orthodox Jewish community. New Life Baptist Church uses the concept of a house church very effectively, to reach traditional Christians in the city of Nazareth, many of whom have moved from Galilean villages to new housing projects in the growing city.

How do you begin a cell group, for example, among Muslims? What type of study materials would you use? I start every Muslim who comes to me with the basics. If you build a house, you dig four main foundations. So I use the *Four Spiritual Laws* translated and adapted into Arabic to begin this spiritual house. Amazingly, Muslims respond as readily as traditional Christians to these simple transferable concepts. The booklet is also available in Hebrew. Then I find it wise to lead new Muslim believers in a study of the Sermon on the Mount, in Matthew, chapters 5 to 7, since it lays the basic foundation for prayer and moral living. Those who respond favorably can continue with a study *New Beginnings*, a programmed discipleship series which takes a new believer through a new life in Christ, including Bible study, prayer, and daily life in the world and the church. Somewhere around lesson 15 of the 50 lessons, they are ready to make a full commitment to Christ, or to leave the study.

New Beginnings was first created in the Philippines, probably patterned after the successful church planting of Charles Brock, who designed a basic discipleship series *Good News for You*, a pre-salvation study of the Gospel of John, and *I Have Been Born Again, What Next?* a pre-church study for new believers. These are available in English, Arabic, Russian and other languages.[9]

The *Seven Christian-Muslim Principles* provides a resource for those who want to use a "contextualized" approach to those Muslims who can only be reached through use of the Quran. This tool, developed for the Navigators in Lebanon, written in both Arabic and English, presents a topical study of the plan of salvation using verses from the Bible and the Quran, together. The seven lessons can be divided to use as a fourteen lesson series. Those who are not comfortable using the Quran at all may prefer not to use this tool. But I have found that many verses in the Quran emphasize man's depravity and God's judgment, and combined with Bible verses can speak to the heart of some Muslims.

Use of *New Beginnings* encourages participation by each person present. The programmed texts give a Bible verse and then a question, with a blank. Each person takes a verse and gives an answer to the question. I found this breaks down barriers between men, women and children in the Muslim family. Otherwise, only the man will lead and learn. Patterned after my simple, indirect leadership, the man of the family can still continue leading the study in my absence. Each person pays for his or her own programmed workbook, which covers most of the cost. Simple Bible chorus sheets, with an accompanying cassette, provide the music. These are easily memorized. Usually, one of the children or young people leads out. At the end of each section of about twenty lessons, each person receives a simple certificate verifying their successful completion and the hours spent in study. One advantage of such studies in the Muslim sector is they can be identified to the outsider as a "study" rather than as a religious meeting. But a word of caution, avoid using commentary except to answer specific questions. Let the Scripture speak for itself. Commentary can lead to dispute and confusion. Commentary models a level of sophistication that others may not be able to attain, therefore limiting its transferability.

New Beginnings is actually the foundation study of a series of discipleship tools which can be used to train and disciple new believers. *Survival Kit* is another discipleship tool my wife used successfully in discipling English speaking Jewish ladies in Galilee. More advanced believers can study *Masterlife,* which is available in the major local languages.

The True Furqan is a recently published book that can be used as an effective tool for pre-evangelism with Muslims. It uses Quranic Arabic and specific vocabulary to critique the Quran and popular Muslim attitudes toward Jesus and ethical living. *The True Furqan* is becoming increasingly popular among Muslim leaders and will soon be available on the Internet.[10]

Empower Local Leadership

Persons gifted with leadership become apparent as you progress in the Bible studies. Share more responsibility with them as they grow spiritually. Use them as advisors to your church planting team. Take them on home visits with you. Encourage them to witness to relatives and friends who may be open to spiritual matters. Let them pray during meetings, and eventually lead. Be careful not to embarrass them, but consult with them privately about matters which concern you in their spiritual growth. Every church planter, cell group leader, or house church pastor should have a disciple whom he is mentoring for leadership, so that he can move on and start new groups.

Several programmed courses provide leadership development for maturing new leaders. *Master Life* is now available in Arabic, Hebrew and English. Make sure those who participate have a strong foundation of studies in Scripture, since *Master Life* is very demanding. It requires a person to covenant with the group to spend adequate time each week in preparation. College credit is offered for successful completion of *Master Life I & II*.

Experiencing God is another programmed training tool, which is less academically demanding, yet proves effective in inspiring a love and vision for outreach. *Experiencing God* is available in English, and Russian. It also recently aired over the radio in Arabic. All these training tools are generic and do not require a particular denominational affiliation.

Other discipleship and leadership training materials can be obtained from Hagefen Press, Operation Mobilization, International Correspondence Institute (ICI) of the Assemblies of God in Haifa, and International Institute of Biblical Studies of the Baptist Convention in Jerusalem. The Israel College of the Bible, Caspari Center and Bethlehem Bible College also offer leadership training courses.

Studies conducted during church planting in the Philippines revealed that a leader without proper materials could conduct a new Bible study for only six months before a crisis point occurred. A leader with materials could last another six months. Leaders need specialized training to carry the group further, until the organization of a church, which usually takes fifteen months from the beginning.[11] The average time to start a church is probably longer than fifteen months in the Holy Land, however. Nevertheless, training of lay leaders and having proper materials is necessary for the continual growth of any group. Due to the needs of growing cell or house groups, a church planter needs to train a group of core leaders. Jesus' pattern of training his disciples serves as our model. We need to place strong emphasis on training core leaders, who will in turn teach others. Empower local leaders through strong training. The best training is caught, not taught; so an intern learns by doing, alongside his mentor in the daily rounds of church planting. The best church development manual is the New Testament, especially the Book of Acts.

Becoming a Church

There may never be agreement among church planters, as to when a group becomes a church. Some sponsoring organizations require a certain number of members and various steps accomplished before they recognize a group as a church. Our association of churches also has many pages of policy for formation of a church. This usually involves making a constitution, calling a pastor and holding an official service recognizing the new body as a church, in most denominations.

I find that new groups often consider themselves a church long before most of the mechanics are in place. Spiritually, an embryo church exists wherever two or more believers gather in the name of Jesus. It functions like a church in society, when there are ten or more men involved with their families. Charles Brock may be closer to reality when he says: "When a group is baptized, they become a full-fledged church. They are not a house church, store church, market church, or a mission point." Programs, buildings, and services to constitute a new church, and dedication of new buildings, may come later, and do have their place, "but a church they do not make."[12] If we allow a group to express themselves as a church as soon as they feel ready, we may save ourselves much labor. We can then begin to turn our attention to starting other groups.

One problem involves how much control a sponsoring church or body exerts over the new church. I found that new churches can act much like teenagers. They resist control and want to do their own thing. Independence requires patience and wisdom on the part of a church planter and the sponsoring body. Occasionally a new church or congregation hesitates to identify with a known group or denomination, because they fear family and community pressure. They may choose to adopt a generic name rather than a church title. Those who oppose such trends need to be aware that this is a common practice among many large community churches in the West.

A characteristic of all groups, whether Arab, Jewish, Russian or English-speaking is their "optimum size." Usually, when a group reaches 40 to 60 people, they either have to divide or you must provide more leadership and a larger meeting space. Each group reaches a natural plateau. Proper leadership training equips gifted leaders who can be responsible for a growing group. A wise church planter will anticipate these normal thresholds and will train leaders in advance, to share the load of shepherding an expanding flock.

Balanced Ministry

Encourage a new church toward a balanced ministry. That means a total ministry which includes worship, fellowship, witness, nurture and ministry. A strong triangle of body life includes first, cell groups or small home groups for discipleship and fellowship. It includes second, formal teaching, preaching and worship on a community or congregational level. Finally, it includes celebration. Celebration can be the joyous coming together of many cell groups, or congregations, for testimony, praise and prophetic exhortation from the Word. Cell groups and local worship helps members bond to each other. Celebration also helps them bond to the larger body of believers, on a regional basis. It can be ecumenical in nature, that is, including other like-minded churches and congregations. The first can be done on a daily basis, the second on a weekly basis, and the last, celebration, on a monthly basis. If any of these three is lacking, your members will most likely find another group to fill that need.

The triangle of small group community fellowship, teaching, worship/celebration provide a strong superstructure for witness and ministry in the unbelieving world. Believers live daily in the real world, especially in the Holy Land. They interface with people who are hurting, hostile, or inquisitive. New believers in congregations must be trained, from the beginning, to relate the Gospel to people's felt needs. Love, made practical, attracts people who are hurting and looking for direction in life. They see the wholeness that Jesus brings to the lives of ordinary people with problems similar to theirs.

The believing community becomes a family for new believers from Jewish and Muslim and traditional Christian backgrounds. He or she may find that their families reject them for their newfound faith. Their reaction differs, depending on the home setting and the attitude of the new believer. They could be evicted from the home and even face threat of death, in some extreme cases in the Muslim community. A church or congregation becomes a spiritual family for many new believers. They depend on other believers to provide fellowship and help their social needs. A church planter bears the burden of encouraging fellowship and caring on the part of the congregation, as well as being a wise and patient witness to the new believer and their family of origin.

A word needs to be said about people who come to your group who always seem to have great need. Occasionally you will get a person who is a professional beggar, manipulator or time waster.

Israel seems to have a fair share of this variety. Leadership of various congregations should coordinate ministries to these people. Sometimes it is wise to designate one person to deal with such people, rather than waste the time and energy of many. Such persons can sow confusion in the fellowship, if left unchecked. It is also best to coordinate with others in cases of genuine need, to avoid a waste of time and resources. Persons in real need deserve a listening ear and sound advice, at the right time. We dealt with persons in the past whom we learned had files several inches thick in the social welfare office! They never seem to solve their problems. Sometimes the only real solution is to take the advice of Paul: "If any one will not work, let him not eat." [13]

Preservation of newly baptized believers remains a responsibility for the church planter. Studies show that post-baptismal discipleship training is a key element in making a believer an effective church member. Also, research in the USA suggests that when someone has six friends in a church, within six months of joining, there is likelihood they will stay members. The fewer friends they have during this crucial period, the less likely they are to remain.[14] New members should be paired with more mature members for fellowship and discipling. The believers in the Book of Acts met daily for fellowship, worship and prayer. Many new believers in the Holy Land exhibit the same desire and enthusiasm.

Stewardship of Life

A believer's outlook on life receives new orientation through his exposure to God's word in scripture, prayer, worship and fellowship with others whom God also changed. Spiritual formation takes place as the demons of lust, drugs and materialism leave and fruits of the Spirit appear in their place. Memories are healed as wounds are confessed in sharing and prayer. This process usually takes time and trial. Few people become saints overnight.

New believers need to know the ownership of God over all aspects of life. Jesus is Lord over all, or he is not Lord at all. Stewardship means Christ, the Messiah in me, the hope of glory. He remakes me into God's image, for which I was created through an infilling of the Holy Spirit and by the cleansing of the Word. My natural response should be, "My all for Him!" That means my life and all that I possess. A heart full of the joy of salvation issues forth praise, service, generosity and witness. This is the maturity to which church planters need to bring every believer. It is like a birth process, as Paul describes: "My little children, with whom I am again in travail until Christ be formed in you." [15] It may also take much pain. Church planting is hard work, but the reward of seeing others grow into maturity in Jesus makes it worthwhile.

This birthing and maturing process requires much nurture and discipline. A church planter in the Holy Land will face a variety of challenges in nurturing new believers. Many Arabs and Jews come with the traumas of rejection, occult practices, multiple marriages, continual indebtedness and a multiplicity of other problems. They bring these negative lifestyles with them into the new fellowships. Spiritual formation requires nurture in the Scripture and modeling. We are naive to expect new believers to be perfect. Alan Schreck expressed it well in his article on Twelve Principles of Church Renewal: "There never was an ideal, sinless church, even after the coming of Christ and Pentecost. The apostles, even after Pentecost, were not perfect, and neither were the churches they founded."[16] Your patience and wisdom will be tested when new believers depart from the New Testament norms of morality. Clear Bible teaching from the beginning, about marriage and morality, is the best preventative. A church planter should not allow their identity and self worth to be bound too closely to failures of new believers. Be patient and wise. Scriptures provide adequate and relevant guidance in the use of discipline and subsequent restoration of deviant believers.

Another practical aspect of the stewardship of life in the Holy Land is the use of money. How a person treats money indicates the state of their heart. Jesus' parables often dealt with the wise use of finances. Newspapers in Israel report daily on the unwise and often illegal use of money by government and religious officials. Church leaders are not exempt from a general spirit of distrust in the use of money. Basically, no one trusts anyone in the Holy Land when it comes to money. Therefore, a church planter needs to lead new groups, from the beginning, in the wise use of money, which is part of biblical stewardship.

Assuming you teach new believers the biblical commands regarding tithing, how will you handle money that people donate to the new church or congregation? First of all, a church planter is wise not to be responsible for keeping or disbursing money. It is best to let the group designate two persons to count all offerings and record it in a journal. A third person, designated as treasurer, can to be responsible to put the money in the bank and keep necessary receipts. Help them understand that this protects everyone involved. Needless problems can arise if money is not handled wisely. Make sure that the person designated as treasurer has the time, along with a wise and generous heart, to be responsible. They must be willing to distribute funding as the group designates, without controlling its use. A church planter needs to train the treasurer to make a simple budget and report periodically to the group on the financial status. Money means control, and its wise use is essential to the morale of new churches. The most productive money for church planting is that which is raised by a local congregation, from its own tithes and offerings.

Banking laws in Israel require that all organizations opening bank accounts hold Friendly Society, or *Amuta*, status, which is similar to non-profit status in many countries. This means the Society is responsible to the bank for legal liability. Two private persons can open a joint account in their names, but this is not advisable. Past experience dictates against it. If one of the two decide they do not want to sign for the money, it is frozen in the bank.

I strongly advise new congregations to find a sponsor who is a legal Friendly Society and is willing to open a local currency account for them. They can limit the indebtedness of the account and designate two out of three believers from the new congregation to sign all checks. This requires extensive paper work with the bank and a lawyer's certification, but it enables the group to also deposit local and foreign gifts. Money not used currently can be placed in a short-term closed account, to draw interest that offsets inflation. Our association assists their new churches in this procedure, which encourages financial independence.

One of the last groups we assisted as church planters applied for Friendly Society status, received it, and opened their own bank account, without my even suggesting it. A leading family in the congregation operated their own business and knew the various procedures needed. This group bought their own piano, sound system, and paid their pastor a partial salary from their tithes and offerings. Six of their members enrolled in seminary extension courses and paid their own tuition. Most had completed *Master Life* in the past and were maturing believers. This kind of initiative cheers a church planter's heart!

I personally believe a church planter would be wise to donate his/her tithe to a variety of congregations, instead of to only one congregation, especially if you are an expatriate and receive your support from abroad. You should not overwhelm the budget of one developing congregation with your tithe and cause it to become dependant on you. Look to the day when you will no longer be present. I have known congregations that have been thrown into a financial crisis on the departure of the church planter. Some organizations recommend that none of the church planter's tithe go into the budget of any church he/she is planting. Whatever we do with money, it should be done wisely and according to the local income standards, as a method of modeling that can be reproduced by the local people.

Linking Congregations

Associations of congregations and churches network continually around the Holy Land today. Hebrew congregations link to other like-minded groups in their areas of the country. The Episcopal Province in the Middle East, with the Bishopric in Jerusalem, has maintained unity of its many churches since its establishment in 1976.[17] Baptists and other like-minded evangelicals coordinate ministries of sixteen churches and a number of centers. The Assemblies, Brethren, and Churches of Christ each have networks of churches that associate with one another. Many of these groups link together in the United Christian Council in Israel (UCCI), for mutual fellowship and defense of religious liberty. Churches in the Palestinian territories of the West Bank and in Gaza also join together for fellowship and encouragement. Messianic Jewish believers link through regional leadership for major celebrations. Most new congregations can find a compatible group of churches or congregations with which to fellowship.

It is natural for believers to want fellowship with other believers. They share common burdens and opportunities for outreach. They defend each other in times of external pressure. Formation of the Messianic Action Committee (MAC) to oppose proposed legislation against evangelical witness is a good example of this. New churches can establish connections with the larger body of believers through their sponsoring church. It helps the group of new believers to know they are not alone in the country and in the world. Ties do not necessarily have to be formal. Association with other believing groups encourages fellowship, mutual support, celebration and witness.

Each Church Plant a Church

A healthy church reproduces other churches. The law of the harvest applies in the Holy Land and around the world. New believers naturally share their faith with others. A new church reproduces its own kind. Some will bless those of other language or people groups in cross-culture church planting. Israel-Palestine, the Holy Land, is a small country, housing many people groups. It is a microcosm of the rest of the Middle East. The salvation of this nation will come through a church planting movement, as congregations multiply other congregations. God will not allow churches to grow fat on his Word. The Word must be shared with others, or it will become a sword dividing from within.

How do we recognize a God-initiated church planting movement in the Holy Land, and other places in the world? Erich Bridges gives us some clues. It is:

1. *"Indigenous*—God uses a church planter or other outside agent to get things started, but the movement quickly becomes self-generating.
2. *Lay-led*—Not anti-clerical, but characterized by strong lay leadership and growing too rapidly for seminary-trained pastors to keep up. It is, by and for the people.
3. *Out of control*—It quickly grows beyond buildings or single denominations, even if it starts in one group. It's often characterized by home and cell groups.

4. *Passionate*—about evangelizing and reproducing disciples and congregations.

5. *Powerful*—Often, reports of supernatural acts of God accompany the spread of the gospel, particularly where strong opposition exists."[18]

Those who bear the name of Jesus the Messiah, Savior and Lord in the Holy Land serve as a "light to the nations" and a "city set on a hill." That light which lights the heart of every man cannot be kept under the bushel in each local congregation. It is destined to spread throughout Jerusalem, Judea, Samaria, and into the uttermost parts of the world. It is returning back to Jerusalem in this age. It cannot remain there. The Holy Land today is a virtual Pentecost where people speak almost every major language on the earth. The evangelical faith which has come back to Jerusalem will go out through ambassadors of reconciliation, sent out by strong local churches to bless the entire world.

The future of the church in the Holy Land depends on our vision agreeing with the vision of God for the church. The New Testament pictures the church as the bride of Christ (Rev. 21:2). Section Three encourages us to sustain a vision for the church in the Holy Land which will lead to church planting movements. What are the factors that lead some congregations to turn inward and eventually split under the pressure of the law of the harvest? Appendix B provides us with living models of how churches are planted or split in the Holy Land, as the Gospel comes back to Jerusalem.

Vision for a Church Planting Movement

chapter nine

What is Your Vision?
(Matthew 10, Luke 9, Acts 1:8, 2:17–21)

What is your vision for your work in Israel? Each of us had a vision when he or she came to the country. My vision was to see a Baptist center or church in every town and village of Galilee. I knew it was an unattainable goal. It was frustratingly impossible. But a thrill wells up in my heart every time I drive through Galilee and tell others of this vision. It could be that a miracle will happen and this vision could be a reality before I retire. Admittedly, I relegated it to only a dream. Many other things blurred the vision. There was so much struggle in the earlier days to find a plan which would satisfy the Convention and the Association. We laid aside our strategy studies as we struggled to set down an operating plan for church development on which we could all agree. It took five to ten years to develop a new center of work. I wearied and settled back to accept the inevitable. But now, with much of that behind us, I get the feeling I should renew the vision.

What about you? What was the vision you had when you first came? Is it not time to renew that vision? New things are happening in the country. There is a new receptivity. There are many more Jewish believers and even a few Muslim believers. Christian Arab young people are catching fire for the Lord. The Jewish and Arab student movement is moving ahead. New couples are coming who are better trained and oriented. They want to move out and get with it. Let's renew our vision!

Vision is Essential for Mission

"Where there is no prophetic vision the people lack restraint. They just let their hair down and go wild!" (Translation mine) Proverbs 29:18—In Hebrew: *b-ain chazon yipara' 'am*

I fear if we do not have a vision for the future of our work, we will fritter our time away on committees, meetings, paper work, and talking to each other, rather than getting out into the harvest field! Without vision, we will let the "status quo" become "fait acompli." Let's begin to dream of new centers of work. Let's begin to see our national brothers as responsible before the Lord, and share our vision with them. Let's begin to encourage and affirm each other in the calling the Lord has given to each of us.

May I share my renewed vision with you? Would it not be great if we could share such a vision with our national leadership? I wish we could challenge each church and center to begin at least one new Bible study fellowship by 1987. And then, each church and center could start a new center of work by 1990. We could set a goal of doubling our membership by 1995. It could be possible to have a Baptist or other believing witness in every city and village of Israel by the year 2000! Now the problem with my setting goals is they may be less than what the Lord would have us envision.

Jesus Had a Vision

Jesus had a vision, and he had a strategy. He spent thirty years getting ready to do the task. Some of us chafe to think we have to spend even two years in language study. Yet we need five just for a good *foundation!* We cannot improve on Jesus' model and strategy:

1. *Sending the Twelve*—Matthew 10—He sent them out in pairs.

2. *Sending the Seventy*—Luke 9—He gave basically the same authority and instructions to both groups:

3. *Concentration*—Matt. 10:5-6—"to the lost sheep of the house of Israel"- Don't be afraid to center in one town, village, community or "peoples group." Set up a model ministry and others will follow. I am doing that in Yaffa and Rumani. I think it will work. We do not have enough time to do everything. Work through the locals. Jesus was willing to trust them. He knew them better than we do! He was willing to spend two to three years preparing them.

4. *Simple Life Style*—v. 8-10—No big money or excess of clothing. We need to dump much of our excess baggage. This is hard to know how to interpret, when the local people are just as, or more, materialistic than we are! But, we need to determine what is essential for ministry and what is not.

5. *Wisdom Where to Start*—Luke 10:6—find a "son of peace." Find a person who receives your word and who is respected in the community. We suffered fifteen years in one village because we did not have a "son of peace," but a contentious man, as the founder of the work. We are just now overcoming. "Do not go from house to house." It will cause jealousy and division. If you have a respected person, others will come

to him. "Eat and drink what they give you." It is a compliment to the Jew and Arab when you eat with him.

6. *Wisdom in When to Stop*—Luke 10:11-12—"wipe the dust off your feet." Do not be insulted if they do not always receive you. There will be others who will listen. We need a discerning spirit to know when people are listening from sincere motives and when they are listening only for some form of material gain. Other nationals can help us know this. Be as "wise as serpents and harmless as doves." Ask the Lord to give you wisdom to know the hearts of men.

7. *Reliance on the Holy Spirit*—Matt. 10:19-20—It is possible that some of us will have to pay with our lives in the task for which God called us. It is more likely that some of our local brothers and sisters will have to pay the ultimate price. But, it is fruitless and unbiblical to develop a "martyr complex." He taught the disciples to flee to another town when they were persecuted. He also promised the Holy Spirit will give us the words when we are called before the authorities to declare our faith. It is altogether likely that we will be involved in an automobile accident rather than be martyred. So, drive safely, and do not tempt the Lord your God!

8. *Trust the Lord to Bring Results*—Luke 10:22—Jesus promised us that God uses a selection process which is different than ours. He chooses to reveal Himself to some. All are called but few are chosen. This is a mystery. We are the seed sowers, the cultivators, the nurturers, but God gives the increase. Do not be angry with the Lord because "His time" has not come. Maybe He delays it lest we fall into pride for the ones "we won."

I heard some years ago of a church planter in Pakistan who found some villages open to the Gospel and others closed. He could not understand why. An older and wiser person explained to him, "The ones open to the Gospel were the ones where 'praying Hyde' worked, labored and prayed for, many years ago." We enter into the labor of others. Trust the Lord to bring the harvest. He told the twelve: *"Assuredly, I say to you, you shall not have gone through the cities of Israel before the Son of Man comes."* Maybe we need to claim this verse for the new century and take courage from it.

Keep Your Vision Clear! —Luke 10:23–24—

Jesus says, "Blessed are the eyes which see the things that you see!" What a privilege we have in this age of the Holy Spirit. We can see in hindsight many of the mysteries the disciples may have missed. But, we have to keep our vision clear. Are there things blurring your vision?

1. Failure to pray, to study the Word, and to unite with a local fellowship.
2. Failure to give at least a tithe to the work of the Lord.
3. Failure to get out among the people to which you were called.
4. Failure to really count the cost, Matthew 10:36-39. It is possible to put parents and children before the call of God. Not that we do not have obligations to them. But we can loose perspective if we allow them to manipulate us out of the will of God.

During the bombardment and curfew in Beirut, Brother Gerias Delli's wife died. He could not get out, but remained in the next room translating *Masterlife*, knowing perhaps that his time was also short. He was not turned aside by circumstances.

Brother Jameel Safuri also remained faithful in proclaiming the Gospel to his Muslim neighbors in Beirut, though he was warned it may cost him his life. His relatives in Cana pled, "Do not return to Beirut, they will kill you!"

He replied, "Then I will be with Jesus." He did return, and they did kill him. This November I met a man from Cana who came to the Lord though "Uncle Jameel's" example.

Count the cost. Keep your vision clear. Know the Lord will honor you in life and in death. It is glory to serve him. And it is more glorious to be with him in eternity!

The Reality of Your Vision

Your vision of your work must be tempered with reality. Every vision has its limitations. Jesus himself had to send others ahead, so they could prepare for his coming. It is the same today. Jesus cannot come to people until someone prepares the way. A vision can begin with a limited target and then expand. The Lord first sent out twelve, then he multiplied to seventy. Then after Pentecost, when he was no longer limited to the flesh, he began working with thousands!

Maybe from this we need to learn to hold lightly to our authority over local brethren. Teach them. Support and encourage them. Then step aside and let them run! Jesus is in them with the power of the Spirit. Even he had to step aside in the flesh and remove himself physically, in order to turn the power of the Spirit loose in the Church. This is the power that will fulfill your vision and mine. Like Paul, be obedient to the Heavenly Vision, and trust God to bring it to pass!

Note: This vision message was presented as a devotional to the Baptist Convention in Israel. Between the years 1986 and 1996 the number of congregations related to the Convention increased from seven to fifteen, or 114%. The number of members increased from 596 to 1,139 or 91%.

chapter ten

Conclusions

The Keys

Models and surveys in the Appendices reveal the keys God uses to plant churches in the Holy Land. These keys undoubtedly apply to other locations in the Middle East and around the world. We can take, for example, the development of the Shefrarm Bible Center and detect those factors which are common to many other new church plants:

Vision— on the part of a congregation or leader to open a new work.

Timing— Local baptized believers needed a church fellowship to grow spiritually. A dedicated lay person returned from Bible school. A gifted evangelist-church planter, an elder with a vision, and an expatriate church planter shared the vision and worked together in God's timing. God uses even dramatic political events and persecution to prod his people to growth.

Inspired leadership—A God anointed pastor or lay person faithfully visited and nurtured potential members. They were fed spiritually and mentored. Leaders formed interest groups to encourage one another. They involved others with expertise, to supplement where they were lacking.

Local Involvement—A local believer made his new building available. The congregation paid partial support to their pastor. They chose their own name, took steps to become a non-profit organization and opened a bank account.

Sponsoring Group—The mother church, the Association, and the local leadership took the initiative to provide advice and encouragement to the new believers, but left them free to choose their identity.

Overcoming Obstacles—Some evangelical ministers and workers in the area had serious questions about starting a new congregation. Spouses of believers objected to their being involved in a non-traditional church. Some believers did and some did not come from Charismatic backgrounds. They worked through their problems and decided on a generic name for their congregation. They also decided not to join a denominational group, so as not to offend the traditional churches in the community. But they still fellowship with other believers at conferences.

Prayer—The pastor and members met almost daily, sometimes early in the morning, for prayer. They shared burdens, plans, new prospects and received the Lord's guidance. Spiritual warfare was accomplished both in the Holy Land and abroad as Satan was bound and strongholds were broken down in the hearts of men and women, boys and girls. Prayer was often accompanied by fasting and weeping over those bound by Satan, until they were loosed. Victory did not come easily, but it often came dramatically.

The Maayan Congregation also confirmed these keys to church planting. One member of the sponsoring group received a vision of a new congregation, moved and began to win and gather other believers. The sponsoring congregation endorsed the vision. The timing of two-year cycles took effect in leadership training and congregational growth. Timing was also essential in the purchase of the new building. Local members took the initiative in prayerfully seeking a name and tithing their incomes to support the pastor-elder and the building fund. They overcame obstacles of lack of space and the need for a new building with ingenious fund raising. They continue their original vision now by sending out leadership and funding the start of new congregations.

New Life Baptist Church modeled the concept of a house church, meeting from house to house, without a central building. The Church of Samaria also utilized methods common to cell churches, to nurture its members in a hostile environment.

Churches which neglect to use the "keys of the kingdom," to unlock doors of opportunity and reach out in church planting, end in stagnation or division. Nazareth Baptist Church, once the mother church of a number of village centers, found itself embroiled in inner division when it moved into its new building. Had church leadership seen the young couples, student groups and home meetings as a ready opportunity to open new centers of work, it could have avoided needless pain.

Nazareth Brethren Church experienced the same crisis in leadership when it entered a new building. Three new groups split off from these formerly dynamic churches, because the leadership lacked "church planting eyes," and tried to maintain control of various factions meeting in the same building. Man cannot control what God designs!

What does all this say to us? God is at work in Israel-Palestine, the "Holy Land," and around the Middle East. He is planting His church. The Gospel message has come back to Jerusalem for a reason. The gates of Hell will not prevail against a church or congregation which takes the keys of the Kingdom to unlock the hearts of thousands of Arabs and Jews waiting for a word from God. Obviously, only the Messianic congregations and a few Arab groups have a purposeful plan to plant new congregations. The rest are at "ease in Zion," or protecting their own turf, and will face the judgment of God if they miss this moment to join God in His story.

Where are we using all of our resources and energy if we are not following the mandate to plant churches which reproduce other churches? What could happen if all evangelical churches and congregations with one mind and heart chose to follow God into the ripe harvest field of the Holy Land and the Middle East? You and I, who are part of the harvest force and the prayer force, need to answer these questions. We will be held accountable. A great window of opportunity has opened before us. Now is the time to set ourselves to the task of reaping the harvest among the unreached people groups of the Holy Land. People from all backgrounds are turning to the Lord. If discipled and sent out again from Jerusalem, they could be frontline harvesters in this 21st century and catalysts for church planting movements worldwide. It is a time our predecessors prayed to see. We are working against the clock. Let us be good and faithful mentors of harvesters for that fateful day, and let us bring in our sheaves rejoicing!

"So shall my word be that goes forth from my mouth;
it shall not return to me empty,
but it shall accomplish that which I purpose,
and prosper in the thing for which I sent it."
Isaiah 55:11

"God's work, done in God's way will never lack God's supply."
Hudson Taylor

Church Growth Survey—Galilee

September 1, 1991

A church growth survey of Galilee (Northern District & Haifa Region) revealed a population of 1,400,000 inhabitants in 1990 divided into these major religious groups:

Jews	840,000
Moslems	400,000
Christians	80,000
Druze & others	80,000
Total	1,400,000

Sixty cities and towns in Galilee have populations of over 5,000 inhabitants. Evangelicals meet in only twenty-two of these localities, or one-third. The population of these twenty-two localities is 560,000 or again one-third of the population. If we consider each of our congregations a "Gospel presence," we witness in only one-third of Galilee, leaving two-thirds virtually without witness.

What is the evangelical presence among the religious groups in Galilee? We congregate in eight cities, with Jewish population totaling 355,000 inhabitants, or one third of the Jewish population in Galilee. Evangelicals meet in eighteen cities and towns where 123,000 Muslims live, or less than one third of the Muslim population. We have four churches in towns where 20,000 Druze live, or a small percentage of the total Druze population. The majority of our membership is from the traditional Arab Christian communities. At least two-thirds to three-quarters of Galilee is outside the range of evangelical witness.

There is one secret group of Bedouin-Druze believers of unknown number. There are about forty congregations (from five to 200 members, nine of which are Baptist) totaling 1,200 members, of which 400 are Jewish believers, 600 Arab believers and 200 expatriates. Altogether, evangelicals constitute one-tenth of 1%, or one in 1,000 people in Galilee. Our religious community, including children of believers and students in our schools, would be about three or four times that number, or approximately 5,000.

Lest we become discouraged by these statistics, there are hopeful signs I found in the survey:

First, there is freedom to witness in Galilee, if the witness is given in a culturally sensitive way.

Second, there are signs of moderate growth in Baptist, Brethren, Pentecostal and Jewish believer congregations.

Third, the influx of Russian immigrants gave rise to two new congregations in Galilee.

Fourth, each year approximately 300 people correspond with the Middle East Television (CBN), asking for Bibles, many of these Muslims.

Fifth, 6,000 Muslims corresponded with a Bible Correspondence School. 10% indicated a decision for Christ and need follow-up.

Sixth, congregations interviewed indicated about fifteen points of outreach for Bible study.

Seventh, youth and student organizations show renewed vitality.

Finally, three target groups for evangelism are: 1. Students, 2. Bedouins, 3. Druze.

Selected Models for Church Planting in the Holy Land

The following evangelical churches and Messianic congregations in the Holy Land represent a broad spectrum of what God is accomplishing in church planting. I present them as models to assist the prospective church planter to "get a handle" on what can be done and what may be improved on for the future. I deliberately give examples of older churches and newer churches. I also provide examples of Arab, Jewish, and expatriate congregations, the entire "harvest field" in the Holy Land. Some have continued the vision of church planting while others have lost theirs.

We have drawn the necessary conclusions in the final chapter above. These serve as candid subjects for those who pray for the 10/40 Window and commit themselves to spiritual warfare to loose captives from bondage.

Assemblies of God

Former blacksmith Edward Tannous leads one of the fastest growing Arab congregations in the country. Tannous moved to Haifa in 1962, from the northern Galilee village of Gish (Gush Halav). He became a believer under the ministry of Wadia (Abu Hannah) Saloum, on December 12, 1981. One month later, after prayer, he experienced the "baptism in the Holy Spirit" and prayed in other tongues. "I was a wicked sinner and the Lord baptized me without my asking!" he said.

He met with Dr. Dale Thorne at the Haifa Baptist Center in 1983, and the small building filled to overflowing. Tannous began meetings in the home of Samir Barakat, and the group felt the blessing of the Spirit. Rev. Ross Byers, Assemblies of God representative from the USA, assisted them in renting a former Catholic Church in the *Hadar*, downtown section of Haifa.

Tannous left his secular work in 1987 and devoted full-time to ministry. His wife supported his ministry through her work as an accountant. He prayed every morning at 4:00 a.m. and met with other believers for prayer in the afternoon. He soon began opening new meetings around the country, with the assistance of lay leaders in the Haifa congregation.

The Assemblies mission opened Galilee Bible College at the church in Haifa, to train Arab and Russian leaders for outreach. The congregation grew to 120 members. Students from the Bible College and other members opened two meetings in Nazareth, with a total of 50 members. Other meetings were opened in Beini, Fasuta, Shefrarm, Rama, Ramla, and Jappo of Tel Aviv. Total membership of all the Assemblies of God Churches, including Ramallah in the West Bank, is over 400.

Tannous believes the secret of success is the baptism in the Holy Spirit as a second blessing, after belief in Christ and water baptism. He has a vision to reach all the towns and villages of Israel, which includes Arabs and Jews. "I found that when we sent out leaders to open new work that the Lord filled their place with new believers, and even more!" explains Tannous.[1]

Baptist Village Congregation

Baptist Village Congregation started in 1960 and serves English-speaking internationals in the Sharon Plain area. In 1965, it hosted the first meeting of the newly-formed Association of Baptist Churches (ABC) in Israel, and its pastor, an Israeli lawyer Dr. Joseph Alkahe became the first chairman of the ABC. About 100 embassy personnel, foreign professionals and others now attend weekly Sabbath services, along with their children. Recently, the congregation attracted a number of members from Filipino, African and Russian backgrounds. The former pastor, Rev. Bob Bradley, served in Hong Kong and ministered to Chinese. The present pastor, Rev. Robert Rogers, is a retired chaplain and the first supported full-time by the congregation.

Members of the congregation started a new worship group among embassy personnel living in the Hertzlia area. The congregation provides for all of its own financial needs and contributed in past years to projects in Arab Baptist churches in Galilee. Services held in English attract occasional Jewish and Muslim believers from the area who desire fellowship. The congregation owns land at Baptist Village and plans to build a new worship facility in the future.

Carmel Assembly

Carmel Assembly was founded in 1991 by David Davis, a former Broadway actor. He moved to Israel with his Jewish wife Karen, a singer/musician, in 1989, following a "Macedonian call" through an Arab woman, who told him about the drug epidemic in Israel. The Davises were sent out by Times Square Church in New York, which, under the leadership of David Wilkerson, reaches out to drug addicts, the homeless and needy people, bringing them a direct message of the gospel and an opportunity for help through Teen Challenge ministries.

David, ordained by World Challenge, came to Israel with a vision to set up a residential, Bible-based "Good Samaritan" center for Jewish and Arab addicts and alcoholics. Following a year in Jerusalem, the Lord directed David and Karen to Haifa, where they began this work, called "House of Victory," in a property vacated due to the Gulf War. A nucleus of a congregation soon grew up in this center, meeting initially one evening a week in the Davises' living room for worship, Bible teaching and prayer. Following an invitation from the leadership of Stella Carmel, Isfiya, a ministry of ITAC, the group moved to begin a weekly Shabbat meeting in the chapel at the Guest House. Carmel Assembly had a membership of 200 in 1998 and a leadership team of three, with Peter Tsukahira and Reuven Ross joining David, to form a pastoral team.

Their new worship center is built on a piece of land located on the highest point of the Carmel mountain range. This "One New Man" community strongly emphasizes discipleship and intercessory prayer. They have hosted several Prayer Summits with leaders in Northern Israel. The ministry of praise and worship, led by Karen Davis, is also seen as central to the calling of this congregation, in proclaiming the Lord Yeshua from the high places in Israel.[2]

Christ Church

Historic Christ Church, located at Jaffa Gate in the Old City of Jerusalem, remains one of the most vibrant evangelical witnesses in the Holy Land. Christ Church's first pastor, Michael Solomon Alexander, a Jewish believer, laid the cornerstone in 1842. The church ministers to 250 internationals in three Sunday meetings, under the leadership of Reverend Neil Cohen. A Messianic congregation of around 150 meets on the Sabbath. A small group of about 40 Filipino nurses and domestic workers meet on Sundays.

Recently, a congregation of around 160 Romanian construction workers also began meetings.[3] Christ Church opens daily to tourists and pilgrims for a tour of the historic building. It serves as a center for numerous inspirational conferences, weddings and events for the Christian community in Israel. Christ Church is part of the Anglican Communion. These congregations sponsor a school for children of Messianic and Muslim believers, a bookshop and a snack bar. Christ Church started *Shoresh*, a Messianic tour company, and expanded its facilities in 1998, to accommodate overnight study tours that emphasize the Jewish roots of Christianity. More of the history of Christ Church is covered in Chapter One.

Grace and Truth Congregation

Grace and Truth Congregation was founded in 1978 in Rehovot, in fulfillment of the vision of Baruch Maoz and other Messianic Jews in the area. Despite opposition of Orthodox Jews in the area, the group grew to about 70. Then a rift developed in the congregation and leadership in 1982, over the role of the Mosaic law. Most of the members left, leaving only about five of the original members. They were forced to close their congregational meeting by a court order, but continued to meet in local homes and in the nearby forest. The congregation later moved to the new quarters of HaGefen Publishing (CWI Israel) in Rishon LeTsion. The group grew to about 30 in 1983. They initiated a national social aid fund to assist needy believing families in 1991. Then they grew to 180 in 1996, largely due to Russian immigration. Now the congregation buses members from Ashkelon and Ashdod for Sabbath meetings, and they are presently looking for larger facilities.

Grace and Truth has fraternal relations with an Arab congregation in northern Galilee. They also sponsored outreach into the Muslim villages of the Central Sharon area. They are involved in the Messianic Action Committee (MAC) which defends religious rights of Messianic believers in the country. A congregation in Holon developed from Grace and Truth.[4]

Haifa Baptist Church

The Haifa Baptist Church first began meetings in a home on Mount Carmel in 1965 under the leadership of Dr. Dwight Baker. It moved to newly purchased facilities of the Christian Service Training Center (CSTC) and began to gather Arab and Jewish believers for worship. After the 1967 War, the Jewish believers formed their own group under the leadership of Rev. Peter Gutkin, a Messianic Jew of Polish origin. The church partnered with ministry in Acre for many years. During the Lebanese war in the 1970's, one of its members, Rev. Ibrahim Siman, conducted refugee relief work for wounded Lebanese. Another member, Rev. Edward Suiti, formerly pastor in Acre, started a congregation for Russian Baptist immigrants. The church reorganized in 1983 under the leadership of Dr. Dale Thorne along with Rev. Siman and Rev. Suiti.

Rev. Philip Saad became pastor in 1986. Rev. Saad, originally from Turan village near the Sea of Galilee, graduated from the Mid-America Baptist Theological Seminary. He began a dynamic preaching and visitation ministry. The church quickly grew to over 60 members and rented the larger Elias Lutheran Church for weekly meetings. The church invited lay evangelism teams with Global Missions Fellowship from the United States in 1995 and 1996 to participate in door-to-door visitation in Haifa and Mt. Carmel. Two new home Bible studies started as a result.

The Haifa church continues to grow but is limited due to lack of space in this very expensive metropolitan area. In 1991 the congregation purchased a residence owned by the Baptist Convention, to be used as a parsonage. Rev. Saad discipled his congregational leaders through tutoring them in courses with the International Institute of Biblical Studies. He also introduced courses from Bethlehem Bible College. The church ministers to professional people in Haifa and has an active youth ministry. It is growing toward financial self-support. The church recently opened a Filipino ministry.

Ha Maayan Congregation

Ha Maayan Congregation in Kfar Saba developed from the vision of the Bet Emmanuel (Emmanuel House) Congregation in Jaffa of Tel Aviv, in 1987. One of the elders, Tony Sperandeo, felt led of the Lord to move to Kfar Saba and begin a home group. The initial three families grew in nine months to twenty-five adults, plus children. The elders of Bet Emmanuel endorsed the vision which gave birth to "Ha Maayan" in April, 1989. The name was chosen after prayer. It means in Hebrew, "the well, or water source." The group grew in size and began meeting once a month at Baptist Village. The congregation grew quickly to 50 adults plus children and necessitated the renting of Baptist Village facilities, on Sabbaths in 1991. God spoke to the group as they met in homes during the Gulf War in 1991 and told them He would give them their own house of prayer.

They started a building fund with $8,000 donated by members. The congregation grew to 100 adults plus children by 1996. The need for adequate facilities for worship, children's classes and office space led them to send out two women to "spy out the land" and bring reports back about possible building sites. The congregation settled on an unfinished building in the hi-tech industrial zone of Kfar Saba. The owner asked for $550,000 plus value-added tax, or a total of about $660,000. The congregation had $200,000 in their building fund for the first payment. They signed the contract on faith on the eve of Rosh Hashanah, the Jewish New Year, on September 24, 1996. The members gave another $20,000 from their own limited incomes. They printed vouchers with the Hebrew letters of *khay* or "life" which had the numerical quantity of 18 and sent them around the world to friends. Each donated 18 or 180 in their own currency. Each payment of $100,000 was made on time, due in part to delays in finishing the building.

Appeals were made to the pastors in the twin-cities of Kafr Saba in Holland, Germany and Costa Rica. The final payment of $200,000 came in miraculously when a friend of a member of the congregation sold their home and made the payment. Now the group meets in two floors of the finished building and practices an austerity budget in order to maintain it.

Spiritual development parallels financial development in Ha Maayan. The pastor develops leaders in a two-year program of personal relations, prayer and study. They now have two elders, three deacons and four house group leaders. When they mature, they move on to start new ministries, where preaching emphasizes character more than gifts. The congregation practices tithing and took responsibility for the pastor's support from the beginning. They also send a tithe of their income to other ministries, like Pro-Life. One deacon is a full-time worker. They send members for summer missions to the Shelter in Amsterdam and also support a ministry to Israelis in Los Angeles.[5]

Ha Sharon Congregation

Ha Sharon Congregation was started by Ari and Shira Sorko-Ram of Maoz Ministries and Arni and Yonit Klein. It began on *Rosh Ha Shanna*, Jewish New Year, in September 1996. For the previous seventeen years, the Sorko-Rams had led groups in Herzlia Petuach, Nathanya and Ramat Ha Sharon. As a result of a successful music and drama outreach in Diezingoff Center in Tel Aviv, from 1994 to 1995, and because of hundreds of people responding in a Messianic coffee house at Dugit, they saw an immediate need for a new congregation, to disciple so many inquirers. They purposed to have a congregation that was aggressively evangelistic, Hebrew speaking without translation, Messianic Jewish in essence, not Christian, but Spirit-filled, with freedom for the gifts of the Spirit to be practiced and used to build up the Body. The congregation was started for sabras, or native born Israelis. Music and praise was led by Arni

Klein, now of Emmaus Way Ministries, and others, who provided a fresh new sound that was attractive to native Israelis.

The congregation grew to over 100, stretching the basement facilities of the home in which they met. They have now acquired a larger building facility in the heart of Tel Aviv. Their program is to: 1) finish and furnish the new building, which will include a worship and intercession center, 2) prepare Hebrew discipling materials for new believers, and 3) train new believers using the technique of cell groups. They have faced the challenge of a number of English speakers attending their meetings and have plans to start an English speaking fellowship, along with a Russian fellowship, in addition to normal Hebrew services.[6]

Kafr Yasif Local Church

The Kafr Yasif local Church started in 1940, under the spiritual leadership of Saleem Shihadi, "Abu Fawzi," a police officer in the Acre Prison. It continues today under the capable leadership of Rev. Yusif Odeh, Rev. Esa Said Dahir and laymen, trained by the International Institute of Biblical Studies (IIBS) which held a seminar weekly in the church house. The Kafr Yasif local church owns a building and finances its ministries by the tithes and offerings of its members since all the leaders earned their living through secular work. The church joined the Association of Baptist Churches after a period of revival when forty people were baptized in one month in 1972. These were discipled and trained by the Christian Service Training Center, which later became the Theological Institute and the IIBS.

Rev. Ashraf Ghaly moved to Kafr Yasif in 1990, to assist the congregation in planting a new congregation in Shefrarm, an Arab city between Haifa and Nazareth. The Kafr Yasif congregation built a social hall with a parsonage above and repaid a loan from the Association building fund ahead of schedule. There are now about 60 adults in the congregation, which meets on Thursday evenings for praise and Bible teaching, and on Sunday evenings for the "breaking of bread" or communion. Offerings are placed under the communion table cloth by members; no public offerings are taken. Rev. Odeh and members of the congregation publish a popular Arabic evangelical magazine *Misbah al-Haqq*, The Lamp of Truth, which is distributed around the world.

Kafr Yasif Brethren Meeting

The Brethren Meeting, or assembly, in Kafr Yasif, started in 1970 under the inspiration of Brother Nofel, a former Druze. Nofel fled Syria as a young man and became a believer in Sudan, after reading the Bible. He visited the traditional Christian churches but was dissatisfied with their doctrine. He finally found a Brethren Assembly which taught Plymouth doctrine. Returning to Israel, he worked in the refinery in Haifa, married an Orthodox Christian and began to visit regularly in Druze and Christian Arab villages.

Nofel took early retirement and went into full-time itinerant evangelistic ministry after a serious fall at the refinery. He gathered a group of believers around him, some former Communists, who became dedicated to spreading the Gospel around Galilee. They now have congregations in Haifa and Kafr Smeah and carry on an active ministry to college students.

The assembly practices closed communion. They do not observe Christmas, which they consider of pagan origins. Most members will not participate in weddings of non-believers. Women are not allowed to speak in their meetings and must always cover they heads. Their strict manner causes some people in Galilee to shun them, but their devotion to the Gospel is undeniable.

Keren Yeshuah Congregation

Keren Yeshua Messianic Congregation began in January 1990, in fulfillment of the vision of three graduates of Dallas Theological Seminary. Noam Hendron, Avner Boski and Jim Sibley envisioned a biblically based, evangelistic oriented and culturally sensitive ministry to reach secular and traditional Jews in Israel. They concentrated on the homogeneous unit of Jews in the Greater Tel Aviv area, contextualizing their meetings in accord with I Corinthians 9:20 to minister to Jews. They used Hebrew for the language of worship, focusing on Israelis rather than expatriates or tourists.

Meetings began in an apartment above the Dugit Art Gallery in Tel Aviv, with 17 people in attendance. Limits in space and complaints from the neighbors who did not like to hear the singing forced them to move to other locations in Jappo and Ramat Aviv. Finally, in June 1991, they rented a room in a youth hostel to accommodate the approximately 40 adults and 20 children who attended: all are members who commute from the Tel Aviv area. The congregation pays for its own expenses. Leadership raises their own support, totally independent of the congregation. They have also started a Russian language work and a house group in the Ramla-Lod area.[7]

King of Kings Assembly

King of Kings Assembly is the Sunday evening event for many internationals and Israelis in the Tel Aviv-Jerusalem area. It began as a home meeting in August, 1983, with 17 people, and was first called the "Jerusalem Christian Assembly." They outgrew the home in less than two months and moved to a lecture room in the YMCA, in West Jerusalem. Then the group grew from 60 to 250, after they rented the YMCA auditorium.

Pastor Wayne Hilsden made a decision to turn the meeting into a local Messianic congregation in 1988. They changed their name to "King of Kings Assembly" and began incorporating Hebrew and Messianic terms into worship. Soon, cell group Bible studies began meeting in homes. Training for Messianic leadership increased when Dr. Ray Gannon led in the establishment of King of Kings Colleges, in 1990, with campuses in Tel Aviv and

Jerusalem. Two Israeli believers, Ilan Zamir and David Friedman, led the college, which received accreditation from the Asian Schools of Theology in 1996. Pastor Chuck Cowen, an Israeli, assumed leadership of the congregation with Pastor Hilsden in 1989. The congregation grew to two Sunday meetings, with 500 people attending. Fifteen to twenty small groups meet weekly, usually in homes. King of Kings eventually planted three Israeli, Hebrew-speaking congregations in the Jerusalem and Tel Aviv area, with a combined membership of 150.[8]

Narkis Street Baptist Congregation

Narkis Street Baptist Congregation started in 1933 on the outskirts of West Jerusalem. Today, it is surrounded by a Jewish residential community. The congregation grew under the charismatic leadership of Dr. Robert L. Lindsey, a New Testament Hebrew scholar, after 1948. The little chapel expanded in the early 1970s, to accommodate a growing congregation of English and Hebrew speaking believers. Arsons burned it to the ground in 1982, and Lindsey constructed a temporary "tent" in the parking lot. Then the congregation grew from about 70 to over 200, as a result of the larger space. They raised over $1,000,000 worldwide to construct a new worship center, which was dedicated finally in 1996, after Dr. Lindsey's death.

A large group of over 250 English speaking expatriates and Israelis still meet every Sabbath, under the leadership of Rev. Charles Kopp. Rev. John Anthony began a Sunday service by popular demand from the Christian community. A Hebrew speaking congregation of 100 Israeli believers met under the leadership of Rev. Pat Hoaldridge. Recently, an Israeli Messianic believer accepted a call as pastor to the Hebrew congregation. A Russian congregation of about 45 also meets. The congregation often reaches out into the community through the Baptist House adjacent to it. They host conferences and encouraged the ministry of Baptist House Book

Shop, which sold many of Dr. Lindsey's books and other scholarly works, along with current Christian books. The Book Shop was closed in 1999.

Nazareth Baptist Church

Nazareth Baptist Church started under the ministry of Rev. Shukri Musa Bishuti in 1912. Illinois Baptists supported it until the George Bottoms family of Texarkana, Arkansas donated money for a building, which was completed in 1928. Then the congregation scattered in World War II and the 1948 War.

Dr. Dwight Baker revived outreach and eventually the church called Rev. Fuad Sakhnini as pastor, who ministered for over forty years. Nazareth Baptist Church served as the mother church to most of the Baptist Churches and centers in Galilee, through the ministry of dedicated laymen and pastors who grew up there. Most of its outreach ministries in the last twenty years took place through the Association of Baptist Churches, of which Nazareth Church is an active member. It became financially self-supporting in the 1980s. Many of its leading members are teachers at Nazareth Baptist School next door.

They tore down the old church building in 1992 and replaced it with a modern three-story structure designed by Riad Haddad, a young architect and son of the chairman of deacons. The pastor took unofficial retirement several years back, but remained as pastor. Today, income is used to pay off debts on the new building. A number of younger members left in 1992 and started New Life Baptist Church, which meets in homes around the city. The deacons now have a separate meeting in Nazareth Baptist School, which became the Local Baptist Church in April, 1998.

New Life Baptist Church

New Life Baptist Church began in 1992, as a couples meeting, in Nazareth Baptist Church, started by Rev. Jack Hodges, Southern

Baptist Representative, and Suheil Saad, a public school teacher and former youth leader of the church. Hodges taught courses on Covenant Marriage and child development. Five young married couples received a vision for outreach into homes not yet reached by the Nazareth Church. They shared their vision for this new ministry with church members, but the idea was not endorsed by the pastor and some of the leadership. So they began separate meetings in various homes of young married couples throughout the city. These resulted in 15 baptisms of new believers. But continual limited space was a problem in homes, as meetings grew to 40-50 in attendance. They cooperated with other evangelical churches in Nazareth and held occasional meetings with the Nazarenes, Brethren, Orthodox and Copts, as well as in neighboring villages.

Eventually they invited Global Missions Fellowship to send an evangelistic visitation team to the Old City of Nazareth, which resulted in 30 people receiving the Lord in 1996. New Life Church applied for membership in the Association of Baptist Churches and was admitted into fellowship in January of 1996. Now the church meets twice weekly for Bible study and worship and once monthly to observe the Lord's Supper and to receive tithes and offerings. They also continue to meet in homes and promote the vision of every leader opening a new work.[9]

Peniel Fellowship

Peniel Fellowship near Tiberias started in 1982, to serve the employees of Galtronics, an electronics company started by Baptist engineer Ken Crowell. He developed the company as a place of employment for a growing number of Messianic Jewish believers in the northern part of the country. They met originally in a hotel in Tiberias but were driven out by Orthodox Jewish protest. The hotel subsequently burned. A growing congregation met in the forest above the city, until the rainy season came.

Thankfully, they accepted the offer of Turan Baptist Church to use their facility during winter months. Peniel then rented a Youth Hostel for meetings on the Sabbath. Attendance grew to the place where the hostel doubled its meeting space. A group of elders leads the congregation, along with Danny Lahav, an Israeli. At least two evangelist church-planters went out from that congregation to start ministries in neighboring cities and kibbutzim. In 1993 the congregation numbered 200 adults and 50 children.

Galtronics grew to be the largest employer in the city of Tiberias. They opened The Galilee Experience on the Tiberias waterfront, with a multimedia-slide presentation of the history of Galilee, a bookstore, and a snack bar. Galtronics won the Ministry of Commerce award in 1994, to the consternation of its detractors in the area. Today, Galtronics employs Arabs as well as Jews, which gives the Peniel congregation valuable contacts among Bedouin villages in the area. The congregation participates in semi-annual fellowship picnics with Arab congregations in Galilee.

Church of Samaria

Muslims in the West Bank area of Samaria began receiving the Lord after the Gulf War in 1991. Years of studying the Bible and correspondence courses, combined with the uncertain economic and political situation during peace negotiations between Israel and the PLO, led some to follow the Lord in believer's baptism. The first informal meeting was held in the ruins of an ancient church on Mt. Gerizim above Nablus, hence the name, "The Church of Samaria," chosen by the little group of believers.

The group grew from family to family and village to village as men shared their faith. It was nurtured by the tireless work of David Ortiz, who lived in Ariel, an Israeli settlement near Nablus. The group invited Dr. Ray Register to move from Galilee to the central area of the country, to assist in discipling believers living inside Israel.

Meetings are decentralized and cell-church structured. They meet in homes, in the fields, under trees, in cars and construction sheds or wherever two or three can gather. They attend formal meetings of other churches who will receive them. Ten members and friends, along with 20 children, gathered for a Christmas celebration in 1997, representing about half of the scattered fellowship at that time. Some members experienced family rejection, interrogation and imprisonment by authorities, and difficulties with multiple marriages. By 2000 their number has grown to several hundred in Israel and the Palestinian territories. They continue to grow in number, as the Lord gives increase.

Shefrarm Bible Center

Shefrarm Bible Center began in 1992 as a joint project of the Kafr Yasif Local Church and the Association of Baptist Churches (ABC). A number of believers in Shefrarm requested baptism after revival services held by Rev. Ashraf Ghaly, an Egyptian evangelist of Baptist-Pentecostal background.

The ABC provided partial support for Rev. Ghaly and obtained a new-work grant to rent a meeting space. Then a local believer who studied Bible at the First Baptist Church in Bethlehem offered the ground floor of his new partially constructed house for the meeting place. The new-work grant provided necessary funds to finish the meeting place and provide chairs. About 20 people received baptism. The building filled on the first meeting and subsequent meetings were also well attended. Six members and believers from other churches enrolled in Bethlehem Bible College courses and IIBS seminars held at the Center and paid their own tuition.

The Center chose a generic name rather than a denominational title, in order not to offend members of traditional churches in the city. They did not officially join the ABC for the same reason, though they fellowship at conferences and exchange visits with other churches in Galilee. Leaders took the initiative to apply for Friendly Society (Amuta) status and opened their own bank account. They also purchased a piano and sound equipment and now pay Rev. Ghaly a partial salary for his ministry. Meetings are held several nights a week, in addition to regular visitation in the city. Plans include a larger meeting place in the future. An Assemblies of God group that meets across the street has similar intentions, since Shefrarm is a city of over 25,000 and has only one evangelical church, aside from these two small ones.

Observations

The above congregations experienced the law of the harvest. When they sowed generously, they reaped generously. Church planting is God's most efficient method of extending the Gospel in the Holy Land. He gets the task done, even without us planning it! The DAWN survey in 1993 revealed 92% of the 25 new congregations planted by those surveyed were started in the five years previous to the survey. All of the eleven new Messianic congregations were also planted during this five year period. The number of new congregations increased 66% in the five years following the DAWN survey.

The above models do not include Churches of Christ, who added eight new congregations in five years for an increase of 57%. The Assemblies of God added four new congregations, an increase of 80%. Churches of Christ multiplied home Bible studies, whereas the Assemblies multiplied community-style meetings. No other churches added similar numbers, with the exception of Church of God, which added two new congregations, increasing 40%.

A survey conducted in 2000 found about 300 congregations and house groups scattered throughout the Holy Land, or an increase of 65% in the number of congregations and house groups in the last four years—over 50% of these in new cities and villages!

There are now congregations or home groups in sixty of the seventy largest cities in the country. These figures include 70 Arab congregations and home groups and 120 Jewish congregations and home groups. There are at least 30 international congregations or home groups.

The group making a directory of congregations in cities and villages of the Holy Land is calling for concerted prayer during the "Year of Jubilee," that congregations and home fellowships start in all of the 70 largest cities.[10] The increase in the number of congregations and home fellowships is so rapid that it is almost impossible to keep up-to-date statistics on their growth.

Church Growth Indicators[1]

BAPTIST CHURCH MEMBERSHIP

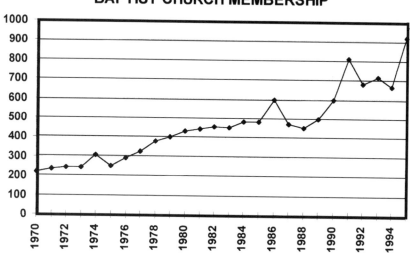

Baptisms

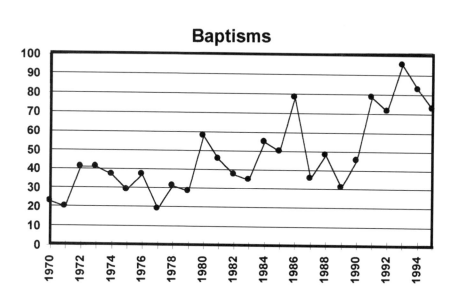

MESSIANIC CONGREGATION MEMBERSHIP (Estimated)

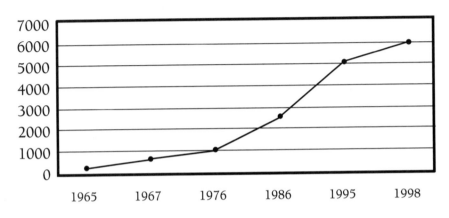

Messianic Congregations and House Groups (Estimated)

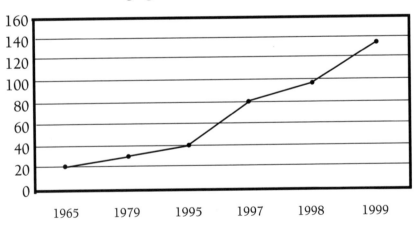

CHURCH OF SAMARIA MEMBERSHIP

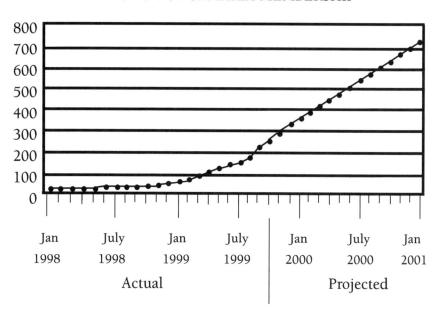

Jan	July	Jan	July	Jan	July	Jan
1998	1998	1999	1999	2000	2000	2001

Actual | Projected

Baptisms

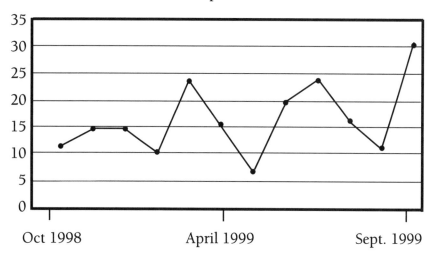

Oct 1998   April 1999   Sept. 1999

Endnotes

Introduction

1. Tom Houston, "The End is Not Yet," *World Evangelization*, Vol. 18, No. 64, September 1993, p.6.
2. Luis Bush, Ed. *AD 2000 Beyond Handbook*, January 1992.

Chapter One

1. Matthew 16:18
2. Judith Lieu, "Early Christian Origins and Relation to Judaism," Lecture, Tantur Ecumenical Institute, Jerusalem, April 7, 1994.
3. Desmond Sullivan, "The Church and the Synagogue of Capharnaum," *Christian News from Israel*, Vol. XXV. no. 1 (17), Autumn 1974, 38-42.
4. Sarah Moore, "Avdat: A Christian City in the Desert," *Jerusalem Christian Review*, Box 24097, Jerusalem, Israel, Vol. 1, Issue 8, p.4.
5. Jane Taylor, "Masters of the Desert," *Eretz*, The Geographic Magazine from Israel, No. 39, March-April 1995, p.47.
6. Robert L. Wilken, *The Land Called Holy*, (Yale University, 1992), pp. 89-94.
7. Dennis E. Groh, The Religion of the Empire, *Christianity and Rabbinic Judaism*, (Washington, DC: Biblical Archaeology Society, 1992), pp. 295-303.
8. Abraham Rabinovich, "Rock on which Virgin Mary rested found near Bethlehem," Jerusalem Post, Monday, November 10, 1997, p. 1.

9. Barnavi, Eli, General Editor, *A Historical Atlas of the Jewish People,* London: Kuperard, 1998, pp. 68-69.

10. Wilkens, op. cit., p. 161. quoting from Sidney Griffith, "Stephen of Ramlah and the Christian Kerygma in Arabic in Ninth-Century Palestine," *JEH* 36 (1985):23-45.

11. Sylvia Mann, "The Mount of Olives, the Mountain of Everlasting Life, *Christian News from Israel,* p. 19.

12. Philip Hitti, *History of the Arabs* (London: Macmillan, 1963), p. 152.

13. Groh, *Christianity and Rabbinic Judaism,* op. cit., p. 302.

14. C.H. Malik, The Orthodox Church, *Religion in the Middle East,* A.J. Arberry, editor (Cambridge: University Press, 1969), Vol. 1, p. 300.

15. Hitti, op. cit., p. 220.

16. Quran 17:2, translation mine.

17. See *Shorter Encyclopaedia of Islam,* (E.J. Brill, 1961), Mi'raj, pp. 381-383 for the various interpretations of the Night Journey.

18. Hitti, op. cit., pp. 620-621. This explains why, when you visit the Church of the Holy Sepulcher today, you find a more modern, ornate pillared tomb build over the spot of the original tomb.

19. Philip Hitti, *The Arabs,* A Short History (Princeton University Press, Gateway Edition, 1970) p. 220.

20. Bernard Lewis, quoted by Gwynne Dyer, "Guilt trip," *The Jerusalem Post,* Monday, July 3, 1995.

21. Hitti, *The Arabs,* p.222.

22. Encyclopaedia Britannica, 1973 ed., "Saint Francis," Vol. 9, p. 708b, "Ramon Lull," Vol. 14, p. 173b.

23. Hitti, *The Arabs,* p. 228.

24. ibid., p. 230.

25. ibid., p. 232.

26. Kenneth Cragg, *The Arab Christian,* A History in the Middle East , (Louisville: Westminster/John Knox, 1991), p. 23.

27. Matthew 25:52.

28. Eli Mizrachi, *Two Americans Within the Gates,* The Story of Levi Parsons and Pliny Fisk in Jerusalem, (Hagerstown, MD: MacDougal, , 1995), p. 385.

29. Kelvin Crombie, *For The Love of Zion,* Christian witness and the restoration of Israel (London: Hodder & Stoughton, 1991), pp. 1-24.

30. ibid., p. 16.

31. ibid., p. 81.

32. Lyle L. Vander Werff, *Christian Mission to Muslims*, The Record (Pasadena: William Carey Library, 1977), p. 155.

33. Crombie, op. cit., p. 81.

34. Vander Werff, op. cit., pp. 155-159.

35. Arberry, *Religion in the Middle East*, Vol. 1, p. 534.

36. Vander Werff, op. cit., p. 161, quoted from Julius Richter, *A History of Protestant Missions in the Near East* (Edinburgh, 1910), p. 253.

37. Arberry, op. cit., p. 541.

38. Bertha Spafford Vester, *Our Jerusalem*, An American Family in the Holy City, 1881-1949 (Jerusalem: American Colony, 1988).

39. Crombie, op. cit., p. 77.

40. ibid., p. 97.

41. C. H. Malik, The Orthodox Church *Religion in the Middle East*, Edited by A.J. Arberry., Vol. 1, pp. 300-311.

42. ibid. p. 311.

43. I am indebted in this chapter to pioneer Baptist representative, Dr. Dwight L. Baker for his mimeographed history, *Baptist's Golden Jubilee*, 50 Years in Palestine-Israel, A Short Commemorative History (Nazareth, Israel, May 16, 1961) pp. 1-16.

44. Ray G. Register Jr., *Clothed in White,* (Nashville: Broadman, 1991).

45. The *intifadha* is the name given by the Arab population of the West Bank and Gaza to the uprising against Israeli Army occupation of their territories. The word means a "shaking off" in Arabic.

Chapter Two

1. Hebrews 4:12a.

2. John 12:23.

3. C.H. Malik, The Orthodox Church, *Religion in the Middle East*, Vol. 1, pp. 320-21.

4. John 2:5.

5. Acts 5:33-39.

6. E.P. Sanders, The Life of Jesus, *Christianity and Rabbinic Judaism*, (Washington, DC: Biblical Archaeology Society, 1992), p. 73.

7. Howard C. Kee, *After the Crucifixion—Christianity Through Paul*, p. 95

8. James Parkes, *A History of Palestine from 135 AD to Modern Times* (London, 1949), pp. 47-48.

9. James H. Charlesworth, Christians and Jews in the First Six Centuries, *Christianity and Rabbinic Judaism*, pp. 312, 324.

10. The Messianic Action Committee, "Anti-Freedom Legislation-Report No. 44, March 1998, PO Box 75, Rishon LeTsion, 75100 Israel.

11. Interview, David and Jean Dorris, Jerusalem, November 25, 1997.

12. Khomeini used cassette tapes from his exile in France to inspire the Muslim Shiites in Iran to revolt against the Shah in Iran.

13. "Special Release," Reports in the Western Media, Palestine, the PNA, and Religion, Palestine Ministry of Information, December 23, 1997.

14. See Qur'an 33:27-28, 59:3-7 where the "People of the Book" refers to the Jews.

15. See John 10:30, I Corinthians 4:23, 15:28, and I Timothy 2:5 that stress the spiritual union of Christ and God, and that God is the all in all.

16. See my book, *Dialogue and Interfaith Witness with Muslims*, pp. 43-46, and Qur'an 3:55, 4:159 , 5:120, 29:33. The one controversial verse, 4:157-8 simply says the Jews did not crucify Jesus.

17. See Qur'an 5:119.

18. Charles H. Kraft, "Conversion in Group Settings," *Handbook of Religious Conversion*, Edited by H. Newton & Samuel Southard (Birmingham, Alabama: Religious Education Press, 1992), Chapter Sixteen, pp. 269-275.

19. See John 11:45-52.

20. See Quran 3:111-113.

21. *Guide to Inter-religious and Intercultural Activities in Israel*, 1995-1996, Inter-religious Coordinating Council in Israel (ICCI), Jerusalem, Dr. Ron Kronish, rabbi, Editor.

22. Such is the case of Charlotte, North Carolina, my home town, during the late 1940s and early 1950s, done with the motivation of separation of church and state.

23. Thomas Friedman, *From Beirut to Jerusalem* (London: Harper Collins, 1993), Chapter 12, "Whose Country Is This, Anyway?"

24. See Jesus teaching about "rendering unto Caesar" in Matthew 22: 21 and Paul's admonitions in Romans 13:1-7 about government authorities.

25. Kenneth Scott Latourette, *A History of Christianity* (New York: Harper and Brothers, 1953), p. 126.

26. Naim Stifan Ateek, *Justice and Only Justice*, A Palestinian Theology of Liberation (Orbis Books, 1989), pp. 77-78.

27. ibid., p.79.

28. ibid., p. 80.

29. ibid., p. 84.

30. ibid., p. 85.

31. Naim Ateek, "The Earth is the Lord's: Land, Theology, and the Bible," *Mishkan*, Issue 27/1997, p.80.

32. Luke 12:34.

33. *Culturgram* '97, State of Israel, (Publications Division of the David M. Kennedy Center for International Studies, Brigham Young University, POB 24538, Provo, UT 84602-4538), p. 4.

34. *Culturgram*'97, West Bank and Gaza, p. 4.

35. "A foreign problem," Editorial, Wednesday, August 14, 1996, *The Jerusalem Post International Edition*, No. 1868 Week Ending August 24, 1996, p. 10.

36. David Weinberg, "Not so holy land," *The Jerusalem Post*, Sunday, January 18, 1998

37. George Jennings, *Welcome into The Middle East!* (Le Mars, Iowa 51031: Middle East Missions Research, POB 632, , 1986), pp. 26-27.

38. Jennings, p. 101.

39. Matthew 19:4-5, *The Holy Bible*, New International Version (Nashville: Holman, 1986).

40. ibid., pp. 182-183.

41. ibid., p. 105.

42. Matthew 10:11, Contemporary English Version, (New York: American Bible Society, 1995).

43. Statistics taken from Patrick Johnstone, *Operation World*, OM Publishing, 1993, pp. 312-314.

44. Morroe Berger, *The Arab World* (New York, 1964), p. 139.

45. Jennings, op. cit., p. 144.

46. Quran, 2:106.

47. Jennings, op. cit., p. 239.

48. George Otis, Jr., The Last of the Giants (Grand Rapids: Chosen, 1991), Chapter 9.

49. A *Dunam* is part of an acre.

50. *Holy Bible*, Contemporary English Version, (New York: American Bible Society) p. 1223.

Chapter Three

1. Dwight L. Baker, *Baptist Golden Jubilee, 50 Years in Palestine-Israel*, p. 7, written for *Royal Service*.

2. Jack Hodges, E-Mail, Nazareth, Israel, October 12, 1996.

3. William David Taylor, Director, Missions Commission, World Evangelical Fellowship, Arab World Evangelical Ministers Association, April 27, 1993. p. 1.

4. AWEMA "Partnership in the Gospel" Conference, Church Planting Working Group, (London: April 1995). Highlighting mine.

5. Communiqué, Arab Evangelical Leaders Conference, Jerusalem, July 28, 1995.

6. Matthew 5:14.

7. A sabra is a native born Israeli. The word means the cactus pear, which is prickly on the outside and soft on the inside. The word also indicates patience.

8. *Maoz Israel Intercessors Network*, Letter No. 53 October 6, 1997, Ramat HaSharon, Israel.

9. Jeanne Kimmel, "Musalaha, A Family Reunion," *Ministry of Reconciliation, In the Footsteps of Our Father Abraham*, Ed. By Salim J. Munayer (Jerusalem: Musalaha, 1993) p.9.

10. Salim J. Munayer, "Jesus Inside and Outside the Camp, The Challenge for Arab and Jewish Believers in Israel Today," *Ministry of Reconciliation*, pp. 45-47.

11. *The Bible and the Land: An Encounter*, Edited by Lisa Loden, Peter Walker & Micheal Wood, (Jerusalem: Musalaha, 2000).

12. Elias Chacour, *We Belong to the Land* (HarperCollins, New York, 1990).

13. Roger Elbel, Global Mission Committee, U.C.C.I. Jerusalem, Israel, Report on Billy Graham "Global Mission," March 16-18, 1995.

14. Ray Register, *Church Growth Survey-Galilee*, Unpublished paper, September 1, 1991, Nazareth, Israel.

15. Dr. Stephen Nash, DAWN, London, UK, August 13, 1996.

16. Kai Kjaer-Hansen & Bodil F. Skjott, *FACTS & MYTHS About the Messianic Congregations in Israel 1998-1999*, Mishkan 30-31/1999 (UCCI: Jerusalem, 1999) p. 50.

17. *Freedom Report* No. 67, November 15, 1999, Messianic Action Committee, PO Box 5462, Herzliya 46100, Israel.

18. *Freedom Report* No. 65, July 13, 1999, MAC, PO Box 5462, Herzliya, 46100 Israel.

19. Bishara Awad, Letter, August 1996, Bethlehem Bible College, POB 127, Bethlehem, West Bank, via Israel.

20. Dr. Ray Pritz, Caspari Center, e-mail, February 21, 1997.

21. Paul Shalom Treat, Center of Religious Pluralism, POB 301, Nahariya 22012, Israel, E-Mail, 23 October 1996, pp. 7-8.
22. Jim R. Sibley, North American Mission Board, SBC, e-mail, Wed., 15 January 1997.
23. "Dome of Rock gets $200,000 in carpets," *The Jerusalem Post International Edition*, Week Ending December 21, 1996, page 4.
24. "MK Katz: Israel partially responsible for Palestinian refugee problem," *The Jerusalem Post*, Monday, November 22, 1999, page 1.

Chapter Four

1. David J. Borch, *Transforming Mission* (Maryknoll, NY 10545, Orbis Books, 1991), pp. 447-449.
2. Matthew 9:17, NRSV.
3. Sherwood Lingenfelter, *Transforming Culture* (Grand Rapids, Michigan, Baker Book House, 1992), p. 210.
4. Bosch, *Transforming Mission*, pp. 452-455.
5. Norman E. Thomas, Ed. *Classic Texts in Mission & World Christianity* (Maryknoll, NY 10545, Orbis Books, 1995), pp. 68-69. Excerpts from Rufus Anderson, *Foreign Missions* (New York: Charles Scribner, 1870), 1, 109-115, 115, 117-19.
6. Helen S. Coan Nevius, *The Life of John Livingston Nevius,* (New York: Fleming H. Revell, 1895), p. 441.
7. John L. Nevius, *Planting and Development of Missionary Churches* (Grand Rapids, Michigan: Baker Book House, 1958, reprinted from the *Chinese Recorder,* 1885), p. 15.
8. Roland Allen, *Missionary Methods: St. Paul's or Ours?* (London: World Dominion Press, 1956).
9. Bosch, *Transforming Mission*, p. 450.
10. Lyle L. Vander Werff, *Christian Mission to Muslims* (Pasadena CA: William Carey Library, 1977), p. 204.
11. ibid., footnote 59, p. 339.
12. Dr. Cal Guy, Fletcher Visiting Professor of Missions, Southeastern Baptist Seminary, in phone conversation, Sunday, January 26, 1996.
13. Melvin L. Hodges, *The Indigenous Church* (Springfield, Missouri: Gospel Publishing House 65802, 1971), p. 95.
14. Nevius, *Planting and Developing of Missionary Churches*, pp. 34, 40.
15. Bosch, *Transforming Mission*, p. 451.

16. David J. Hesselgrave, *Planting Churches Cross-Culturally*, A Guide for Home and Foreign Missions (Grand Rapids, Michigan 49506: Baker Book House, 1980), p. 328.

17. ibid., p.418.

18. Nevius, Planting and Developing Missionary Churches, pp. 23-24.

19. William L. Wagner, *North American Protestant Missionaries in Western Europe: A Critical Appraisal* (Bonn: VKW, Druck & Verlag M. Wehle, 1993), p.126-128.

20. Hesselgrave, *Planting Churches Cross-Culturally*, pp. 162-164. Quoting from Raymond Firth, *Elements of Social Organization* (Boston: Beacon Press, 1963), p. 30, and Donald McGavran, *Understanding Church Growth* (Grand Rapids: Eerdmans, 1970), pp. 85-87.

21. Mark 16:15, RSV.

22. Donald K. McKim, "The Mainline Protestant Understanding of Conversion," *Handbook of Religious Conversion,* edited by H. Newton Malony & Samuel Southard (Birmingham, AL: Religious Education Press, 1992), p. 124.

23. For an excellent coverage of the debate around the resolution see *Mishkan,* issue no. 25, 2/1996, From the Israeli Press, *The Baptists are Coming! The Baptists are Coming!* by Sean Osborne, pp. 76-78.

24. I Corinthians 10:33.

25. David J. Hesselgrave & Edward Rommen, *Contextualization,* Meanings, Methods, and Models (Baker, 1989) p. 1.

26. *Al-Injeel*, al-tarjima al-qudsiya lil-injeel al-suniya (Box 21795, E. Jerusalem, Israel).

27. Salim Munayer & Phil Goble, *The New Creation Book for Muslims* (William Carey Library, 1989), Arabic version, 1991.

28. TORAH, PROPHETS, BOOKS, AND NEW TESTAMENT(Hebrew) (The Bible Society in Israel, P.O. Box 44, Jerusalem, 91000 Israel, 1991).

29. *Hebrew/Russian Bible* (The Israel Association for the Dissemination of Biblical Writings, P.O. Box 31, Jerusalem, 91000, Israel, 1991).

30. Jerry Rankin, "Mobilizing for Missions in the New Millennium, Part 10: What Can I Do?, *Intercom, supplement.* (Richmond: International Mission Board, SBC) December 1999.

31. Jim Montgomery, *Dawn 2000:7 Million Churches to Go* (Great Britain: Highland Books, 1990) pp. 108-109.

32. Charles Brock, *Indigenous Church Planting, A Practical Journey* (Church Growth International, 13174 Owens Lane, Neosho, MO 64850, 1994), p. 113.

33. ibid., p. 55.
34. John Gilbert, *FMB Thesaurus Definitions,* document of the International Mission Board, SBC (Richmond VA:1994).
35. I Peter 2:9.

Chapter Five

1. See my book for a description of the project in ministry to Muslims, *Dialogue and Interfaith Witness with Muslims* (Multi-Language Media, Box 301, Ephrata PA 17522).
2. Erich Bridges, "Like Wildfire, Out of Control," *the Commission*, Richmond: International Mission Board, SBC, February 1999, p.51.

Chapter Six

1. Jeremiah 5:23, *New American Standard Bible*, The Lockman Foundation, 1960, 1962, 1968, 1971.
2. Isaiah 53: 5-6, King James version.
3. Charles Brock, *Indigenous Church Planting, A Practical Journey* (Church Growth International, Neosho, Missouri, 1994), pp. 74, 77.
4. James B. Slack, Church Growth Principles Basic To Church Planting, Chapter 2 of *Handbook for Effective Church Planting and Growth*, Compiled by: Jimmy K. Maroney and James B. Slack, Edited by: Ellen Libis (International Board, SBC, Richmond, Virginia, nd.), p. 17.
5. Lynne L. Abney , Communication Resource Specialist, International Mission Board, Nicosia, Cyprus, email, July 14, 1997.
6. Slack, epicit, p. 30.
7. Lucy Shahar & David Kurz, *Border Crossings, American Interactions with Israelis* (Intercultural Press, 1995), pp. 154-156.
8. Matthew 10:37, 19:29.
9. I Timothy 5:8.
10. Proverbs 5:18-19.
11. Brock, *Indigenous Church Planting*, pp. 72-73.
12. Associated Press, "Atlanta, American children dying more by murder, suicide, gunfire,"*The Yuma Daily Sun*, Yuma, Arizona, Friday, February 7, 1997, p. 19.

Chapter Seven

1. Gene Mims, *Kingdom Principles For Church Growth* (Convention Press, Nashville, TN:1994), pp. 88-90.

2. Nadia Shamsedin, e-mail, 10/6/97 in which she credits the start of spiritual mapping to George Otis, Jr.

3. *MAOZ* Newsletter, Dallas, Texas, November 1995, p. 5.

4. Tom White, *Breaking Strongholds* (Ann Arbor, Michigan: Servant Publications, 1993).

5. C. Peter Wagner, *Confronting the Powers* (Ventura, CA: Regal Books, 1996)

6. John Dawson, *Healing America's Wounds* (Ventura, CA: Regal Books, 1994)

7. Maps may be secured from *Survey Of Israel*, Post Office Box 14171, 61141 Tel Aviv, Israel.

8. Claylan Coursey, Discovering Responsive People and Places, *Handbook For Effective Church Planting And Growth* (International Board, SBC, Richmond VA, n.d.) p. 31.

9. Luke 9-10.

10. Robert Coleman, *The Master Plan Of Evangelism* (Grand Rapids, Michigan: Fleming Revell:1972) pp. 30-31.

11. David J. Hesselgrave, *Planting Churches Cross-Culturally* (Baker:1980), p. 185.

12. Charles L. Chaney, *Church Planting At The End Of The Twentieth Century* (Tyndale:1991), p. 198.

13. Stuart Christine, *Guidelines for the Planting Team, Planting Tomorrow's Churches Today* (Monarch, Great Britain:1992), pp. 235-242.

14. James B. Slack, Church Growth Principles Basic to Church Planting, *Handbook For Effective Church Planting And Growth* (International Board, SBC, Richmond, VA: n.d.), p. 30.

15. Greg Livingstone, *Planting Churches In Muslim Cities, A Team Approach* (Baker:1993), pp. 100-101.

16. I am indebted to Donald A. McGavran for this expression, found in his *Understanding Church Growth* (Eerdmans, Grand Rapids, MI: 1970, 1980, 1990), preface p. x.

17. One case we witnessed is of our son-in-law, who expired of renal shock in the old Hadassa Hospital in Tel Aviv, but was revived through prayer.

18. Matthew 10:11.

19. Hesselgrave, op. cit., p. 164.

20. Charles Brock, *Indigenous Church Planting*, pp. 115-121, 146.

21. ibid., pp. 122-123.

22. Wolfgang Simson, *Houses that Change the World, Toward a Re-Incarnation of Church,* (Madras: 1998).

23. ibid., pp. 126-130.

24. Chaney, op. cit., p. 109.

Chapter Eight

1. 1 Corinthians 4:15b-16, 11:1.
2. Baptist Convention in Israel, 1995.
3. John Gilbert, FMB Thesaurus Definitions, (International Board, SBC, Richmond VA 23230:1994).
4. Charles L. Chaney, *Church Planting At The End Of The Twentieth Century* (Tyndale, Wheaton IL:1991), p. 38.
5. James Slack, *Church Growth Principles Basic to Church Planting, Handbook For Effective Church Planting And Growth*, p. 29.
6. Tim Matheny, *Reaching the Arabs, A felt need approach*, (William Carey Library: 1981), pp. 146-152.
7. TAFTEE, *House Groups,* Bangalore, India. This excellent resource on house groups has been adapted and translated into Arabic by PTEE, POB 1931, Amman (11118), Jordan.
8. New Wine-Cell Church Seminars, Conceptual Building Blocks, copied from Bill Beckham/Ralph Neighbor of Touch Ministries, PO Box 19888, Houston TX, USA. Ministry Cassette No. NW 22A&B available from ICC, Silverdale Rd., Eastbourne, East Sussex BN20 7AB, England, email: icc@mistral.co.uk.
9. Church Growth International, 13174 Owens Lane, Neosho, MO 64850, USA.
10. *The True Furqan* (Enumclaw, WA 98022: WinePress Publishing, 1999).
11. Claylan Coursey, Discovering Responsive People and Places, Chapter 3, *Handbook for Effective Church Planting*, pp. 58-61.
12. Brock, *Indigenous Church Planting*, p. 202.
13. 2 Thessalonians 3:10.
14. Martin Robinson, The Impetus of Church Growth, *Planting Tomorrow's Churches Today*, p. 99, note 7.
15. Galatians 4:19.
16. Alan Schreck, "*Twelve Principles Of Church Renewal,*" (reprinted and adapted from *Faith and Renewal,*) *The Christian Educators Handbook on Spiritual Formation,* (Wheaton: Victor Books, 1994), p.156.
17. Information received over the Internet.
18. Erich Bridges, "Like Wildfire, Out of Control," *the Commission,* (Richmond: International Mission Board, SBC) February 1999, p. 51.

Appendix B

1. Rev. Edward Tannous, interview, Haifa, Israel, August 14, 1997.
2. David Davis, Haifa, Israel, e-mail, February 20, 1998.
3. Rev. Ray Lockart, Jerusalem, Israel, e-mail, February 11, 1997.
4. Baruch Maoz, Grace and Truth Congregation, Rishon LeTsion, Israel, e-mail, March 24, 1998, and "20 years of mercy, Grace and Truth," 1996.
5. Rev. Tony Sperandeo, interview, Kafr Saba, Israel, September 17, 1997.
6. Ari & Shira Sorko-Ram, Emails November 24-25, 1988, and telephone interviews 1999
7. Noam Hendron, interview, Baptist Village, Israel, August 6, 1997.
8. Rev. Wayne Hilsden, Jerusalem, Israel, e-mail, February 20, 1997, *King of Kings Assembly Bulletin,* January 1996.
9. Suheil Saad, interview, East Jerusalem, July 25, 1997.
10. *2000 Directory* Congregations-Home Groups in the Cities and Villages of Israel including West Bank and Gaza.

Appendix C

1. Statistics courtesy of the Global Research Division of the International Mission Board of the Southern Baptist Convention for Baptist Church membership.

Selected Bibliography

Bush, Luis, ed. *AD2000 and Beyond Handbook,* Colorado Springs: AD2000 & Beyond Movement, 1993

Allen, Roland. *Missionary Methods: St. Paul's or Ours?* London: World Dominion, 1956

Arberry, A.J., Ed. *Religion in the Middle East*, 2 Vols., Cambridge University Press, 1969

Ateek, Naim Stifan. *Justice and Only Justice, A Palestinian Theology of Liberation.* Maryknoll, NY: Orbis, 1989

Baker, Dwight L. *Baptist Golden Jubilee, 50 Years in Palestine-Israel.* Nazareth, Israel, 1961

Berger, Morroe. *The Arab World.* New York, 1964

Borch, David J. *Transforming Mission.* Maryknoll, NY: Orbis, 1991

Brock, Charles. *Indigenous Church Planting, A Practical Journey.* Neosho, MO: Church Growth International, 1994

Building Effective Church Planting Teams, A Handbook for Team Leaders and Mentors, The Fellowship of Church Planters, 467 Armistice Blvd., Pawtucket, RI, 02861, USA (n.d.)

Chacour, Elias. *We Belong to the Land.* New York: HarperCollins, 1990

Chaney, Charles L. *Church Planting at the End of the Twentieth Century.* Wheaton: Tyndale, 1991

The Christian Educator's Handbook on Spiritual Formation. Edited by Kenneth O. Gangel & James C. Wilhoit, Wheaton: Victor Books, 1994

Christianity and Rabbinic Judaism. Washington, DC: Biblical Archaeology Society, 1992

Coleman, Robert. *The Master Plan of Evangelism.* Grand Rapids: Fleming Revell, 1972.

Cragg, Kenneth. *The Arab Christian, A History in the Middle East.* Louisville: Westminster, 1991

Crombie, Kelvin. *For the Love of Zion, Christian Witness and the Restoration of Israel.* London: Hodder & Stoughton, 1991

Culturgram '97. State of Israel. Provo, UT: Brigham Young University, 1996

Dawson, John, *Healing America's Wounds,* Ventura, CA: Regal, 1994

Friedman, Thomas, *From Beirut to Jerusalem,* London: Harper Collins, 1993

Five Till Midnight, Church Planting for A.D. 2000 and Beyond, Tony Cupit, Editor, Atlanta: Home Mission Board, SBC, 1994

Garrison, David. *Church Planting Movements,* Richmond: International Mission Board, SBC, 1999

Groh, Dennis E. "The Religion of the Empire," *Christianity and Rabbinic Judaism.* Washington: Biblical Archaeological Society, 1992

Handbook of Religious Conversion. Edited by H. Newton & Samuel Southard, Birmingham: Religious   Education Press, 1992

Hesselgrave, David J., *Planting Churches Cross-Culturally.* Grand Rapids: Baker, 1980

—Rommen, Edward, *Contextualization.* Grand Rapids: Baker, 1989

Hitti, Philip. *History of the Arabs.* London: Macmillan, 1963

—*The Arabs, a Short History.* Princeton University Press, 1970

Hodges, Melvin L., *The Indigenous Church,* Springfield: Gospel, 1971

Jennings, George. *Welcome Into the Middle East!* Le Mars IO: Middle East Missions Research, 1986

Johnstone, Patrick, *Operation World,* Grand Rapids: Zondervan, 1993

—*The Church is Bigger Than You Think,* Great Britain: WEC & World Focus 1998

Kjaer-Hansen, Kai & Skjott, Bodil F., *Facts and Myths About the Messianic Congregations in Israel,* Jerusalem: UCCI &Caspari Center, POB 71099, Jerusalem 91000, Israel, 1999

Kronish, Rabbi Ron, Ed. *Guide to Inter-religious and Intercultural Activities in Israel, 1995-1996,* Jerusalem: ICCI

Latourette, Kenneth Scott. *A History of Christianity.* New York: Harper, 1953

Lingenfelter, Sherwood. *Transforming Culture*. Grand Rapids: Baker, 1992

Livingstone, Greg. *Planting Churches in Muslim Cities, A Team Approach*. Grand Rapids: Baker, 1993

Lowe, Chuck, *Territorial Spirits and World Evangelization?*, Bristol, Great Britain: PMF, 1998

Malik, C.H. "The Orthodox Church," *Religion in the Middle East*, Vol. 1. Cambridge University Press, 1969.

Matheny, Tim, *Reaching the Arabs, A felt Need Approach*. Pasadena: William Carey Library, 1981

Maroney, Jimmy K. & Slack, James B. *Handbook for Effective Church Planting and Growth*, Edited by Ellen Libis, Richmond: International Mission Board, nd.

McGavran, Donald A. *Understanding Church Growth*. Grand Rapids: Eerdmans, 1970, 1980, 1990

McKim, Donald K., "The Mainline Protestant Understanding of Conversion," *Handbook of Religious Conversion*. Birmingham: Religious Education Press, 1992

Mims, Gene. *Kingdom Principles for Church Growth*. Nashville: Convention Press, 1994

Mizrachi, Eli, *Two Americans Within the Gates*. The Story of Levi Parsons and Pliny Fisk in Jerusalem. Hagerstown, MD: McDougal Publishing, 1995

Munayer, Salim J. *Ministry of Reconciliation, In the Footsteps of Our Father Abraham*. Jerusalem: Musalaha, 1993

— & Goble, Phil, *The New Creation Book for Muslims*. Pasadena: William Carey, 1989

Nevius, Helen S. Coan. *The Life of John Livingston Nevius*. New York: Fleming H. Revell, 1895

Nevius, John L. *Planting and Development of Missionary Churches*. Grand Rapids: Baker, 1958

Maroney, Jimmy K. & Slack, James B. *Handbook for Effective Church Planting and Growth*, Edited by Ellen Libis, Richmond: International Mission Board, nd.

Otis, George Jr., *The Last of the Giants*. Grand Rapids: Chosen, 1991

Parkes, James. *A History of Palestine from 135 AD to Modern Times*. London, 1949

Piper, John, *Let the Nations Be Glad! The Supremacy of God in Missions*, Grand Rapids: Baker, 1998

Planting House Churches in Networks, A Manual From the Perspective of a Church Planting Team. The Fellowship of Church Planters, 467 Armistice Blvd., Pawtucket, RI 02861, USA, revised 1998

Register, Ray G. *Dialogue and Interfaith Witness with Muslims.* Ephrata, PA: MLM, 1979, 1995 (Box 301, Ephrata, PA 17522)

Robinson, Martin & Christine, Stuart. *Planting Tomorrow's Churches Today.* Great Britain: Monarch, 1992

Shahar, Lucy & Kurz, David, *Border Crossings, American Interactions with Israelis,* Maine: Intercultural Press, 1995

Simson, Wolfgang, *Houses that Change the World,* Madras: Simson, 1998 (PF 212, CH-8212 Neuhausen 2, Switzerland)

TAFTEE, *House Groups.* 13 Hutchins Rd., Bangalore 560005, India. Adapted and translated into Arabic by PTEE, P.O. Box 1931-Amman (11119), Jordan. Available from PTEE in English photo-copy

The Bible and the Land: An Encounter, Edited by Lisa Loden, Peter Walker, & Michael Wood, Jerusalem: Musalaha, 2000 (POB 52110, Jerusalem 91521, Israel)

Thomas, Norman E. Editor, *Classic Texts in Mission & World Christianity.* Maryknoll: Orbis, 1995

Vander Werff, Lyle L. *Christian Mission to Muslims, The Record.* Pasadena: William Carey Library, 1977

Vester, Bertha Spafford, *Our Jerusalem, An American Family in the Holy City, 1881-1949,* Jerusalem: American Colony, 1988

Wagner, C. Peter, *Confronting the Powers,* Ventura, CA: Regal, 1996

Wagner, William L. *North American Protestant Missionaries in Western Europe: A Critical Appraisal.* Bonn: VKW, 1993.

Warren, Rick. *The Purpose Driven Church* Grand Rapids: Zondervan, 1995

White, Tomas B., *Breaking Strongholds,* Ann Arbor, Michigan: Servant, 1993,
—*A Believers Guide to Spiritual Warfare,* Ann Arbor, Michigan: Servant, 1990

Wilkens, Robert L., *The Land Called Holy.* New Haven: Yale University, 1992

Index

About the Author—

Dr. Ray Register has served as a representative for the International Mission Board of the Southern Baptist Convention in Israel for thirty-five years. Thirty of these years he served in Galilee as a church planter-developer and as Field Representative of the Association of Baptist Churches in Israel. He developed and directed the International Institute of Biblical Studies and served four years as Chairman of the United Christian Council in Israel. For many years he was also a board member of the Children's Evangelical Fellowship.

He lived a year in Jerusalem, while doing pre-doctoral studies at the Overseas School of the Hebrew University on Mount Scopus, attended lectures at the Tantur Ecumenical Institute in Jerusalem as Christian advisor to the Center of Religious Pluralism and was active in the Israel Interfaith Committee.

Dr. Register lectured on Islam and interfaith witness with Muslims for the YWAM School of Frontier Missions in Jerusalem. He presently serves as acting president of the Academy of Theological Studies in Jerusalem. A graduate of the University of Virginia and Hartford Seminary Foundation, he also earned a M.Div. and D. Min. degree at Southeastern Baptist Theological Seminary, where he taught as Fletcher Visiting Professor of Missions in 1996.

Dr. Register has authored two books, *Dialogue and Interfaith Witness with Muslims and Clothed in White, The Story of Mavis Pate, ORN.*

For your comments concerning

Back To
Jerusalem

and/or
Inquiries for information
concerning
Prayer needs and projects
in the Holy Land,

Please contact:

IAM Partners
P.O. Box 463045
Escondido, CA 92046-3045

or

email: 104276.1403@compuserve.com

To order additional copies of

Back To
Jerusalem

Have your credit card ready and call

(877) 421-READ (7323)

or send $19.95 each + $3.95* S&H to

WinePress Publishing
PO Box 428
Enumclaw, WA 98022

Website: www.winepresspub.com

*add $1.00 S&H for each additional book ordered